I0819019

Romp!

Romp!

A Journey Through the Natural History of Otters and Why They Matter

Heide Island, PhD

TARCHER
an imprint of Penguin Random House
New York

Tarcher
an imprint of Penguin Random House LLC
1745 Broadway, New York, NY 10019
penguinrandomhouse.com

Book design by Shannon Nicole Plunkett

Map and illustrations by Alexis Seabrook

Library of Congress Cataloging-in-Publication Data has been applied for.

ISBN 9780593855034
Ebook ISBN 9780593855058

Printed in the United States of America
1st Printing

For my teachers, Tom, my mom, and the otters.
And in loving memory of my dad.
Here's looking at you, kid, wherever you are.

Contents

Deception Pass
State Park
Strait of
Juan
de
Fuca
Naval Air Station
Whidbey Island
(Ault Field)
WHIDBEY ISLAND
Skagit
Bay
Strawberry
Point
Oak Harbor
Crescent
Harbor
Lake
Pondilla
Fort Ebey
State Park
Penn Cove
Outlying
Landing
Field
Coupeville
CAMANO
ISLAND
Point
Partridge
Coupeville
Ebey's
Landing
Crockett
Lake
Admirals
Lake
Saratoga
Fort Casey
Admiralty Bay
Admirals
Cove
Keystone
Fort
Worden
Port
Townsend
Greenbank
Passage
Fort Flagler
MARROWSTONE
ISLAND
Holmes Harbor
Goss
Lake
Langley
Possession
Sound
Bush
Point
Freeland
Mutiny Bay
Deer
Lagoon
Admiralty Inlet
Useless Bay
Deer
Lake
Clinton
Glendale
Beach
Mulkilteo
Puget Sound

Introduction

For the Love of Otters

Every explorer I have met has been driven—not coincidentally but quintessentially—by curiosity, by a single-minded, insatiable, and even jubilant need to know.

—JACQUES-YVES COUSTEAU

When I was eight, my dad, a commercial fisherman, recruited me to join him during the summers as his deckhand. "Well, kid," he said, "we need more than one person to run the boat." This was the year I first learned to "drive," though my driving lessons were in his 26-foot Tollycraft, the *Blue Zephyr.* My dad was a sturdy man, with brown hair past his ears and a red scar under his left eye from a childhood dog bite. He was an imposing figure and my absolute hero. He could do no wrong, and I could not have had a greater motivator than to be entrusted with such an adult responsibility.

I learned to pick fish, make TV dinners in a hobbit-sized gas oven, and use the boat's VHF radio. I was always scanning channel 16, hoping the Coast Guard would call us for confirmation of permits, life jackets, or anything else so I could use the NATO alphabet and call signs I had practiced: "This is the *Blue Zephyr*, Alpha, Bravo, Echo, 7-2-7-8. Yes, we are a permitted vessel."

Dad and I took turns watching the net while it soaked for the four-hour sets. Always on the alert for orcas, porpoises, or sea lions drawn to the smell of fish, he diligently avoided entanglements, even if that meant an early haul. If he spied a single dorsal fin, he'd power up the hydraulics and reel the net onto the rolling drum mounted on the deck while I picked fish from the net, narrowly avoiding the scavenging cetaceans. On calm mornings, we'd see the exhalations of humpback whales returning to feed in the summer months, their breathy vapor rich with the reek of krill and baitfish. Their massiveness was juxtaposed with a gentle grace that felt paradoxically otherworldly and familiar. Toward Berners Bay, we often saw moose or grizzly bears wandering the intertidal zone bisected by glacial-fed freshwater creeks teeming with the crimson-and-green bodies of spawning sockeye salmon.

In Alaska, hunting and fishing are, among many people, a sustainable way of living. This is especially true among First Peoples like the Tlingit and Haida of southeast Alaska, though longtime "sourdoughs" and newly arrived "cheechakos" can also appreciate the importance of conserving and preserving the wild spaces that supply food for their tables. My early indoctrination to the outdoors nurtured in me a lifelong affection for nature and the natural world, the Tongass National Forest and the Inside Passage acting as my earliest teachers.

There is no place like Alaska. No matter where you are there, you're in nature; there is no urban or suburban, only human-occupied and not. There are days without night at the summer solstice and nights without day in the winter. The viridescent aurora borealis shimmers in sheets of scarlet, violet, or peridot. When I learned the aurora was caused by solar flares, my enchantment was not diminished by my science education. Rather, the more I knew, the more mysterious, special, and even spiritual it seemed.

The same is true of my enchantment with otters. And my fascination with these animals is not singular; many zoologists, conservation biologists, and behavioral ecologists study the fourteen global otter species. Nor am I unique among the public. In gift shops and online, you can buy otter stickers and socks, otter plush toys and T-shirts, otter artwork and jewelry. Otter puns are abundant—how otterly cool. Few animals at zoos and aquariums have conjured curiosity and delight the way the otter has.

But, as we do with any hero, we tend to distill their complex natures into caricatures. We think of otters as cute and cuddly, but in reality, they're carnivores from the same family as the wolverine and the honey badger—they're no pushovers. Male sea otters, for example, have been known to drown pups. River otters, on occasion, attack people. These intelligent, adaptive, problem-solving, tool-using athletes are so much more interesting than the cartoon version of them we put on merchandise.

Otters play an enormous role in helping us understand and preserve our natural world. For example, they serve as an *indicator species*, meaning regional otters' fitness and behavior are indicators of the health of the watershed and ecosystem. Some otters are also *keystone species*, which means their contribution to the natural environment plays an essential role that all other local biological systems benefit from and rely on. Sea otters, for instance, maintain the health of kelp beds by eating urchins, thereby protecting a habitat that supports a variety of fish and offers vulnerable harbor seals protection from sharks. Additionally, otters act as ecological chemists, fertilizing plants with marine-derived nitrogen through their scent-marking and latrining behavior. In other words, otters pack a considerable environmental punch. They're valuable citizens of the natural world.

The word *romp* is one of the many collective nouns used for a group of otters, along with *tangle*, *raft*, *bevy*, *school*, and *family*. This book is about a specific romp of North American river otters I studied on Washington state's Whidbey Island, but it's also about otters in general—their behavior, adaptability, habits, diet, diversity, and ecology. It discusses the scientific research surrounding otters as well as our complex relationship with them, and what we can do to coexist with them by preserving their habitat and ours.

This book is not intended to be a comprehensive review of all fourteen otter species, although I do discuss each one when relevant throughout the book—not just North America's river otters and sea otters but also species you may never have heard of, like the heavily poached hairy-nosed otters of Southeast Asia or the lesser-known Congo and Cape clawless otters in Africa. (For a more authoritative and academic survey of the world's otters, consider Hans Kruuk's 2006 book, *Otters: Ecology, Behaviour, and Conservation*, or Grace and Paul Yoxon's 2014 guide, *Otters of the World*.)

Our perception of otters has historically been one-dimensional, based on what they offer us as humans, whether it was their fur in centuries past or their value as symbols of conservation in more recent decades. In this book, I'm excited to offer a more three-dimensional perspective of the wondrous, delightful, baffling, and sometimes appalling characteristics of the otters with which we share the world.

1.

Where Are the Otters?

Searching for Signs

When you're gifted a year to study river otters in the field, one crucial prerequisite immediately emerges: knowing where they are. And I thought I did. North American river otters are in, well, North America. They can be found in every state except Hawaii, and aside from Prince Edward Island, they are also found throughout Canada.

I even observed them in the community of floating homes where I used to live on the Columbia River in Portland, Oregon. One spring, as I walked up the gangway connecting my floating home to the shore, I noticed my two dogs staring at something on a neighbor's boat. I knew they were eyeing a critter, but I expected to see a nutria or beaver. Instead, to my surprise, I saw two adult river otters grooming their fur on the boat's transom. When they spotted the dogs, they launched off the step, dove under the dock, and then, in a heartbeat, popped their heads back out of the water.

Just on the perimeter of snatching distance, the otter pair peered curiously up at Gracie, my golden retriever, and Addie, my cocker spaniel. There they were, dog and otter, almost nose to nose. There was a resemblance between them: perhaps the shape of their heads, or maybe just the sentient expressions on their faces. Both Gracie and Addie were inquisitive, with ears perked and tails raised, as if to ask, "What kind of water dog are you?" They didn't bark. They just stood transfixed for several minutes. It was as though both otters and dogs forgot for a moment to be fearful. But the moment passed, as moments do, and the otters lost interest, ducked back into the river, and headed west toward Astoria.

I lived in that floating-home community for well over a decade, yet that was one of only a handful of interactions I had with otters on the Columbia, a success rate indicative of the challenge in consistently viewing river-foraging otters.

The word *river* in the name *river otter* is a bit misleading, as these semiaquatic mustelids (members of the same family of carnivores as ferrets, minks, weasels, skunks, wolverines, and badgers) can be found in any type of aquatic area—lakes and ponds, streams and rivers, brackish and freshwater marshes, estuaries and bays. North American river otters, also called Nearctic otters, occupy coastal waters, too. They're amenable to whatever prey is available, including fish, birds, snakes, frogs, salamanders, small mammals, and invertebrates. They may even dig for grubs.

Yet ocean environments often provide more nutritious and caloric food options, like oil-rich fish and easily harvested shellfish. Because coastal areas provide a reliable food source in a relatively stable area, *marine-foraging* river otters—river otters who hunt for food in the sea, not to be confused with sea otters—that live along bays and inlets typically have a narrower home range, around 1 to 3 square miles. *Freshwater-foraging* river otters, in contrast, must contend with fish migrations and adapt to dramatic seasonal changes in water level and temperature. All of that influences the expansiveness of their home range, which can be upward of 30 square miles.

Living in the floater community, I also had a home range of about 30 miles, as I went back and forth from my home in north Portland to my job as a professor at Pacific University in Forest Grove. Even at five in the morning, without traffic, my commute was an hour. One winter, when a storm made road maintenance impossible, it took ten hours to get home. My husband, Tom, and I had moved there in the early 2000s because it was affordable and felt like an oasis in the city. I often came home to find a heron on my deck or a displaced sea lion passing through, heading up the river to The Dalles for an easy meal. Although I loved living on the river, I felt trapped by the long commutes, encased in my car for hours a day as I drove to and from my job, the store, the gym, and—when conducting observational research with students—the Oregon Zoo.

By 2018, I needed a change. Having just paid off our floating home, Tom and I started looking for a second property in the Puget Sound area to buy, rent out, and ideally retire to one day.

I also had a yearlong work sabbatical coming up, during which I planned to spend two weeks each month studying the behavior of river otters in the wild. And I thought I knew just where to find them: on Blakely Island, one of the 175 islands in the San Juan archipelago in the inland sea known as the Salish Sea that straddles Washington state and British Columbia at the confluence of Puget Sound, the Strait of Juan de Fuca, and the Strait of Georgia. Although Puget Sound, with its 110 marine protected areas, is home to many marine-foraging river otters, the private and remote Blakely Island—with its land area of only 7 square miles, a saltwater bay, and two freshwater lakes—is even better river otter habitat. There are no roads, ferries, or services to the island beyond local water taxis. In fact, before stepping foot in the harbor, you have to obtain an invitation from one of the few dozen residents or through the Blakely Island Field Station, part of Seattle Pacific University.

For the last decade, my research had focused on animal wellness, specifically that of the resident river and sea otters housed at the Oregon Zoo. Now I hoped to observe Blakely's river otters as comparators.

When I arrived at Blakely in June 2018, I found a serene field station perched amid tall stands of conifers, with an unusual blend of architecture—part Swiss chalet, part English stone cottage. On my first night, I was so eager to check out the bay and harbor for otters that I missed the community dinner. To my surprise, LeRoy, one of the station's caretakers, handed me the keys to his truck and a VHF radio. "You can use this while you're here," he told me. LeRoy reminded me a bit of John Wayne, and I found myself responding to him with a straight-backed "Yes, sir" or "No, sir."

And so, each morning, I rose in the predawn and, with the help of LeRoy's truck, searched the island's likely otter haunts. I looked in culverts, slogged through the mud on lake trails, and scrambled up logs. I scampered across rocks in the intertidal zones and walked the dock in the harbor until dark. But there was no scat, no observable denning areas, and no obvious couches (the places where otters nap during the day, displacing and trampling down vegetation). There were no food leavings, either—no mounds of fish parts neatly piled on the beach, no crab carapaces, shells, or feathers. Absolutely nothing.

Every day, after I returned from my first round of searching, I joined the station's caretakers to collect my lunch.

"Did you find any otters today?" LeRoy might say as he snacked on a piece of salmon jerky.

"No, sir, no otters today."

So out came the infrared cameras. I planted fifteen trail cameras near likely otter hangouts, where freshwater met estuary or bay, and visited them daily. After the first few nights, I saw footage of black-tailed deer, several dogs, and a northern flying squirrel, but no otters. In the mornings, I solicited information from Blakely's summer research students as they collected dragonfly specimens or counted deer. They saw no otters, no scat, and no other signs that the otters were still there.

Instead of joining everyone for evening meals, I began taking a small plate to my room to eat as I reviewed camera footage. I held my breath as I watched each frame, hoping to see the humped torso and awkward gait of a river otter. Aside from an endless parade of photobombing insects and the occasional flyby from a bat, I had nothing. Nada.

The station's director, Dr. Tim Nelson, mentioned that in the thirty years he'd been supervising student research, there had always been otters on Blakely Island. But in the summer of 2018, there was no sign of otters at all. The island was tiny. Surely, if there were otters around, I would have found *some* evidence. Where could they have gone?

After my first two weeks on Blakely, Tom came to pick me up from the marina in Anacortes. I missed him, but I dreaded the thought of telling him about my trip on the five-hour drive back to Portland—not only because there were no otters on the island but also because it was clear I'd have to figure out something else to do with my sabbatical year. I had monthly trips scheduled to Blakely

Island for the entire year. But I couldn't just drive LeRoy's truck around, hoping the otters would show. I'd have to pivot and revise my research site or even my whole sabbatical plan.

As my water taxi from Blakely pulled up to the mainland, Tom stood at the slip, waiting for me. I hoisted my backpack onto one shoulder, my camera bag on the other, and stepped onto the dock. He enfolded me in a hug.

"So, while you've been chasing otters—"

"Searching for otters," I corrected.

"Right, while you were *searching* for otters, I checked in with our realtor and expanded our search to Whidbey."

I nodded. In our search for a second property, we'd been outbid on our last two offers in Hood Canal, an area of Puget Sound south of Blakely. It made sense to start looking on Whidbey, another island in the area—in fact, the largest island in Washington state.

Although securely in midlife, Tom seemed boyish. He had the kind of bubbly energy you might expect of someone taking you to a surprise party. But I hate surprises.

"What is it? What is that expression?" I asked.

"Well," he said as we got in his truck, "I found a cabin on the water! And we close today!"

I blinked. "What do you mean we close *today*?"

"It's a pocket listing. The realtor told me about it early this week. I didn't want to worry you while you were in the field. Plus, your cell reception on the island was crap, so I decided not to wait."

I could feel myself getting warm. "That's a pretty big decision. A decision that should have included me."

"Just give me a chance, Heida," he said, using my grandfather's nickname for me. He knew that would work. "I followed all our criteria. And the market has been bonkers. If I didn't act quickly, we would have lost this house, too."

I had to concede this was all true and that if he'd gotten ahold of me, I would've told him to go for it. But still. It seemed nuts that we were about to close on a house neither of us had seen in person.

Instead of heading to Portland from Anacortes, we drove over the Deception Pass Bridge onto Whidbey Island to see our new house.

As we moved south, we left the dense forests of Douglas fir, Sitka spruce, and western hemlock. Past the big-box stores in Oak Harbor, the road became a two-lane highway along the water, a boundary between grazing pastures and the ocean. It was stunning—verdant and agricultural on one side, coastal and Olympic on the other. We followed the winding road past state park signs down through Coupeville, where the Sandra Bullock movie *Practical Magic* was filmed in the nineties. I could see the Hollywood appeal: old-timey shops with classic pastel-washed facades or weathered cedar shake, narrow walking streets, and a craggy wharf along the protected cove.

As we passed the ferry terminal a little farther south, a green-and-white ferry pulled away from her slip. My stomach churned like the prop wash in her wake, but Tom beamed over at me and squeezed my hand. "We're almost there," he said.

We turned onto Keystone Spit, a thin piece of land separating Admiralty Inlet from Admirals Lake. Driftwood was piled along the beach by houses too close to the ocean for today's building codes. The older homes, including the cabin, were built in the early 1960s.

Tsunami signs punctuated the path beside it—not exactly reassuring.

Suddenly, from a culvert on the ocean side of the street, four wet, dog-sized mammals with elongated bodies and weasel-like faces bounded across the road in front of the truck.

Tom stomped on the brakes, and we screeched to a halt. We sat frozen, our mouths open, as four river otters loped across the road. The one in the front, the largest of the four, was dragging an extravagantly large flatfish. It paused, looked up at us, and readjusted the catch in its jaws. Then all four otters dashed from the road into the adjacent bulrushes along the lake. I resisted my impulse to bolt from the cab, camera in hand, and crash into the brush after them.

"You're a magician!" I said, hurling my arms around Tom.

"Well, I guess I don't have to sell you on this cabin."

"Nope," I said. "I know where I'll be spending my sabbatical."

We drove on, and finally, there it was: our new home. The cabin was situated on ocean rock and stones just above the supratidal zone—known less formally as the splash zone. Its dingy shag carpet smelled like mothballs and old socks. The drafty windows were either delaminated by the corrosive salt of the ocean spray or missing panes entirely. The planed cedar logs that made up the interior walls were coated in dust, and the fireplace was crusted in baked-on soot. As soon as we walked in, Tom pronounced it "fantastic!"

Tom is a home inspector and a contractor, and one of his many talents is the ability to see the potential of a place. Having lived with him for over two decades, I got what he saw: the strong bones and the beauty in the materials. The logs were heartwood, no knots, only clean grain. The original mid-century fixtures were charming and nostalgic. Tom was already mentally measuring for replacement windows, wood flooring, and new countertops. What mattered to me was the cabin's most magnificent feature: the breathtaking ocean view.

And, fate willing, the otters.

By September, after a flurry of renovations, Tom heads back to Portland. Now he'll be the one commuting each month: three weeks at home in Portland for work and one week off with me in Whidbey, where I'll remain for the year.

Today, as on most days, I'm already dressed in thermals in the blue hours before sunrise. The clock on my coffeepot says 3:40 a.m. I tuck into a pair of Xtratuf rubber boots, add a wool jacket, and gingerly cradle my Sony camera, ensuring the extended rain sleeve fits over the 400-millimeter lens. Outside, the brisk air is heavy with the fragrance of green ribbon seaweed, bull kelp, and sea lettuce. There is a slight hint of something decaying, fishy, and sulfuric—something I will no doubt have to bathe from Gracie's and Addie's fur. The dogs' snouts skim the ground, a scent leading them down the short steps of the deck onto the shore.

I sit on the first step, facing the bay, sipping my coffee. It's too dark to see anything in detail beyond the reflection of bright stars on the sea. I close my eyes and wait, straining to hear the soft echo of chirping through the coastal sounds. I am listening for the alarm chirp of an otter pup—or, more precisely, *three* otter pups.

During this morning ritual, I often hear them: the

otters that crossed the road in front of our truck just two months ago. Otter pups chirp to locate their mother and siblings. When they've been separated for more than a few minutes, those chirps transition to urgent, high-pitched whistles. Extend the separation longer, and the whistles transform into urgent shrieks, wraithlike and spooky. In the dark of the early morning, pups frequently get lost. Even now, as the dark shifts to dawn, I generally hear the pups before I see them.

River otters are crepuscular, meaning they're most active during dawn and dusk. Though they don't keep to a precise schedule, these are the most reliable times to see them. During predawn, as the world sleeps, the otters are already out fishing.

I frequently see couches or resting areas, as well as scrapes from digging or marking around Admirals Lake, which is less a lake and more a residential pond within Admirals Cove, fed through seepage from Crockett Lake. The otters move between Admirals Lake and Admiralty Bay through a tide gate, an outflow pipe that connects the two bodies of water via an underground drain. After the otters fish the ocean, they pass through this culvert, emerging back into the lake. Sometimes they take their food to go, running with a fish from the bay into the culvert to finish their breakfast along the lakeshore. Other times, they eat their catch in the pipe itself, especially if the neighborhood eagles or herons are also awake and hunting; the large predatory birds have no reservations about stealing the otters' hard-earned catch.

Breakfast is followed by an amble onto the grass or the beach, where the family grooms the salt from their fur. They conclude with a butt-wagging, foot-stomping dance to propel a fecal spackling called *spraint* onto rocks and logs. This otter poop dance has a strong social influence—if one otter goes, they all go.

There are two reasons for this behavior. The first is that they often cooperatively fish, meaning they coordinate their hunting. This might look like one otter nosing at the sandy bottom to disturb a flatfish, while another otter swims close behind and redirects the fish into the path of yet a third otter, which swoops in to intercept the fleeing fish. This social foraging is not a drawn-out enterprise, as otters' fast metabolisms require frequent feedings. This is evidenced by the transit time from ingestion to excretion, which is only about two to four hours, depending on the composition of their meal. By comparison, humans need about one to three days. The second reason is to mark territory. River otters don't police their habitat so much as survey it, and their "latrines" provide olfactory and visual cues of their range. The presence of unfamiliar scat also alerts them to other otters occupying or traveling through their territory.

The data-collection value of the latrines cannot be overstated. If I collect the spraint fresh, that biological sample can be used to answer questions about diet, hormones, and genetic information, including the sex of the otters and how they're related to each other.

Ideally I would confirm sex by genetics, but environmental DNA analyses are expensive, and fortunately, these otters are not modest. On several occasions, they've *hauled out*, or rested, on the beach in front of the cabin to take a break, eat a recently caught starry flounder, and groom themselves or each other. Before returning to the ocean, they roll around in the exposed sand from the tidewater and let fly. Genitalia are often hard to see among North American river otters, but the angle of urine can be an identifier. A male otter's urine stream points forward, toward the head. Among females, the urethra is close to the base of the tail, so the stream projects downward and toward the tail. I've been lucky enough to catch digital images of these angles, so I'm confident there are three females and one male in the family.

Just as a group of lions is called a pride and a group of crows is called a murder, there is a special name for a group of river otters: a romp. The Admirals Cove romp is a kin group of a mother and three pups. If they were all adults, I wouldn't need to pay so much attention to urine angle; their size could help me distinguish males from females. Virtually all otter species exhibit *sexual dimorphism*—differences in shape or size depending on an animal's sex. Male North American river otters weigh 15 to 35 pounds and are 2.5 to 4 feet from nose to tail, while female adults are, on average, about 25 percent smaller.

Like many adult river otters, the matriarch of this romp has a unique pattern on her muzzle. I start calling her Patches after the trio of large dark spots that lies slightly to the left of her nose. Biologist Scott Shannon has alliteratively referred to these as *mustachial* (mustache-like) *maculations* (patterns of spots) after recognizing them among the river otters he observed for twenty-five years in Northern California's Trinidad Bay. They're often lost during a young otter's first molt in late winter or early spring, but sometimes they remain into adulthood, as I gather they have for Patches.

These markings are the only way I can identify her without more invasive methods—the kind in which the animal must be trapped, sedated, and, if physiology trackers are surgically placed in the abdomen, held for recovery. Techniques like tagging, radiotelemetry, and bio-logging, which frequently use transmitters, receivers, or drones in conjunction with GPS, can be a great way to track certain animals. But tagging is difficult with otters. Their ears are far too small for tags, and radio collars often slip off their narrow clavicles and relatively small heads.

So, much like a four-year-old might name a new dalmatian puppy Spot, I name Patches after her most notable physical feature as a noninvasive, if imperfect, approach to tracking her.

This practice is a small act of defiance among some scientists, a way of reclaiming our connection to animals as nameable beings. Ethologists (animal behaviorists) and wildlife researchers have historically assigned the animals they were studying a number, not a name, in order to keep them at an emotional remove. This number usually corresponds with a foot or ear tag. Sometimes researchers use both a number and a name. For example, Southern Resident killer whales in the Salish Sea are given a letter that corresponds with one of the three pods (J, K, or L) and a number that reflects their birth order, but they also receive nicknames. L-25, thought to be the oldest living resident orca at ninety-six years old, is also called Ocean Sun. When you consistently observe animals, you come to know their personalities and histories, so using only a number for identification just feels . . . off.

I'm not tagging these otters, so using some basic identifiers in naming is helpful, but only if there are features that stand out. Not all river otters have unique markings, and those markings don't always persist into adulthood, but at least for now, I can use them to recognize my local romp. Just as I named the mother Patches,

I name the pups Crest, Slash, and Swoosh after their own unique patterns.

Sea otters, the other otter species found in Washington, have no unique markings for identification except rhinarium scars; sea otter fur is so thick that the *rhinarium,* or nose, is often the only place for a courting male to grab a female—or the most vulnerable place to target in a fight with another male. The only otter species with distinctive, lifelong fur markings are the giant otters of South America and the spotted-necked otters of Africa. Giant otters have uniquely shaped patches of white, cream, dark-brown, or black fur along their neck and throat, while spotted-necked otters' markings are, as you might imagine, splotches or spots along their necks. Both types of markings can be used like fingerprints to identify individuals within these two species.

At 5:14, there is still no otter chirping, only the whoosh of the ocean and the piping of a bald eagle. The clear night is giving way to an equally clear morning. I can still see the lights from Port Townsend across the bay and the steam from the local paper mill. The glossy back of a harbor porpoise cartwheels out of the sea and back beneath the waves.

The last three mornings, I was joined in my otter scans by a lone sea lion fishing along the shoreline. His head, doglike with long whiskers, large eyes, and earflaps held just above the waterline, skimmed the shallows as he hunted for surface-dwelling schools of capelin. His pronounced *sagittal crest,* or brow ridge, identified him as a male at least five years old. Occasionally, he gave me a side-eye, monitoring my distance from the water's edge.

I don't see him today as I scan the bay, binoculars in hand. I take inventory of what I do see: thirteen seagulls, five common loons, and a great blue heron balancing on a kelp raft.

Then, there she is: Patches!

She's at the bay's north end, swimming at a fast clip toward the culvert at the southern end. Her lithe four-foot-long body is like a miniature, furred submarine. Only her flat head, with its small ears and broad muzzle, breaks the surface. Her thick tail, a full third of her body length, is a rudder directing her torso's subtle up-and-down flexing, propelling her toward the bay's south end.

Patches is swimming too fast for pups to keep up, and I don't see three little heads trailing in her wake. She is also not diving, which would indicate she was fishing. Instead, she's traveling at what looks like her maximum speed of about 13 kilometers per hour (just under Michael Phelps's fastest recorded swim speed of 14.2 kilometers per hour). This must be a destination-driven swim. She likely grabbed a quick bite in the bay before her pups woke up this morning, and now she's on her way back to them.

I hope she gets there before they realize she's missing. If she doesn't, they'll start calling for her, and the loud chirping can easily be heard across the lake. The otter pups have few predators on the island, but coyotes do share the same habitat, and although an attack on an adult otter would be unusual, a pup would be a boon. But this is likely my anxiety talking. I'm invested in this family of otters now. I'm their person (whether they need one or not).

The word *otter* stems from a Proto-Indo-European root meaning "water creature," but unlike sea otters, river otters do not intuitively know how to swim. Though otter pups start playing at four weeks of age, their mom doesn't initiate Otter Skills 101 until they're eight weeks old—old enough to learn water entry, floating, swimming, and some diving. When the otters are fully weaned at around ten weeks, the mom introduces her pups to solid foods and enrolls them in Otter Skills 102. This involves dive mastery, hunting, and, in some cases, cooperative or coordinated fishing to strategically capture faster prey. During this time, pups also learn to evade predators, scent trouble, identify good territory, and evaluate when it's more prudent to fight or flee in the face of a threat.

This early education lasts from when the pups take their first steps into the water to when the male pups are ousted from the romp to make their way alone. Depending on food availability, this can happen as early as six months or well into a male's first year; girls often stay with their mother longer, anywhere from a year to two years. Patches's pups are in the second set of training and thus are likely four to five months old.

There is enough daylight now to monitor the latrines. I have seven of them to visit in Admirals Cove: four along the lake and three on the bay, in the upland forested canopy. I put the dogs back inside, collect my field bag, and head out the door to the beach.

With scat collection, you want the freshest samples, but with four otters and daily visits to the latrine, that's a whole lot of crap. How do you know which sample is the most recent among all the piles? To be certain, you have to remove all feces the day before collection. The first time I did this, it broke my heart a little—all that data, just tossed. But eliminating all spraints compels the otters to return the following day to re-mark, providing a wealth of new data. I've wiped all seven latrines clean, providing a clear dance floor for the next day's poo party. I know I'll be tempted to collect *all* the fresh samples, but some judiciousness is required, as each scat pile costs around $90 to analyze.

It is a low ebb tide right now, so I walk along the compacted sand at the tidal edge. As I trudge past the outflow from the lake to the bay, I see Patches's tracks from the bay into the drainage pipe. They are the tracks of an otter in a hurry. River otters, like other semiaquatic mammals, are elegant swimmers, but rather awkward on land. Their legs are short, with five digits on each webbed foot, so on land, they move in a walk, bound, or gallop rather than a run. Patches was definitely bounding from the bay to the drainpipe, judging by the reversed sequence of her footprints. A walking pattern involves a step with the front right foot, followed by the hind right foot, and then the left front and hind feet. These tracks, on the other hand, show paired, simultaneous strikes, with the hind feet in the lead and the smaller front feet following in the rear. I leave the prints to the tide and continue on.

I'm heading for an old snag, a naturally felled tree that lies debarked and bleached by sun and salt water on a game trail barely visible from the beach. This is my visual marker for what seems to be one of the otters' favorite latrines. Patches is gone now, but last night, around six in the evening, she and her pups were fishing at twilight. Perhaps they entered the bay at the trail rather than the culvert. If so, I can expect some "sign"—tracker parlance for the precious poop I need to collect as well as for scrapes (otter-trodden vegetation near latrine sites), holts (fully protected, underground, or covered shelters), couches, and any other ecological evidence of their presence.

When I arrive, there is indeed a fresh series of clustered spraints, eight in total. Otters' strong jaws pulverize their meals—bones, scales, feathers, and whatever else they've eaten—into tiny pieces that look a little like crushed ice among the dark gray spraint piles. I pull on black latex gloves, searching for the best samples. I am discriminating, picking the largest, freshest two I can find and using disposable bamboo spoons, one for each sample, to scoop them into the same kind of collection jars you might use to give a urine sample during a hospital visit. One of the remaining scat piles has a film of opaque yellow material called *scat jelly* blown over the top. I collect it as well, then sprinkle the remaining uncollected scat piles with biodegradable glitter made of eucalyptus cellulose and the mineral mica. Unlike regular craft glitter, it contains no microplastics. It's food-grade—you could eat it, though not after it's been used for my purposes.

I can't help but smile to myself as I tap the garish pink sparkles over the uncollected, now fancy feces. Old spraint quickly decomposes to just bleached bones and scales, a white, crumbly, amorphous pile. If spraints are even a couple days old, particularly in the Pacific Northwest with its high humidity and constant drizzle, it can be tough to tell their age. The glitter makes it easy to distinguish the old fecal deposits from the new.

I'll freeze these samples until I have a big enough batch to warrant processing. Then the spraint samples will be analyzed for diet data, while the scat jellies will be used for hormone analysis.

As I make my way toward the lake, I feel good about my sabbatical plans, maybe even a little smug. Reliable freshwater and saltwater sites for marine-foraging river otters? Check. A place to stay at the new field site? Check. Bonus: I can afford to remain for the full year without weeks off or breaks in data collection. Today, it's not even noon, and I have fecal specimens settling in the jars of my field bag. I've already spotted an otter, and not just any otter, an otter I know. An otter that, for right or wrong, I've claimed in the same way I would a friend or favorite place. It is a protectiveness. She is "my" otter.

The sun rises over the bay, and just as it does, I see a line in the water that looks like the letter V, with three small heads trailing behind. At the tip of the V is Patches. She has returned to fish with her pups.

She dips her head below the surface, and the force of her momentum temporarily lifts her body out of the water. Her muscular tail thrusts up, pushing her farther below the surface. The three pups follow suit, one after the other. Their heads duck beneath the waves, and with a final push of their tails, they're all under the sea. Thirty seconds later, their heads pop back up closer to me.

Two of the four were successful in their dives: Patches and Crest, the largest female pup. Both of them are chewing, heads tilted back and open-mouthed, in the same way human children are often discouraged from doing. Their chewing is loud. I can hear it from the shore, where I watch, camera in hand. The male pup, Swoosh, dives back down, while Slash trails her sister. Slash looks in my direction, and I focus on her through the camera's viewfinder. There is an awareness and a sentience in her eyes.

I watch her as she watches me. She utters a little chirp and then plunges headfirst below the water.

Like semiaquatic spies, the otters disappear and reappear from out of nowhere. Their sneaky approach and departure remind me of the tale of the Kóoshdaa Káa, or Land Otter People, told by the Tlingit and Haida of southeast Alaska. I don't recall where I first heard about the Kóoshdaa Káa while growing up in Juneau. Maybe it was from friends who learned it from their parents or their Tlingit community elders. Or maybe I heard about it at summer camp or during one of the Alaskan Native studies programs taught at my elementary school.

As the story goes, if you're out in the woods hunting or gathering wild blueberries, take care. You may have the uneasy sensation you're being watched, or you may hear a voice, a haunting whistle, or the sound of an infant crying, compelling you to seek its source. If you feel that pull to move farther into the forest, stop your foraging and run back to safety, or you could be taken by the Kóoshdaa Káa. Though these spirits may appear like otters, they are, in the words of cultural anthropologist Frederica de Laguna, "really transformed persons." They "capture those who drown, who are lost or who wander in the woods, and such unfortunates are taken by these Land Otter Men to their homes or dens, and unless rescued in time . . . are in their turn transformed into land otters."

In his book *Haunted Inside Passage*, Bjorn Dihle interviews Alaskans who report run-ins with the Kóoshdaa Káa. They describe seeing people who weren't there, hearing eerie noises, and feeling "like you're being watched but you never see anything." One interviewee, Ethel Lund, "an eighty-four-year-old Raven of the

Kiks.ádi (Frog) clan and the Sun House," says, "I grew up in a Tlingit household and they used to threaten you if you didn't behave—a boogeyman that comes around. And then I saw these little otters, I don't know if that was what they were referring to."

When I consider the two Alaskan otter species that likely inspired the story of the Land Otter People, the northern sea otter and the North American river otter, it's not difficult to imagine seeing humanlike qualities in both. Sea otters spend most of their life in bays, floating on their backs atop the water. In the thick marine layer of twilight, along nearshore rocks and kelp beds, you might see what look like fur-bundled babies in brown pelts with round, flat faces and forward-facing eyes. River otters, meanwhile, are seen swimming belly-down, like a snake, until they reach the shore and bound up the beach. Then what may resemble a childlike figure on all fours disappears into the forest ferns, and perhaps the Kóoshdaa Káa story is born.

Land Otter stories are not unique to Alaska. They were also shared farther south among the coastal tribes of the Salish Sea, including the Skagit, the Snohomish, and the Clallam, whose traditional lands include Whidbey Island, also known as Tscha-kole-chy. In Salishan traditions, though, the Land Otter didn't necessarily share the sinister traits of the Kóoshdaa Káa.

In Japanese folklore, the Yōkai are spirits or monsters that assume the form of all kinds of different animals, including otters. According to folklorist Michael Dylan Foster, the Yōkai are

> creatures of the borderlands, living on the edge of town, or in the mountains between villages, or

> in the eddies of a river running between two rice fields. They often appear at twilight, that gray time when the familiar seems strange and faces become indistinguishable. They haunt bridges and tunnels, entranceways and thresholds. They lurk at crossroads.

This is fitting: In ecology, these transitional areas between habitats are referred to as *ecotones*, and they are where river otters are most reliably observed.

2.

Whiskers in the Waves

Otter Senses

It is early December, and although the air is crisp in the winter chill, the sun is warm, and the wind is uncharacteristically absent. It's as if the universe peeked into my planner and, recognizing my unease, decided to help me out. Today is dive day, and I'm a little nervous. I've spent time scuba diving in the South Pacific, both for recreation and for research, but I haven't dived in cold water for over a decade.

Luckily, I'm in excellent hands; a NAUI master scuba instructor is joining me, the same one who certified me to dive over thirty years ago. He's also my favorite dive buddy, and he happens to be my uncle, Jim Larsen. Jim is among the three men who influenced my love of the ocean, alongside my dad (a former commercial fisherman and an accomplished diver himself) and Jacques Cousteau, the diver and creator of the docuseries *The Undersea World*. A good sport, Jim has traveled the three and a half hours from Vancouver, Washington, to Whidbey Island just to accompany me.

I solicited Jim's support to help me gather data on the fish and invertebrates in Admirals Lake and Admiralty Bay using underwater video scans, a viable, nonlethal alternative to traditional fish-sampling techniques like electrofishing, seining, trapping, and netting. Since I'm only using noninvasive methods, in order to spare Whidbey's already delicate ecology, we'll have to collect several hours of video for validity. Later today, during a slack tide—the brief window at the peak of high and low tides when the current is almost stationary—we also plan to explore the "otter line," the north–south track the otters regularly make in their fishing excursions, approximately thirty feet from the low-water line in front of my cabin.

I'm hoping our dive surveys will provide a clearer

picture of the otters' foraging and fishing options between Admiralty Bay and Admirals Lake. When the Patches romp fishes the lake, they often catch saltwater fish, like small sculpin and flounder, hinting at the lake's brackish ecosystem and tidal inflow. Any fish in the 11-acre lake—more of a pond, really—would come either from the Crockett Lake Preserve, a 281-acre lake and marshland to the west, or from the inflow of salt water from the bay through the tide gate that partitions the Pacific Ocean from the roads.

Unless I check out the otters' hunting grounds for myself, it's tough to know where their lakeside meals originate. If they can get the same kind of fish in the lake and the bay, why go to the bay at all, risking dangerous tides, deeper water, and rip currents? But there may be an easy explanation for their fishing patterns: *Demersal*, or bottom-dwelling, fish like sculpins and flatfish are more active during high tides. If the clever otters have figured this out, they might prefer fishing the bay at low tide, when these fish are least active and therefore easier to catch.

Early winter in the Pacific Northwest is an excellent time to scuba dive in the sea. The shorter days limit the amount of phytoplankton, so the water is clearer, with visibility of fifty feet or more. But that's the sea, and we're starting our dives in the lake. Today, as on most days, Admirals Lake is algal green.

Scuba gear is awkward. With a Gore-Tex outer layer and a fleece onesie within, the dry suit already feels oversized, and that's before adding the 35-pound air tanks, 18-pound weight belt, neoprene hood, mask, snorkel, fins, buoyancy compensator, regulators, pressure and depth gauges, and GPS—oh, and don't forget the video equipment. As I make my way effortfully toward the water, my equipment shifts, swings, and tries to knock me down. Sweat starts to bead inside my dry suit.

Side by side, Jim and I walk through widgeon grass into the lake. Once we're clear of the sedges, we use each other's shoulders for support as we don our fins. We also put on masks in order to see clearly underwater. Otters don't need masks; they have an extra transparent, semi-permeable eyelid called a *nictitating membrane,* which traps air along the cornea, managing some of the underwater visual distortion. It's like a built-in dive mask for each eyeball. They also have strong circular muscles around their irises, allowing more light into the eye while they're submerged. But unlike me, their *nares,* or nostrils, close underwater. I can still exhale through mine, fogging the glass on my mask. To prevent this, I have to give the lens a spit and swish to prevent fogging before strapping it to my face with the snorkel.

Unfortunately, the mask does little to improve the clarity of the lake, which is the color of strong green tea. There's a tug at my hip. My emergency regulator, or "octopus," is dragging a streamer of filamentous algae from the surface. It's remarkable: We have gear for visibility, gear for flotation, gear for propulsion, gear for breathing, and gear for conserving heat, and yet we still have but a sliver of an otter's comfort, mobility, and visibility underwater.

Jim uses diver signals, a sort of underwater sign language, to communicate with me. He gives me the OK signal with his thumb and forefinger joined together in a circle. It means: *I have no gear problems.*

I signal back the same OK sign. *No gear problems here, either.*

He gestures a thumbs-down. *I'm ready to descend.*

I sign a thumbs-down in return. *Copy that. Descending.*

Relinquishing spoken language is not the only sacrifice we make during a dive. Despite our expansive tackle, we have nothing to aid us with touch. Our hands, like our heads, are tucked into neoprene. Every square inch of surface is covered in clothing. We have to trade touch sensitivity for heat conservation, as our sparse body fuzz and the 90,000 to 150,000 hairs on our heads offer little in the way of insulation.

River otters, in contrast, sport no fewer than 300,000 to 400,000 hairs per square inch all over their bodies, save for their noses and the pads of their feet. Sea otters are even more lavishly furred. In fact, they have the densest fur of any mammal in the animal kingdom, at 850,000 to 1 million hairs per square inch. For perspective, that's 1 million hairs in an area the size of a postage stamp. This thick, lush fur has always made sea otters a target of hunting and trapping. During the maritime fur trade from the mid- to late 1700s into the early part of the twentieth century, European and American trappers nearly wiped them out, reducing them to just 1 percent of their historic population.

Like the coats of most mammals, river otter coats have two main hair types: the long, stout outer guard hairs, which protect against debris and moisture, and the thin, short inner hairs, or underhairs, which are often described as downy. When adequately groomed, the guard hairs lie flat against the body and are coated in sebaceous secretions, or oil, providing waterproofing. The inner hairs serve as insulation, much like the fleece onesie inside my dry suit. The insulating hairs, collectively known as the *integument*, stay dry partly because of the way the follicles interlock. The hairs' specialized anatomical adaptations, referred to as *fins* and *petals*, trap air bubbles, holding the warmed air close to the otters' skin and keeping water out—provided they can keep their coats clean of debris, pollutants, dirt, and salt. My dry suit lacks these Velcro-like structures, so the pocket of air that keeps me warm has to come through valves that open to the tank.

The *pelage*, or fur coat, is especially important because none of the otter species have much subcutaneous fat. This means that—unlike, say, whales or seals—sea otters, the smallest of the marine mammals, have no blubber to keep them warm, though they spend over 90 percent of their life in temperatures between 0 and 16 degrees Celsius (32 and 60.8 degrees Fahrenheit). To compensate, they've evolved a three-layer pelage with intermediate hair, and skin twice as thick as that of other otters.

In one way, we are alike, the otters and I: Their sparse body fat means they only regulate flotation through the air trapped in their fur, just as I do with the air in my suit. But I require a lot of gear that has to be adjusted differently for salt water and fresh water. Meanwhile, the lithe river otters can transition from fresh to salt water without changing a thing, and still swim, see, and feel better than I do in their aqueous world.

All otters are expert divers, and like all divers, they have to manage their energy the deeper they dive. The farther down you go, the greater the pressure. As pressure increases against their bodies and the air trapped in their fur escapes, their skin is exposed to the chill. This limits their bottom time, which means they have less time to hunt before exposure starts to affect them. For sea otters, this is all the more salient, since they eat animals that primarily live along the seafloor. To combat this, sea otters have evolved a couple of cool adaptations. Physiologically, they leak metabolic heat from their muscles into their bloodstream. Behaviorally, they spend more time *felting*: blowing air into their pelage as they groom and using their forepaws to press the hair fibers into an interlocking weave.

This means that shallower dives are more efficient for heat conservation and clean fur is an absolute necessity—so much so that wild sea otters spend between 5 and 20 percent of their day grooming, while captive sea otters, with no risk of predators, can spend about 25 percent of their day on felting activities. Mothers in either habitat may spend even longer, as they have to groom their own pelage as well as the *lanugo*, or natal fur, of their pups, who won't begin to groom themselves until around one to two months of age. This grooming generally occurs in the water, like most sea otter activities. It consists of cleaning debris, aligning hairs so the integument can adequately trap air, and waterproofing the skin and pelage by oiling them with sebaceous secretions.

The river otters on Whidbey always follow a foraging or hunting bout with grooming as well. It not only keeps them clean but also strengthens their kin bonds. Mom grooms herself and her pups; the pups groom themselves and each other. This is frequently followed by rolling, nipping, and, of course, the otter scat dance.

How else do otters stay warm in their chilly aquatic or semiaquatic environments? As homeotherms, otters, like other mammals, maintain a constant internal temperature of around 37 degrees Celsius (98.6 degrees Fahrenheit), generating extra heat by using their muscles to move or by reflexive shivering. They can also use *va-*

somotion, the spontaneous dilation and constriction of blood vessels in the feet and the tail, to help balance body temperature and prevent overheating or excessive heat loss.

As Jim and I sink into Admirals Lake, the visibility is not simply poor; it's awful. The lake is shallow, between 4.5 and 6 meters (15 and 20 feet) at its bowl. When we walk into the lake, we stir up the bottom, silt and mud mixing into the algal water. I check that my dive knife is affixed to its lanyard at my side; entanglements are common in diving-related deaths, even in shallow water. The large-leaf pondweed and Eurasian water milfoil around me are already entangling with my regulator and buoyancy compensator. Entanglements are common among marine animals, too, though vegetation is not the usual culprit. Instead, it's human-made detritus like six-pack rings, plastic bags, Mylar balloons, and abandoned fishing nets, called ghost gear.

Visibility is even worse than I thought it would be. I can't see twelve inches in front of my face. We won't be able to collect meaningful video data in the lake today. I ascend to the surface and look for Jim's snorkel. He is already trudging up the bank, his fins hanging by their straps from his gloved hand.

"Hey!" I yell after him, taking off my mask.

Jim turns around. "Do you still have the coffee on?" he asks with a chuckle. He rarely lets disappointment affect his sense of humor. "There's no point in continuing," he adds. "We couldn't see if an otter was directly in front of our faces and feeding us fish, Nicklen-style."

He's referring to Paul Nicklen, the marine biologist

and videographer who, while on an Antarctic expedition for *National Geographic*, recorded a once-in-a-lifetime encounter with a leopard seal. Leopard seals are not like the cute, wide-eyed fur or harp seals whose pups look like cuddly plush toys; they are uber-solitary, massively jawed predators with at least one known mortal attack on a diver. But in 2006, over several days of interacting with Nicklen, a female leopard seal didn't attack; she brought him wounded penguins and modeled how to snatch them in what appeared to be hunting lessons. After several attempts at teaching, she gave up and just brought him a dead penguin, no doubt hoping this poor emaciated leopard seal would finally seize his dinner.

Not for the first time, I marvel at the otters' abilities. They were in the lake this morning, not four feet from where we would wobble in, and yet our limited senses prevented us from collecting any data, while they fed on sculpin they likely caught in just a matter of minutes.

Otters swim during all visibility conditions: murky, clear, day, night, and twilight. How do they do it? Yes, they have that transparent third eyelid to help them visually navigate underwater, but their sense of touch is also extremely sensitive and important for hunting. Like most mammals, otters have *vibrissae*, or whiskers, arranged in a grid, making a mask of sensitive touch receptors scattered across their muzzles. In comparison to the whiskers of terrestrial mammals such as dogs and cats, otter whiskers are longer, stiffer, and denser. The pores that encapsulate their vibrissae include blood vessels, oil-producing glands, and a collection of over 1,300 touch receptors and axons, making them extraordinarily sensitive.

Whisking—the use of whiskers to guide movement,

aid foraging, and boost tactile perception—is essential for otter foraging success. One study of European otters found that they took four times longer to find prey in murky water than in clear water—but when dewhiskered in murky water, they took twenty times longer, suggesting that otters rely on their vibrissae to supplement vision when the conditions are too murky for vision alone. In fact, their whisker complex is so fine-tuned that they may even feel their prey's muscular contractions in the water, actively adjusting their facial muscles so that their whiskers, like movable antennae, are oriented to maximize contact with the target surface. Whisking within the water column or on the bottom of a lake, river, or bay, they anticipate their prey's escape maneuvers.

This whisker specialization may even allow otters with eye injuries to survive. Hans Kruuk, the esteemed biologist and otter specialist, reported that he observed a Eurasian otter in the Scottish Shetlands with milky, opaque cataracts—and yet, despite the apparent blindness, its body condition was excellent. It seems the otter was able to successfully hunt and forage using only its sense of touch.

If our lake dive had any bottom time, Jim and I would need to follow a surface interval, taking time between the two dives to avoid getting decompression sickness, commonly called "the bends." But the visibility was so poor we didn't leave the surface, so Jim and I discuss an early entry into Admiralty Bay. Upon consulting the Tides application on our phones, we see it's now a flood tide, meaning the tide is rising. To make our dive easier, we decide to wait for the neutral current of the slack tide. I imagine we look absurd to any neighbors who might be watching, both of us draping hoses on every available surface as we rinse off the gunk from the lake and get our gear set up for our second dive.

The best entry into the bay is in front of an old buoy made from a used keg. When Tom and I first moved in, I used a range finder to determine it was 30 meters (98 feet) from the low-water line. This buoy has been my marker for data collection and is almost directly in the middle of the route Patches and her crew take to go hunting.

At last, the tide turns, and Jim and I begin our dive. Like the lake, the water is sediment-rich, not the emerald-tinged winter water I might expect given the time of year, but an ochre-brown consistent with the bottom. Still, the visibility is much better here, and what we see surprises me.

Despite its proximity to a celebrated dive site at the Keystone Jetty and a beach of smooth stones, agates, and sea glass, the area under the buoy is a desert of sand and silt, with sparse tufts of sediment-covered eelgrass. Seeing any eelgrass here is heartening; a marine seagrass that once flourished throughout North America, it is increasingly declining across all nearshore ecosystems.

Seagrass meadows perform many important ecological roles. They reduce the force of wave energy on delicate nearshore animals, prevent ocean sedimentation, and protect the shoreline from erosion. And, like forests on land, they *sequester*, or store, carbon, limiting climate change by reducing the amount of carbon dioxide in the atmosphere. When carbon is sequestered in the ocean, it's referred to as *blue carbon*. Blue-carbon ecosystems like seagrass meadows, salt marshes, and mangroves sequester carbon at a rate disproportionally higher than land ecosystems of equivalent size, making them all the more valued as subjects of conservation and close scientific observation.

But, eelgrass notwithstanding, the barrenness in Admiralty Bay is not what I expected. Patches and her pups are good hunters, but based on what we're seeing, it would seem they're also magicians, conjuring fish from sand. I've documented dozens of their foraging bouts, and almost every dive results in sculpin, English sole, starry flounder, crab, or greenling. Where did all the fish go? I wonder if the otter line where Patches and her pups hunt isn't just a little farther north.

When I look north, I realize I can see boulders in the distance—but those rocks don't belong there. As Jim and I get closer, we see they're dislodged bulkhead boulders, the ghostly remains of retaining walls ripped from their abutments by past storms and king tides. Once barricades protecting residential property from sea swells, they now serve as an aggregate of artificial reefs.

We swim to the first boulder. Rounded by the waves and covered with a variety of marine organisms, it looks more like a giant pod or egg. It reminds me of the scene in *Cocoon* when Steve Guttenberg stumbles upon a pool of aliens in enormous chrysalides. Clinging to the contours of this rock are purple encrusting sponges that, at this depth, appear ballerina pink. A forest of frost-colored giant plumose anemones stand at differing heights, each with over two hundred plumed tentacles; their soft bodies have a lit-from-within glow.

I double-check that my camera is on and filming, then shift my gaze back to the rock. Tucked between an anemone and a type of sea slug called a yellow-margin dorid is a four-inch prickly sculpin with a flat head and underbite. The mottled army green of its tapered body makes it appear as though it's wearing military fatigues. Like a little lieutenant on duty, it guards its rock with a sour expression, appearing to challenge me to a fight. I back away.

Although this prickly sculpin is too small to provide much sustenance for the otters, it's in the right genus. Its cousin, the staghorn sculpin, is a common catch for the otters, so we must be getting closer to where they fish. I focus on the sandy sea bottom and an outline appears: a diamond shape with a pair of pebble-sized eyes on its lower right side.

I dump air from my suit and yank Jim's sleeve, pointing down at the sandy outline of the flatfish. I adjust my camera as Jim descends and decorously touches the sandy boundary around the fish's partially buried, fan-shaped tail. In response, it ruffles its fins, dusts off the debris, and undulates like a flying carpet, resettling maybe two feet away. My inner predator comes to the surface: *Really? That's it? I can still see you.* It's an English sole. This is no challenge for an otter. Although female soles can live up to twenty years, this flatfish will not be long for this world.

Jim gives me the *Look* sign, two gloved fingers pointed at his eyes, then points to a checkerboard of twelve more diamond-like outlines—a parquet floor of flatfish in the sand. Bingo! We've found the otter line. I pan the video camera across the fish, almost completely camouflaged save for their outlines and the subtle opening and closing of their mouths as they pull seawater across their gills.

My dry suit starts to vacuum seal, creating a squeeze. I look at my depth gauge; we've descended to 45 feet, well within river otters' estimated maximum dive depths of

60 feet. I take the inflator hose on the buoyancy compensator and give a short, quick blast of air into my suit, but it's too much, and my ascent is swift and uncontrolled. In a flash, my uncle grabs my foot and pulls me down, hard. He burps air from my suit and wags his finger in front of my mask. I'm embarrassed; poor air management is a rookie move. I'm clearly out of practice.

Fortunately, it's not a deep dive, so it wasn't a life-threatening mistake. In the meantime, I've descended into a small school of shiner surfperch, with their bodies so stereotypically fish-shaped they almost look like they were drawn by kindergartners. I regroup and focus on an adjacent boulder, careful not to touch the anemones affixed to it. A skeletal-looking northern kelp crab on long spider legs skitters down the rock and into a shadow, just a flash of orange carapace.

We've been in the water for 45 minutes, 30 minutes longer than Patches's typical foraging bout. As we continue our swim, I adjust my buoyancy to maintain the long, gentle kicks that will let me conserve energy and preserve the remainder of my air. River otter swimming looks rather different from my own. Otter kinetics can involve paddling, diving, undulating, bobbing, rolling, and somersaulting. To dive from the surface, for example, Patches bends her lumbar spine above the tail and gives a strong push with both hind feet, thrusting her tail upward and closing her ears and nostrils as she descends to the bottom. She and her pups are never submerged for long. They're economical with their water time, conserving their energy budget as best they can.

In the mid-1990s, a study of river otter locomotion noted that among six captive river otters, 88 percent of their surface swimming and 86 percent of their submerged maneuvering involved paddling. "Paddling" is not just one thing. It can occur in many different ways: with all four feet, exclusively with the forelimbs, alternating between fore and hind limbs, or hind limbs only. The style of movement varies depending on whether the otter is in a chase, treading water, adjusting its direction, or exploring an object. They deploy the up-and-down, body-to-tail flexions used in an undulating swim during maneuvering when a fish changes direction. This involves spreading the webbing on their front and hind feet so they can be used like fins or flippers.

We're now in 25 feet of water, and the shallow marine noise sounds like a rain stick. You might expect the sea to be a silent, tranquil place, but the wave activity mixes the sediment with the tiny shell particles lifted from the ocean floor, and they audibly tinkle against each other.

I watch for diving otter bodies, thinking how miraculous it would be for our dive to overlap with Patches and her pups' daily fishing excursion in the bay. It is early enough in the day that it could happen, but it doesn't. The otters have never been in the water when the seals or sea lions are close, and with our dry suits on, Jim and I may look a bit like sea lions, even if the suits are "yum-yum yellow," the name divers use for a common scuba suit color that used to be rumored to attract sharks. (It doesn't.) Although I know of no instances of pinnipeds preying on otters, the otters still give them a wide berth.

I wonder if we would have had better odds of diving with otters during low tide. Like most animals, otters are sensitive to changes in weather and season. They exploit food resources based on ease of capture and availability of prey; among behavioral ecologists, this is referred to as *optimal foraging theory*. A study of seasonal variation in river otter diets in California's Humboldt Bay found that otters adjusted their marine-foraging strategies to inland lakes and rivers during winter when tidal activity is highest. In other words, when the bay was rougher, the otters sought calmer waters, where it was easier to hunt. The Patches romp is likely doing the same, fishing between the lake and the bay, depending on which option is least energetically expensive.

It's time to head back to shore. There is no cool way to exit a dive. You're all snot and mask marks, seaweed streamers dangling from every limb like a saltwater Swamp Man in yum-yum yellow. And without exception, I always have to pee. As soon as I exit the water, the urgency hits, and I sprint up the beach. My uncle laughs. "Don't worry, I'll carry your gear!" he shouts after me.

Before dawn the next morning, I start my next excursion. Jim isn't interested in this one—no diving involved. There is frost on the asphalt, and a fog hovers between the houses, enrobing tall stands of hemlock and fir. I expect the Patches romp will fish the lake first, moving from their den on Crockett Lake into the brackish water of Admirals Lake and then to Admiralty Bay just as it reaches dawn during low tide, when hunting conditions become easier: shallower water, less active flatfish, and easier access through the culvert pipe.

I refer to their den on Crockett Lake, but otters may have many dens. An early river otter study using biotelemetry found that among river otters in western Idaho's North Fork Payette River drainage area, otters with implanted tracking devices used 1,283 different resting sites, of which 38 percent were beaver lodges and bank dens, and another 8 percent were snow and ice caves. Additionally, over the 16-month study period, a single otter used 88 different den and resting sites within its home range.

I head to Admirals Lake. The manicured grass and bulrushes along the curve of the lakeshore harbor a fresh otter latrine. I turn on my infrared binoculars and scan for emerging otters. You can't see bodies in the water with night vision, since water blocks most infrared wavelengths, so I focus on the tide gate. But I see nothing. I return the binoculars to the backpack, conscientious to make as little noise as possible. I don't want to spook Patches or her pups if they're out there and I just don't see them. In the twilight, I can't count on my vision, so I close my eyes and focus all my attention on listening.

I hear loons, seagulls, the whisper of waves in the bay. But there are no grunts, chirps, or purrs of otters. Figuring I might as well collect some of the spraints from last night, I pull a fecal collection kit from my bag.

Then I hear it: a soft, low purring, with clear starts and stops, almost like someone is saying the word "him" and elongating the "mmm" sound through closed lips: *hmmm-hmmm-hmmm*. It's coming from the lake's edge, punctuated by several high-pitched chirps.

One of the female pups—Crest or Slash, I can't be sure which in the twilight—pads out of the lake onto the shore. She shakes pearls of water from her fur and throws herself onto the grass. On her back, she worms from side to side, hind legs paddling in the air, scratching an itch on the sod. A second otter—smaller than her sister, so it must be Slash—bounds up the bank and tumbles over Crest, nipping at her right ear.

Both bounce into action. Crest chases Slash, Slash

chirps and swivels away, and they begin wrestling. I'm close, maybe twenty feet from them, but so far, they haven't noticed me. I raise my camera and aim, ensuring they're both in the frame.

Click, click, click, click!

Damn it. I have my shooting mode set to continuous. Ten loud shots snap in succession.

Both otters stop wrestling. They're not alarmed, exactly. They seem more perplexed, as if they've just heard a songbird cluck like a chicken. Crest raises her nose to scent the air. Patches, too, has emerged from the lake and stands stationary, vigilant, watching me. Swoosh is still submerged along the water's edge, holding his position, unsure if it's safe to come out.

This is the fieldwork equivalent of a spy getting burned. But they see me now, so I'm committed. I just have to sit here and see what they do. They can take off at any time, so I might as well get as many photos as I can, gambling that they'll habituate and tolerate my voyeurism. I quietly switch the camera mode to single-shot and take two more photos. *Click. Click.*

As if shaking off the confusion, Crest lurches after Slash, who hisses playfully at her. Patches marches up the bank. She shakes, stops, listens, and plods toward the tide gate. Toward me. I freeze. Does she recognize me? What is she doing?

Swoosh is out of the water now, sniffing at a tuft of pampas grass, unperturbed. He lifts his tail and shoots a spray of spraint onto the ground while alternating his left and right hind paws in a march. His claws grip the grass, and each step sends a clump of soil into the air.

Patches is facing me, ten feet away. She doesn't appear agitated. She just seems curious. She sits on her back legs, nose in the air, eyes trained on me. There is no alarm hiss, no growling. It's just the two of us. I slowly set down the camera. We continue like that, regarding each other. With other humans, I'm usually the first to break eye contact; it makes me feel uncomfortable and vulnerable in some way. But with this otter, it feels intimate and open. She's not judging. She's figuring me out. I am the chicken among her songbirds. Finally, she seems to conclude I'm like one of the many island deer: a big mammal, but benign, acceptable company in her foraging space.

She, too, relieves herself beside Swoosh's leavings and joins her teenagers in a bout of grooming, periodically stopping to hiss as one of the pups clumsily runs into her. I take more photos, turning the knob back to continuous mode to see if the repetitive clicks are now okay. The otters don't look up. All four of them are licking and felting their fur.

I realize I'm between them and the tide gate, their entry point to the bay. How do I get out of their way without disturbing them? I elect to stay put, deciding it's better to let them figure that out than change my position and potentially spook them again. As if in response, they stop grooming. Slash noses her mom, who rubs her face against her daughter.

Then, at the behest of an unknown urging, they all take off toward the bay. They bypass the tide gate and instead bound over the road in a train. Patches is at the head, and, as usual, Swoosh is the caboose. Down the smooth stones of the littoral zone—the shallow, sloped area where the land meets the water—they motor through the driftwood, onto the sand of the beach, past the barnacle-encrusted outflow pipe, and into the bay. It's low tide. The sun is peeking over the Olympic Mountains.

I descend the shoreline parallel to the otters. The wind is picking up; long rollers pull all four otters up the pocket of a wave and over the lip to the backside. I don't see them for a moment. Then I spy a tail flip up into a dive, followed by three more. They're gone, underwater.

A dark brown otter head breaches the surface with a sculpin, the tail dangling from her maw. Given how fast she captured her prey, I assume the otter is Patches. She starts chomping on her catch at the surface, perhaps waiting to see if her young ones are successful. They are. First one, then two, and finally, the lone Swoosh comes to the surface with his smaller fish. A wave curls, and they each duck into the narrow tube. I hurry to anticipate where they will bob up again. We are almost even with the keg buoy. The wind tugs at my hair. The calm of this morning has shifted.

I've been learning about the otters from afar, but now, it seems, they're also learning about me. Even as I attempt to keep my distance, the gap between us is narrowing as they go about their morning ablutions. I'm torn. I'm not a threat, and it feels like I've connected with this family, but for how long? And at what cost to the otters?

3.

Twitch

The Joy of Community Science

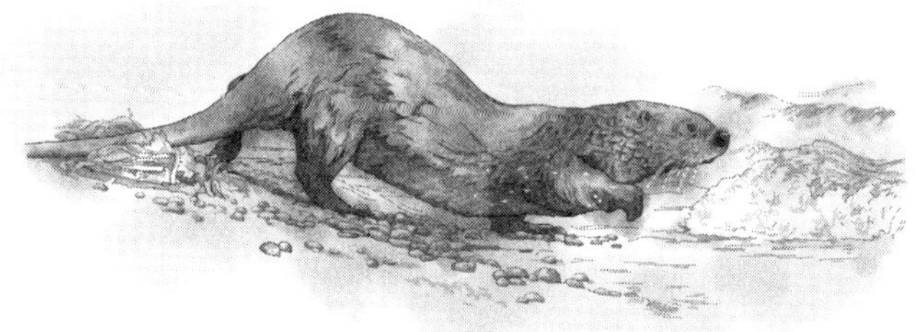

On December 18, 2018, just one week after my uncle and I go diving in Admiralty Bay, a tornado hits Port Orchard, about 65 miles south of Whidbey. It's a 2 on the Enhanced Fujita scale, signifying winds upward of 120 miles per hour—not that bad by Kansas standards, but for Kitsap and Island Counties, it's the largest tornado on record. In the Salish Sea, a tornado is a wind and ocean event, and this one hits during a cluster of extremely high tides known as king tides. Although the tornado misses Whidbey, the high winds do not.

On the day of the tornado, I'm not on the island. I'm not even in the state. I'm in Portland visiting Tom and our families for the holidays. My phone starts buzzing with weather alerts from Island County, texts from neighbors, and news updates. One viral video shows the passenger ferry *Coho* steadily climbing an impossibly tall wave to the zenith and sliding down the slope nose-first into the wave trough as swells break on the deck. A similar video of the Mukilteo–Clinton ferry from the south end of Whidbey airs on the local news.

In Washington state, ferries are an iconic image of stability, persistence, and safety. It's unsettling to see videos of 2,400-ton boats loaded with cars, trucks, and RVs being tossed about in the waves. It's even more unsettling when you know you'll have to board a *smaller* ferry to make the same crossing in the near future.

In Portland, a raging rain beats down on the metal roof of our floating home. But the house is fine, as it always is, rising and falling with the dock, its mooring hooks stoutly secured around four different pilings driven deep into the silt substrate of the Columbia River. The Whidbey cabin, situated on a low-bank beach, is a different story. I decide to head back early to check on it.

Tom loads his truck with flashlights and other emergency equipment. I drive behind him in my Prius with the dogs. The road is a tempest. I wrestle the steering wheel against the wind, careful to stay out of the grooves that might pull me into a hydroplane. My thoughts land on the otters, and worst-case scenarios begin to play out on the stage of my imagination.

I picture Slash caught in an ocean wave, desperately calling for her family. She disappears from view behind the next swell, only to reemerge wild-eyed, chirping, and panicked. Exhausted, she can do nothing more. She is pulled out to sea.

Another mental scene unfurls: four otters, their eyes squinting against the pelting rain, running in a tight cluster across the road. In their haste to get to safety, they don't notice the car. There is a shriek of brakes, and—

Enough. I turn on an audiobook. It's hard to shake my anxiety, but the truth is that river otters—with their thick coats, flexible diets, keen senses, and limited predators—adapt quickly to changes in weather. Patches and her pups are most likely huddled together, warm and dry, in their den or burrowed beneath the residential decks of their human neighbors.

Among coastal California river otters, researchers in Humboldt County found that during storms and other inclement conditions, otters moved inland, where they could find greater cover and more accessible food. They returned to marine areas in late spring, when the weather was better. Whidbey offers no "inland"—it's a long, skinny island, 10 miles across at its widest—but more than 50 percent of the land area is undeveloped, with forests, lakes, ponds, prairies, agricultural areas, marshes, and open bays. The habitat is diverse enough that the otters have a lot of options for where to weather a storm. Washington sea otters also remain faithful to their home ranges, riding out rough weather in sheltered, nearshore areas, often wrapped in kelp or hauled out on land. The mortality risk is highest for the youngest sea otters, as swells, wind, and wave strikes can separate pups from their mothers, leaving them vulnerable to hypothermia, drowning, and predation.

After three hours of driving, we reach Port Townsend, where a ferry will take us and our cars across the water to Whidbey. The crew directs Tom to drive up the ramp onto the first deck of the *Kennewick*. Under normal conditions, the front row is prized for its unobstructed view of the ocean. I'm usually at home on a boat, but today, I feel like a nervous kid boarding her first roller coaster, only to be placed in the front car.

I pull the emergency brake, gather the dogs, and get out of my car.

A crew member in a yellow vest stops me just as I open the passenger door of Tom's truck. "There'll be heavy seas in the channel," he says. "You two need to stay put in your cars for the whole crossing."

"How have the crossings been today?" I ask him, knowing this is a stupid question.

"The rest of today's crossings have been canceled due to wind," he says, wedging black rubber chocks against our tires. "But we have a good captain. Either we make it across, or he turns around. We turned around once yesterday."

I get into Tom's truck.

As the *Kennewick* pulls away from the dock, the sky looks like a Rembrandt painting, oily and atmospheric. The ferry dips as we encounter the first set of big waves in the channel. A sneaker wave glances off the ship sideways, pitching the ferry to the port side. Cables and lines snake out from their stays, clanging against the ship's metal shoulders. The ferry misses an approaching swell just to hit the next one mid-break. Seawater crashes onto the deck, whooshing beneath the truck and through the ferry's scuppers, back out to sea. The usually thirty-minute crossing expands as the captain maneuvers slightly off course.

In the distance, Crockett Lake and the whole of Keystone Spit look wrong, but I can't quite place what's off.

Just then, the captain turns sharply toward the starboard, and we move farther off course for several minutes.

"Aw, man, I think he's turning around," Tom says. "I'm glad we skipped lunch." Tom is an experienced mariner who once held a 100-ton captain's license, though it's now expired. Despite that, I can see he's fighting nausea; his face is colorless as he chews on mint gum.

A voice from the loudspeaker informs us that the conditions will push us into the dock too fast, so we have to enter the harbor at an angle. We aren't turning around, just readjusting for docking. As we pass the Keystone Jetty, the captain reverses the thrusters. One final lurch, and we're docked. I get back into my car before the crew signals us to disembark.

The spit is flooded. Small islands of pavement peek from pools of standing water. We manage to drive past Crockett Lake without swamping my engine, but then we come across a downed power line. There is no getting to the cabin this way. Tom turns left, taking the back road to our house.

As we follow the bend of the highway, I realize why everything looked wrong from the water. There are no lights anywhere. It's dinnertime, yet there's no warm glow from house lights, no flickering of televisions, and no streetlights. The power is out on the island.

The sight as we pull into our driveway is peculiar. One of our kayaks is planted vertically like a blue, plexiglass tree against the cabin's yellow siding. The second kayak appears to have surfed onto the thick rope that serves as a railing on the front deck, its bow sandwiched between the gutter and a deck post.

Tom ushers the dogs into the cabin. It is damp and cold. Using a flashlight, I go room to room, expecting to find broken windows, leaks, or other damage, but somehow the interior is fine. Tom starts a fire in the fireplace, and I light the pilot on the stove to make a pot of tea. The fire instantly cuts the chill.

In the morning, we assess the property for damage. All along Admirals Cove, storm-worn homes are dotted with flotsam, beach wrack, driftwood, weatherworn furniture, and ocean trash like vibrant, plastic flowers. Our neighbors Tipp and Annie have a sailboat that has sailed onto their back deck, likely accounting for at least one of their house's many broken windows. They're not on the island, so I text them photos, attempting to reassure them that the rest of their house seems fine. Our neighbor Theresa is rattled; she'll have to rent a sump pump to empty her basement garage.

I knock on the door of our neighbors Bob and Brenda's house. Bob emerges from his backyard and enfolds me in a hug. He's wearing a tattered Fish and Wildlife jacket from his career as a biologist for the state of Alaska.

Brenda isn't far behind. "Honey, are you two okay?" she asks. "Do you have heat?"

I tell her Tom retrofitted the old fireplace with a gas insert, so we're warm enough and can cook on the gas stove.

"Oh, that's good," she says, squeezing my shoulder. "We have a generator, so we're fine, but some neighbors don't have heat or flashlights. We've invited everyone to the house around six to warm up and share supplies. If you have extra flashlights, please bring them."

Tom and two other men stand above a Bobcat skid-steer loader, a miniature excavator our neighbor rented, looking like children with a new toy. My gaze drifts back to the bay as they murmur words like "loading capacity" and "radial lift."

It's a minus tide, the lowest I've seen on the island. The two bulkhead boulders I explored with Jim during last week's dive are exposed. *Isn't that what happens before a tsunami?* The tsunami warning sign at the entrance to the neighborhood comes to mind. I start mentally ticking off other indications: an earthquake, a rapid tidal drawdown, and a loud ocean roar. There was no earthquake, a negative tide is a natural counter to the king tide, and it's quiet. Confident there will be no big wave, I head down the beach. I notice twenty or more tiny Christmas anemones, their green-and-red-striped amorphous bodies clinging to the rocks, barely above water.

I start walking toward my garden of trail cameras, also called "trap" or "trophy" cameras, just south of the beach in an upland forested area. I'm worried they were uprooted in the storm. I call the dogs and grab my field bag—and a garbage bag. The beach is littered with rubbish: Styrofoam bits, the wet cotton candy of house insulation, several plastic tampon applicators, red shotgun casings, flattened bottle caps, boat fenders. As seagulls pick through beached jellyfish, I walk the shore, gathering trash as I go.

By the time I'm a quarter mile from my camera sites, the garbage bag practically weighs as much as I do. I drag the marine debris up the bank toward the dumpsters by the community pool. The dogs nose around the driftwood piles, pinballing from one scent to the next. Patches and her pups frequently pass through this path in the early dawn or after twilight. It's an incautious route, but once the otters get past the pool's dirt parking lot, the path offers unfettered access from the lake to the beach.

Suddenly, I notice tracks stamped into the still-wet sand: clear impressions of the five teardrop toes and C-shaped palm pads of an otter. River otters' bulbous toe pads on both front and hind feet leave deep compressions in the sand. Sometimes the webbing is even visible, as it is in these tracks. The rear feet look wider than the forepaws, because the hind feet have a dropped pinky toe. Among these tracks, the hind paws are almost even with the front feet; the otter was galloping. Overlapping the tracks are two more sets of prints, indicating at least three otters in this romp. The tracks are fresh, with sharp edges.

As I tread farther up the path, the tracks change direction. In the middle of the crisscrossing prints is a hollow made by an otter rolling and rubbing its feet, head, neck, and torso against the coarse surface of the beach. The rolling may help dry their fur, remove microscopic salt crystals, and even convey play. Their hind feet have plantar glands within whorls of hair, so scratching at the sand also marks the area with their scent. It's otter graffiti: "We were here."

I smile, feeling like an outdoorsy Sherlock Holmes. It has taken me hours of otter observation to be able to parse behavior from footprints.

The dogs hover their noses just above the prints, keenly interested in the scent. I smell seaweed, salt water, and something else—petroleum? Creosote? I wonder what the dogs experience in their olfactory world. Can they smell the otters through the heavy odors in the air?

As a less sophisticated scenter, I have to rely on my dominant sense: vision. I pull my binoculars from my bag and scan the coastline for heads skimming the surface or a tail dipping into a dive.

I surrender the quest for my trail cameras, preoccupied with the possibility of spotting the Patches romp. I scan the sheltered arm of Admiralty Bay's south end up toward the northernmost point of Admirals Cove, called Driftwood Beach. But I see only neighbors searching for missing patio furniture and the skid steer plowing pebbles and beach stones around bulkhead boulders. A few birders have wandered this way, mirroring my posture with their binoculars fitted to their faces. I return the dogs to the cabin and continue walking.

The north shoreline is more exposed than the south, offering little shelter from the easterly winds. And yet, a wet, sleek otter body glides between the breakers onto the shore, appearing as though conjured. It shakes, sending water droplets in an arc from its head to its long, muscular tail. A second, smaller otter missiles onto the beach, less graceful, knocking into the larger one. A wave rolls a third otter onto the beach a couple of feet away, chewing on a fish. The fish head drops from its mouth onto the beach. Unbothered, the new otter plucks the fish from the beach and trundles farther up the shore, shaking water from its fur.

Three otters. Where is the fourth? Did I miss it? Am I too far away?

I look at all the people milling around in their yards. The beach is too active. I can't imagine the otters will stay visible for long, but the culvert is utterly exposed in the minus tide, so there's no cover there, either. Will they run up the bank where they are or enter the bay to use the exposed culvert?

In an instant, the romp runs up the bank.

I run, too, binoculars strapped around my neck, one hand holding them flat against my chest. I keep my distance, careful not to spook them into changing their direction. I know the road is closed due to flooding, so at least I don't have to worry about cars. My backpack whacks against my back as I hightail it up the bank, noticing the birders watching me through their binoculars. I have surrendered all stealth to keep up with the otters. I scramble over the bulkhead, slip on a fugitive snag from the storm, dash through the beachfront of a neighbor's yard, and emerge directly into the flood plain of the road. The salt water swamps my Xtratufs, seeping into my wool socks.

The otters are there on the opposite side of the road, scenting the air, cautiously ambling down the hill into the ditch toward the lake. They stop. Listen.

Can they hear the ridiculous human panting and gasping behind them? I hold my breath, willing myself to be invisible, stealthy—a spy in a green jacket and knit hat.

But I'm not a nature ninja. I am noiseless to no one, not even the birders, who watch me running with curiosity. I wave at them, hoping to convey nonchalance: *Nope, no birds here!* I turn back toward the otters. Three tiny heads, one after the other, tuck beneath the lake's surface, reemerging a hundred yards away in the middle of the lake before diving back under.

Sigh.

I squish my way back toward the cabin in soggy socks and muddy pants. Tom is in the front yard on the skid steer, pushing rocks away from the deck. He turns off the engine.

"Did you see the otters?"

"Yes, they snuck up the beach while I was picking up trash." Sitting down on the deck, I pull my foot loose from my boot with a sucking sound. "I managed to get a couple of photos, but was too far away to confirm that it was Patches."

"Who else could it be?" he asks. "It's always Patches."

"Yeah, but this time there were only three otters. I need to get her muzzle markings to confirm her identity."

He jumps off the Bobcat. "Do you think something happened to the fourth otter?"

I pause, remembering my worst-case scenarios. "I don't know. You hungry? I heard Brenda mention that Callen's is open."

Situated across from the ferry terminal, Callen's is on the main grid, which means it's the only place in the neighborhood with power. The restaurant has an eighty-year history. Originally the Ripp Tide, then the Keystone Cafe, it's now Callen's, named after the youngest daughter of the owners, a married couple who bought it the year prior during a visit to the island on Valentine's Day.

This is not an uncommon story. You talk with Whidbey residents, and you hear the same thing. They moved to the island on a whim, a fluke, or through serendipity. They were visiting friends or attending a conference. They lost their job on the mainland just as a better one on the island became available. They fell in love with the community and left their established life to start over on the island. It's as though Whidbey has a kind of sentience, selecting its people by providing the plot twist in each resident's narrative—a real-life, Pacific Northwest *Fantasy Island*, without the celebrity cameos.

Even the land under Callen's has good mojo. When plans were drawn for the ferry terminal, and the diner—then still the Ripp Tide—was scheduled to be leveled, residents came together to save the building, setting it on logs and rolling it across the street to its current location on Crockett Lake. Today, they're offering locals without power free coffee and use of the Wi-Fi.

When Tom and I walk in, our neighbors Tony and Lindsay wave us over.

"Was Bigfoot chasing you this morning?" Tony asks, raising his eyebrows. "You were on fire!"

"I didn't even see you!" I say.

"You seemed to be focused on the otters."

"I was! You saw them?"

"Yes. I saw them, thought of you, and then, there you were."

"The otter whisperer," Lindsay says with a smile.

"Ha! Hardly. I think I led some birders astray, though. I was surprised anyone would come to watch birds in this weather!"

"Some people were already on the island for the birds and then got stuck here with the storm," Lindsay says. "Maybe birders have bird tales like fishermen, and you just provided the perfect 'one that got away' story."

For three nights, the community crowds around fireplaces and firepits. Bob and Brenda offer rakes, blankets, candles, and flashlights. Tony and Lindsay bring cheese, bread, and honey from their beehives. I pass around a notebook to exchange contact information with folks.

As it happens, Tony and Lindsay aren't the only ones who noted my morning otter chase. My dawn and dusk excursions with clipboards, notebooks, and cameras have made me an object of neighborhood speculation. Luckily, no one has mistaken me for a burglar and called the police, but I'm surprised to learn that many people in Admirals Cove don't know about our resident otters. Others, however, not only know about Patches, they also know people all over the island with their own communities of river otters. They offer me contact information, assuring me it's totally fine to cold-call a stranger about river otter sightings.

When the power is restored, our flashlights and spare batteries are returned, and so is my notebook, slightly battered, with dozens of names in varied handwriting and multicolored ink. *This is where I should have started*, I think. Before applying for permits or planting trail cameras around the island, I should've reached out to my neighbors, the strangers who came together during a storm to check on each other. The hours I spent hiking trails and exploring freshwater marshes were a great way to get to know the island, but if I'd started with networking, I would have had twenty or thirty pairs of eyes watching for Patches and her romp for the last several months. Instead, I've been muscling through it alone—until now.

I've just received permits to place cameras in Fort Ebey State Park when I receive my first "twitch." This is the word birders use for an email or text from another birder alerting them to an uncommon or otherwise notable sighting. I identify with the birders, all of us tucked into wool jackets and rain gear, trudging into the predawn cold with binoculars, cameras, and snark. (One birder I met in the field had a sticker proudly displayed on the rear bumper of his car: *BIRDERS HAVE LOOOONG . . . LENSES*.) So I've come to borrow birder parlance for my otter-sighting alerts.

This twitch comes from Jill: *Hey, three RIOT are in Admiralty Bay*. Birders shorten the names of birds and animals to four-letter codes; RIOT is short for RIver OTter.

Unfortunately, I'm miles away. I text back, *Just 3?*

Yes, John and I have been watching them for 10 minutes.

I'm not alone in recruiting a community to help monitor wildlife. Because river otters throughout North America have different habitats, predators, food sources, den options, and mate availability, they adapt their foraging, diet, territoriality, daily activity, and breeding to accommodate these environmental variables. This makes river otter behavior regionally unique—and the study of their behavior a challenge. To combat this, many scientists enlist help in their communities to track and monitor animals.

The River Otter Ecology Project near San Francisco has an "Otter Spotter" program, where otter sightings can be documented using an online platform. A similar program at Cardiff University uses mapping software to collect Eurasian river otter sightings around Great Britain. I, too, create an online survey where people can report otter sightings, but the twitch texts allow me to respond in real time, like a firefighter ready at a moment's notice—my very own otter phone tree.

The phone tree expands as I get involved in local conservation groups. The same day Jill contacts me, I receive a text from Pam at the Whidbey Camano Land Trust. The Land Trust is one of the most visible nonprofit groups on the island and maintains over 100 properties and 9,100 acres of protected land. They also have an army of advocates, from birders and biologists to environmental lawyers and retailers. The Land Trust protects shorelines, removes invasive weeds, restores endemic plants and habitats, and now connects residents with each other in support of research. Pam, a volunteer for the Land Trust, found fresh otter scat at one of the beach cleanups by her house; when she shared this with the education director, he gave her my email.

After collecting three scat specimens by Pam's home, I impulsively decide to hike an easement the Land Trust acquired along Strawberry Point. At 169 square miles, the island is the fourth biggest in the contiguous United States—not huge, but not tiny, either. With so many hiking trails and wild spaces, I want to learn all its varied habitats. Land Trust volunteers have just begun the labor of clearing the forested understory and establishing a footpath. I'm careful not to step off their trail. I can't tell if they've already begun pulling invasive plants. Some native plants, like the sword and deer ferns, extend their long feathery fronds into the path, brushing dew onto my pant legs.

The canopy opens into a basin prairie. Following the contours of the bowl, it bisects the meadow and ascends back into a thinned forest of Douglas fir, cedar, and pine. A lacuna in the understory offers views of Mount Baker and Mount Erie. With a start, I realize I failed to bring my camera. I thought I was only collecting a quick scat specimen on the beach by Pam's house. I didn't anticipate an impulsive decision to hike a nearby trail alone without a phone or a camera. *Well, that was stupid*, I think.

I turn to go back down the path through the meadow when I notice the quiet. I don't know when the red crossbills and song sparrows stopped chittering, but they're silent now. The hair on my arms bristles. I have the distinct feeling I'm being watched, and I remind myself that there are no nonhuman threats on the island.

Then I see him, peeking his head out from behind a tower of prairie grass, his left eye trained on me from under a cap of brown hair. I take a breath in. He and I have never met, but I know who he is. I'm even with his shoulder at 5 feet, 3 inches, but I'm 125 pounds to his 700. Bruiser, the island's infamous and only elk, is turning to face me.

A senior elk, estimated to be around eleven years old, Bruiser has a reputation as a rather crabby old guy. No one's quite sure how he got here. One of the local theories is that a decade ago, during a low tide, he and his herd swam along Skagit Bay to Whidbey's northwest tidal flats. He had just won the bull elk jackpot for unchallenged territory. But when his herd left, Bruiser stayed behind, and Whidbey claimed another resident from the mainland. From September through October, when elk compete for female attention, Bruiser has no competitors. No bulls to bugle a challenge at, no antler sparring, and no place for that energy to go—just an expansive territory with no cows. And now I've encountered him during rutting season, by myself, with no cell phone.

I have no idea what you're supposed to do when you encounter a lonely bull elk. I revert to the Alaskan hiking etiquette for moose encounters: Avert your gaze and keep him in your peripheral vision while slowly walking backward. Do not turn your back on him. Moose and elk are related. Both are cervids; both are huge and temperamental with humans. Hopefully, the rules are the same.

Bruiser flicks his right ear, still staring at me, and nods his head twice, two quick jerks up and down. Then he stuffs his muzzle back into a clump of grass, apparently confident I pose no challenge. I exhale, realizing only now that I've been holding my breath.

Bruiser is not the island's only local animal celebrity. There's also Ellie, a northern elephant seal who was first documented in 2010, when she came to the island to molt, and then again in 2015, when she came to pup. Ellie has birthed four pups on the island to date. Her son, Ellison, has garnered many fans despite—or perhaps because of—several "assertive" encounters with the public. It can be easy to forget these animals are wild when media attention generates Disney-character personas for them.

In some ways, I've been surprised by the seal family's popularity. In Oregon, where I've lived for over a decade, the fishing communities around the coast don't have much love for pinnipeds, the phylum of marine mammals that includes walruses, sea lions, and seals. But it helps that elephant seals don't typically hunt the endangered salmon, and their distinctive appearance and sounds do tend to pique humans' curiosity. Their repertoire of powerful, reverberating bellows, grunts, and screeches should be familiar for any fantasy buff; vocal recordings of elephant seals from the Marine Mammal Center in Sausalito, California, were used for the orcs' war cries in the Lord of the Rings trilogy.

But it's more than that. Whidbey holds its residents, especially its wildlife, close, because the island has a history of loss. Penn Cove, centrally located on Whidbey, is home to one of the oldest and largest mussel farms in the United States. But on August 8, 1970, it was the site of a different harvest, when more than eighty Southern Resident killer whales were rounded up with boats, planes, and explosives, to be sold to marine parks. Five orcas drowned, and at least thirteen members of one orca family were killed.

Although they're often called killer whales, orcas are members of the Delphinidae family, the largest of the dolphins. Found in all oceans, they're grouped into different *ecotypes* based on differences in behavior, such as hunting strategies and preferred prey. There are two ecotypes in the Salish Sea: (1) the marine-mammal-eating transient (or Bigg's) orcas, named because they traverse a wide geographic range from Alaska to California, and (2) the salmon-eating Southern Resident orcas, named because they live along the southern end of Vancouver Island. Because their main food source is endangered, the Southern Resident orcas are also endangered. They're now protected under the Marine Mammal Protection Act, but that wasn't the case on that day in 1970, when a five-year-old calf called Tokitae or Sk'aliCh'elh-tenaut was among the whales taken in Penn Cove.

For many years, the area's First Peoples, including the Lummi Nation, fought for her return. After a decades-long advocacy effort, the Miami Seaquarium agreed to release her, but it was too late. Tokitae, who had been renamed Lolita, died, fifty-three years to the month after her capture, in the oldest and smallest orca tank in the United States. When Whidbey Island protects its community—its *entire* community—it's with a fierceness born, in part, from grief.

Not all Whidbey wildlife is under such threat. Leucistic black-tailed deer—mottled white deer with splashes of brown, gray, or beige—are perhaps the island's most populous wildlife celebrities. Often mistaken for albinism, leucism (also called piebaldism) is the result of a recessive genetic trait found in about 1 percent of all deer that inhibits melanin and other pigments from being deposited in the skin and fur. Given the dearth of predators and the constrained gene flow typical of an island, these distinctive-looking deer are not uncommon on Whidbey.

Otters are not uncommon on Whidbey, either, yet they haven't achieved the celebrity status of some of the other local wildlife. Their crepuscular schedule and a general shyness toward people have helped them stay under the radar.

4.

What Is an Otter?

Otters' Evolutionary Origins

I kick off my Xtratufs and tug heavy waders with attached boots from my field bag. As I fasten the final coverlet on the bib and push my feet into the attached boots, I marvel at Lake Pondilla, situated about ten miles northwest of Admiralty Bay. It is an ecological wonder, from its ancient geology to its botany—the plush mosses and lichens, the water purslane, duckweed, mare's tail, and the dense evergreens. Waterbirds, mostly ducks, make awkward landings on the lake, disrupting the quiet with quacking that sounds like a nasal laugh. It makes me smile to imagine what a duck joke might entail.

I shuffle into the shallows, feeling like the Creature from the Black Lagoon in my oversized waders. At least they're a cheerful powder blue, so perhaps I look more like his perky cousin. My target is a well-used latrine, supervised by a couple of trail cameras affixed to fence stakes that I hammered into the lake's littoral zone. My Washington State Park research permit grants me access to off-trail areas such as this one.

This lake is much deeper than Admirals Lake. The tannin-colored shallows transition to the hue of dark coffee as the bottom of the lake drops. To my right is a copse of willows. On windy days, the branches sweep into the camera frame, triggering the shutter to record for up to ten minutes, which drains my batteries and creates false positives on the SD card that stores the images. Today, I swap out the SD card, but the batteries are still good, so I leave them to run down until my next visit.

Returning to shore, I step over a rotting snag that smells of wet soil and cedar. I know from the trail cameras' footage that this felled tree is furniture for a family of raccoons. A large raccoon sow perches atop it in the early-morning hours while her hands move beneath the lake, mining the mud for freshwater invertebrates. Her two kits curiously pat the water's surface, chasing each wrinkling ripple with their forepaws as their mother kneads the mud back and forth.

Camera recordings also show a solitary female coyote, probably a yearling, who uses the snag as a shortcut from the willows to a blackberry thicket. Occasionally, it also reveals a brindled male coyote with prominent cheek tufts and a robust chest. The male is about 16 kilograms (around 35 pounds), a healthy weight, with no observable mange or injuries. But he spooks easily, running out of view of the camera shortly after the trigger is deployed, despite its special "no-glow" flash.

There is an otter romp at Lake Pondilla as well, the reason for my trail cameras. For them, the snag is recreational; the juvenile otters use it as a sort of safe zone to avoid feisty siblings who want to wrestle. Like the Patches romp, this is a kin group, with a matriarch, four pups, and two adult females, likely the mother's daughters from the previous year. The camera shows that these two adult siblings come and go, sometimes with the romp, other times just with each other. I call them the Nine-to-Five romp because they're on time and reliable. I can count on them to be among the wildlife the camera captures each day.

This land that the snag rests upon and the lake that I wade through date back to Whidbey's early glacial history, during the late Pleistocene epoch, between 25,000 and 18,000 years ago—around the same time (geologically speaking) that humans began to spread out of Africa into other areas. That may seem like a long time ago, but you have to go back even further to find the first otter.

Twenty million years ago, during the Miocene epoch, a badger-like animal from the genus *Mionictis* genetically split off from other mustelids—the family comprising weasels, badgers, otters, and other similar carnivores—and began wandering the newly evolved grasslands of Europe and North America, quickly expanding into Africa and Asia. This is today's otters' earliest ancestor, from which all members of the subfamily Lutrinae evolved.

At least, that's our current understanding. But as with the origins of humanity, otters' evolutionary lineage is debated among experts in paleontology and systematics. When never-before-seen fossils are unearthed and a new species is pulled from the strata, scientists scramble to identify, track, and catalog its lineage and relationships with other species. What seems like a straightforward question—"What is an otter?"—can shift as new information is brought to light.

To fully appreciate the probability of finding a fossil important enough to cause the reevaluation of a family tree, think of trying to find a needle in a haystack, except the needle is splintered into pieces and hidden in millions of haystacks, and the haystacks and the needle shards are all buried underground. Millions of years later, when erosion exposes a tiny piece of that needle, someone has to recognize that it's something special *and* know enough to call on a paleontologist. Then, if that paleontologist has the requisite funding and the appropriate permissions for the dig location, the fossil can be excavated.

Alternatively, you could catch a lucky break, as in

2015, when a young girl walking a Vancouver Island beach found an unusual rock with what appeared to be bones encased within it. Fortunately, her dad took it to the Royal BC Museum, where the 23-million-year-old bone was identified as the clavicle of a new type of plotopterid, an extinct species of flightless, penguin-like bird named *Stemec suntokum*—the first ever identified on Vancouver Island.

For early birds, the clavicle is the second most meaningful bone to find, after the skull. For mammals, specifically the lutrines, it's the carnassial teeth. These are the teeth located behind the canines and formed by the fourth premolar in the upper jaw and first molar in the lower jaw in most carnivores, which function like scissors, often self-sharpening as they pass each other to shear flesh from bone or shell. If an otter damages a canine tooth, it might affect their ability to seize and kill prey, but the loss of a carnassial means the otter cannot cleave meat from bone. In other words, losing canines is debilitating, but losing carnassials is death.

Carnassial teeth differ between species based on selection pressures from their respective environments, which makes these teeth taxonomic treasures among paleontologists. Some carnivores have carnassials specialized for slicing meat, while others might show adaptations for crushing bones. By examining wear patterns, degree of development, how the upper and lower carnassials fit together, the height of the teeth's ridges, the sharpness of their cusps, and the compression of their root structure, paleontologists can infer an ancient otter species' diet, habitat, and foraging behavior.

Then there are the sea otters, who just had to mess up the elegance of otter *cladistics*, the classification of species based on shared characteristics and likelihood of a common ancestor. Unlike other otters, sea otters do not have carnassial teeth for shearing flesh. Instead, their molars have been modified into broad *bunodont* teeth. With a name deriving from the Latin for "round tooth," bunodont teeth are used for crushing and grinding, consistent with the needs of an animal whose diet consists mainly of hard-shell invertebrates like abalone, urchins, and clams.

Today there are three main branches in the otter family tree: the Old World otters of Africa, Asia, and Europe; the New World otters of the Americas; and the genetically unique giant otters of the Amazon. The Old World otters and New World otters are sister lineages, arising in the evolutionary record around the same time, while the giant otter, the evolutionary elder, has the earliest branching lineage, surpassing those of other living otters.

Let's take a closer look at each group, starting with the Old World otters. Some experts have argued that for simplicity's sake, they should all be categorized in the genus *Lutra*, like the Eurasian and hairy-nosed otters. But for now, they remain divided among several genera as follows:

- Eurasian otters (*Lutra lutra*)
- Hairy-nosed otters (*Lutra sumatrana*)
- African spotted-necked otters (*Hydrictis maculicollis*)
- African clawless otters (*Aonyx capensis*)
- Asian small-clawed otters (*Aonyx cinereus*)
- Congo clawless otters (*Aonyx congicus*)

- Smooth-coated otters (*Lutrogale perspicillata*)
- Sea otters (*Enhydra lutris*)

DNA evidence suggests that the lineage that gave rise to the New World otters split from the Old World otters approximately 9 million years ago; however, the timing of the former lineage's migration into North America remains uncertain. Their expansion into South America, however, likely corresponded to the emergence of the Panamanian land bridge around 3 million years ago, which spurred the well-known Great American Biotic Interchange. These migrant otters evolved distinct morphologies and, through speciation, genetically separated into the following New World species:

- North American river otters (*Lontra canadensis*)
- Southern river otters (*Lontra provocax*)
- Marine otters (*Lontra felina*)
(not to be confused with sea otters)
- Neotropical otters (*Lontra longicaudis*)
- Mesoamerican otters (*Lontra annectens*)

Though they're grouped with Old World otters, sea otters also live in the New World and are evolutionarily distinctive because of the selective pressures exerted by their marine lifestyle. Sea otters have a unique suite of adaptations, including dense fur, flipper-like hind feet, broad tails, highly efficient kidneys, greater lung and blood volume, greater tactile sensitivity, highly dexterous forepaws, and a metabolic rate three times that of their semiaquatic cousins.

The real odd otters out, though, are the Amazon giant

otters (*Pteronura brasiliensis*). They make up a third, solitary branch that's not really part of either the Old World or the New World otters. Mitochondrial and nuclear DNA analyses have shown that they have the highest genetic divergence, meaning they're the least like the other otter species. They're the largest of the extant otter species by length, though not by mass; they can be almost 2 meters (about 6 feet) long with a maximum weight of 34 kilograms (75 pounds), while the sea otter tops out at around 1.6 meters (5.5 feet) long and 45 kilograms (100 pounds).

In 2016, a new species of extinct giant otter was identified: *Siamogale melilutra*, the most recent of the ancient *Siamogale* otters, which lived in China roughly 6 million years ago. Like today's otters, this species was semi-aquatic, living in the marshlands of what is now Yunnan province. Its bunodont teeth could crush shells and bivalves, indicating it preferred the same type of prey as modern sea otters. Larger than its modern cousins, it had roughly the same mass as a wolf.

But the largest of the ancient otters were the *Enhydriodons*, which were closer in size to male lions. Today's sea otters are just a little heavier than my robust golden retriever; the *Enhydriodons* were 450 pounds. Fierce predators, they lived throughout what is now Africa, India, and Pakistan, sharing habitat with early hominids and competing with them for food. As opportunistic feeders, which adapt their feeding behavior as food availability shifts, they may have even preyed upon our early ancestors, though there is no evidence of this in the fossil record. These behemoths appear to be the earliest ancestors of present-day sea otters, and like contemporary sea otters (as well as *Siamogale*), they had bunodont teeth.

As well adapted as those teeth are for liberating mollusks from their shells, they're still subject to fractures, periodontal disease, lesions, and abscesses. Consider for a moment that both Tutankhamun and Ramesses II may have died from an abscessed tooth. Dental damage can be lethal, for humans and otters alike. That's likely why today's sea otters developed a behavioral adaptation to limit wear and tear on their precious porcelains: tool use.

Sea otters have flaps of skin in their armpits where they store stones for cracking open bivalves and urchins. Although they still use their teeth more often than not, modest tool use may spare them from the worst of the damage. It may also explain why they have fewer teeth: thirty-two compared to North American river otters' thirty-six.

In total, I have twenty-two cameras set up to digitally capture otters in multiple locations around the island: Strawberry Point, Lake Pondilla, Penn Cove, Admiralty Bay, Admirals Lake, Crockett Lake, Bush Point, Goss Lake, Deer Lake, a couple private ponds, and the mudflats in Langley overlooking Saratoga Passage. Every evening, I sit at the kitchen table, transcribing the hundreds of images I've collected into usable data.

Identifying the animals and their behavior in those images is tedious. Roughly 25 percent of the trail cameras' photos are false positives from when the sensor detects movement and starts filming but the videos or photos show nothing. Other times, they show humans, curious about the cameras, checking the permit number on my asset tags to be sure they're not for surveillance. I occasionally get an image of someone mugging at or, more jarringly, mooning the camera. At least it cuts the monotony, especially when they include a dance. I've been tempted more than once to save these in a "Goofs" file, but I delete them instead.

Aside from those false positives, I document everything: date, time, GPS coordinates, location names, and environmental variables such as tide, sea state, moon phase, weather, temperature, and other visible species. I also note if the EA-18G Growler jets from the island's naval base were underway or not. I cross-list behavioral observations with photo numbers and attempt to identify otters by physical features: injuries, scarring, approximate size, coloring, muzzle markings (if present), sex (if discernible), and whether I'm seeing a family group, a bachelor group, or a solitary animal.

This is a behavioral as well as an ecological audit. Through this process, scientists learn stories. The data starts to tell the otters' tales. Is there enough available food? If not, why is prey limited? What are the predator pressures? What is the quality, availability, and density of resources within the habitat?

River otters are *bioindicators*, meaning we can learn information about the environment through them because they're sensitive to ecological changes. One prominent source of ecological change is a nasty group of chemicals known as persistent organic pollutants (POPs) because they're extremely difficult to break down. They include many pesticides, lawn fertilizers, heavy metals, pharmaceuticals, and a supervillain of toxicology: synthetic fluorochemicals such as per- and polyfluoroalkyl substances (PFAS) and perfluorooctane sulfonate (PFOS). Since their inception in the 1940s, these chemicals have been used in all sorts of products, from food wrappers and nonstick coating on pans to waterproofing on raincoats and stain guard on furniture. They're often called "forever chemicals" because nothing breaks them down—not heat, not water, not time.

Because they've been used so widely for so long, and because they don't degrade, these chemicals have permeated our environment and our bodies. According to a *New Yorker* exposé, a whistleblowing 3M scientist found them in virtually every blood sample she tested from lab rats, humans, "eagles, chickens, rabbits, cows, pigs, and other animals." Indeed, "nearly all people have at least one forever chemical in their blood, according to the Centers for Disease Control and Prevention." These chemicals are toxic to plants and animals, causing chronic health problems, disrupting the endocrine system, and affecting fertility, among other issues.

In humans, as in most mammals, the liver processes these chemicals and isolates them from the rest of the body by storing them in fat cells. But otters have little fat as a group, and sea otters have almost none. Furthermore, otters are in a high trophic level, meaning they're near the top of the food chain in their ecosystems. Why is this a problem? They eat contaminated animals that eat other contaminated plants or animals, with the contaminants becoming ever more concentrated with each step up the trophic ladder. This additive effect is called *biomagnification*.

The Southern Resident killer whales (SRKWs) of the Pacific Northwest (like Tokitae, the calf captured on Whidbey) are a clear example of the challenges of biomagnification when a population is exposed to POPs. These orcas don't eat marine mammals like seals and sea lions; their diet consists mainly of salmon, and their absolute favorite is the endangered Chinook salmon. In their coastal habitat, Chinook are exposed to pollutants like industrial discharge, urban drainage, agricultural runoff, and any trace medications still present in waste-treatment water. They eat smaller fish that also live in the polluted environment, and those smaller fish eat food from the same polluted environment, and so on. The toxic compounds accumulate in each successive animal's tissues and biomagnify until they reach the orca at the top of the food chain.

Unlike otters, orcas have a dense fat layer, an excellent place to isolate harmful compounds from the rest of the body. But when prey becomes scarce and they become malnourished, the contaminants in the fat are liberated into the bloodstream, and depending on their concentrations, they can overwork the liver and the rest of the body's filtering system, causing illness or death.

In a landmark study of Southern Resident killer whales, researchers used scat-scenting dogs to find and collect 140 orca scat samples, which they analyzed for concentrations of POPs. They found that toxicity concentrations were highest when prey abundance was the lowest, likely because it was coming from fat stores. In most cases, POP bioaccumulation increased with age. Further, if an orca female is pregnant, those contaminants can be transferred to her calf through the maternal blood supply or through her milk, which may explain the high mortality rate of Southern Resident calves in the Salish Sea. An especially troubling finding is that the transfer of POPs from mother to child may be highest among firstborns. In fact, in 2014, when a pregnant female called J30, or "Rhapsody," died while giving birth to a calf, a necropsy revealed the calf's POP levels exceeded her mother's.

In the absence of significant fat stores, this process occurs even faster among otters. The liver must deal with accumulated chemical compounds each time a meal is consumed, and if those meals are exceptionally polluted, the kidneys, liver, and essentially the entire filtering system can fail, and the otter can die. The health of an ecosystem may not be apparent on the surface, but a sick watershed will reveal itself in sick otters. When regional otters experience a die-off unrelated to hunting, trapping, or car accidents, it usually indicates that we're poisoning the waters. And when we're poisoning the waters, we're poisoning everything, including ourselves.

The health and size of the Nine-to-Five romp—seven otters—may be partly due to the pristine waters of Lake Pondilla, one of central Whidbey's twenty-five kettle lakes, sculpted at the end of the last glacial period. All of Whidbey, the San Juan Islands, and the Salish Archipelago were once beneath 4,100 feet of glacier ice. When the glaciers began to melt 12,000 years ago, they left icebergs on the land, which formed depressions, or kettles, that filled with water, creating kettle lakes. There are kettle lakes are all over North America; Henry David Thoreau's Walden Pond in Massachusetts is a famous example.

Whidbey has an entire trail system around the island's kettles, including Lake Pondilla, where I now sit beside a bed of pine cones, fir needles, and coils of wet otter scat arranged in a ring like a fairy circle. I count nine piles in total.

The Nine-to-Five romp leaves the lake at dawn, moving from forest to bluff and bluff to beach along a narrow dirt trail. They bound through sand-loving lyme grass, enter the ocean, and head south to Point Partridge for their morning marine hunt. At dusk, they scamper back up the bluff on rock and sand, past the curtain of tree limbs, and down a trail of forest debris to the shallows of Lake Pondilla. But for all their coming and going, all I have to piece together the breadth of their activity is a series of snapshots from the trail camera, a plastic paparazzo tied to a fence post and painted in fatigue green.

But I'm grateful for the digital recordings. They allow me to see that Lake Pondilla is home base for the Nine-to-Five family, like Admirals Lake is for the Patches romp. They use a lakeside den and feed on the lake's snails, insect larvae, and state-seeded bass. In fisheries, *seeding* refers to the introduction of juvenile fish to ponds or lakes. Seeding fish can be problematic, transmitting pathogens from cultured fish to natural habitats; there's no way for otters to "shop organic" and avoid the farmed fish.

It feels strange that I should know the Nine-to-Fivers' activity so well, especially since, unlike with Patches and her offspring, I've never met them in person. Observing their behavior and activity from digital footage alone feels voyeuristic and one-dimensional, like following an acquaintance on Facebook or Instagram. The Patches family and I are part of each other's community. It is human to want to connect with your subjects, but at the same time, I recognize that connecting with me is not necessarily in the Patches romp's best interest. They don't regard me as safe enough that they would let me get within close proximity of them, but I am familiar and predictable enough that they allow me my creepy habit of following slowly behind them, collecting their poop and saving their hair. Still, I can't help but hope that perhaps they see me as something of a caretaker, if not a guardian, someone who wards off unleashed dogs and shares with curious beachcombers how to observe the otters from afar without disturbing their dinner.

Although otters within the same species may differ regionally in size and weight, most of the time these differences are modest. Even across species, there is very little feature modification. This is a nod to the fact that there was very little, if any, hybridization between otters across evolutionary time. But how can this be? There was extensive hybridization among other carnivores like the big cats, wolves, coyotes, and bears. Even among humans, sexual dalliances existed between our hominid ancestors and the Neanderthals. The likely reason for the otters' non-hybridized genetics is that geographic barriers like continental separation limited the overlap between species, even those within a narrow range.

Just 110 miles northwest of Whidbey, where river otters scamper back and forth from freshwater to coastal bays, sea otters float and forage in the waves along the Olympic Peninsula. Before the maritime fur trade of the late 1700s, their historic range extended from coastal waters throughout the rim of the North Pacific Ocean, from northern Japan to Baja California, Mexico. Today, Mexico is home to North American river otters along the Rio Grande and the Gulf of California, as well as a third otter species, the neotropical otter. Though the neotropical otters have the widest distribution of all the *Lontra* species, from northwest Mexico to Argentina, they look almost identical to their North American river otter cousins, except for their long, flat tails.

In fact, the neotropical otter reveals one of the challenges of charting taxonomic relationships in biology: *cryptic biodiversity*, the existence of two or more distinct species formerly thought to be one single group. In March 2024, a group of scientists mapped the genomes of the three subspecies of neotropical otter: *Lontra longicaudis enudris* in Argentina, *Lontra longicaudis longicaudis* in Colombia, and *Lontra longicaudis annectens* in Mexico. From these extensive genetic analyses, scientists determined that the subspecies found in Mexico was actually its own unique species: the Mesoamerican otter, *Lontra annectens*. This brought the number of global otter species from thirteen to fourteen (though amid all the dramatic news stories of 2024, this remarkable finding received virtually no press).

Although this was big news, it was not the first time an otter species separation had occurred. The Congo clawless otter was once thought to be a subspecies of the Cape clawless otter. After decades of debate, in 2004, it was recognized as a distinct species based on differences in pelage and dentition (Congo clawless otters have smaller cheek teeth). A year later, French zoologists reinforced the distinction after evaluating the systematics, genetics, morphological differences, and distribution of the two species. Thus *Aonyx capensis congicus* became simply *Aonyx congicus*.

So, what makes a new species? Klaus-Peter Koepfli, a senior research scientist at Smithsonian-Mason School of Conservation and one of the authors of the genomic analysis that identified *Lontra annectens*, put it this way to me at a conference:

> Genomics has two camps, the "lumpers" and the "splitters." The lumpers "lump" species into broader categories, while the "splitters" focus on the specific differences characterizing species, creating subspecies to help further differentiate their diversity. For an animal to achieve species status, it must adhere to one of four criteria.
>
> 1. There should be genomic support that the species are truly different, using evidence from mitochondrial, but especially nuclear, DNA markers.
> 2. Morphology should be different. In other words, they should look distinctive.
> 3. The geographic distribution should vary from other species.
> 4. The ecological niche of the two species should differ.

The neotropical and Mesoamerican otters, like the African Cape clawless and the Congo clawless otters, are referred to as a *cryptic species* because they were originally misidentified based on barely distinguishable physical characteristics, but in reality, each was genetically distinct and reproductively isolated. Despite that, there are subtle physical differences that distinguish the Mesoamerican otter from its neotropical cousin. For example, the Mesoamerican otter has a broader, more oval nose, similar to a dog's, while the neotropical otter's is banded, more triangular, and narrower across the nostrils. Because the distinction between the two species is still so new, scientists are scrambling to catalog the other ways in which these otters differ.

The African clawless otters are also very similar in appearance. In fact, they're so similar, the African Otter Network has guide sheets for field researchers to help them parse one from the other. Both species have large, stocky bodies, similar to those of Eurasian or North American river otters, though the reclusive and lesser-known Congo clawless otter is slightly smaller. They both have countershading in which the dorsal (top) surface of the body is darker and the underside is lighter, but the Congo clawless otter has slight grizzling of the dark hair on the top of its head and shoulders (much like grizzly bears' fur has a frosted appearance compared to brown bears'), with ears outlined in white. Both species have dark quadrangles around their eyes—think of the pattern of tear staining in white dogs—but for Cape clawless otters these patches are indistinct, while in Congo clawless otters, they're well defined and look almost like deep brown guitar picks affixed to the otters' buff or white cheeks.

Morphology and genetics aren't the only factors confounding the question "What is an otter?" There is also behavioral flexibility across species. Even within a single species, individual communities of otters may adopt behaviors to exploit their ecological niche. Their daily activity will shift if their hunting grounds are clogged with tourists, if predators are present, if a new otter enters a territory, or if food availability changes.

Even though otters can be active at any hour, the Nine-to-Five romp is strictly crepuscular, active at dawn and dusk. This is likely because of the operating hours of the state park they live in; they leave at daybreak when visitors start arriving and return at sunset when people are no longer around. Patches and her offspring live in a residential community with dogs and early-morning beachcombers, so they also forage and hunt during twilight hours. But other otters on Whidbey can be quite *cathemeral*, meaning their daily schedule can vary, without a specific period of rest or activity.

Then there's den location. Though river otters typically make their homes around freshwater lakes and ponds, a retired couple in Bush Point has observed river otters denning under the deck of their beach cottage for almost a decade, exploiting the Pacific Northwest rain and the brackish water along the bay to cleanse their fur.

As for food preferences, when low tides expose invertebrates, making them the easiest pickings, otters' preferred forage may shift from fish to invertebrates. These preferences can be influenced by season as well. I learned of a juvenile otter who temporarily occupied a pond on Greenbank Farm during the Pacific treefrog's spring breeding season. Rather than hunt at night, targeting the croaks of the nocturnal amphibians' love songs, the little otter spent hours in the middle of the day diving and swimming to gather the dozing frogs among the stands of cattails. It persisted there for four weeks, taking breaks to collapse cattails along the bank into a temporary couch and enjoy a late-afternoon siesta.

Frog feasting is not unique to this otter—the Eurasian otter is known to enjoy a whole array of amphibians—but for the otters on Whidbey, when there are so many more nutrient-rich options, frogs usually rank low on the list. The Greenbank otter likely made this foraging choice out of necessity. If he was male, he may have recently left his family romp along Holmes Harbor and discovered that this pond just across the street was the most convenient alternative hunting spot in the vicinity.

Typically, marine-foraging river otters have smaller home ranges, as the abundance of fish reduces the need to go searching for food. This is especially true for female otters, who limit their coastal range to 8 to 16 kilometers (5 to 10 miles), whereas males venture a little farther afield, 24 to 32 kilometers (15 to 20 miles). Point Partridge, where the Nine-to-Five romp forages, is only around 19 kilometers (12 miles) from Admiralty Bay, where Patches and her family hunt, and the deck-denning otters in Bush Point are just 8 kilometers (5 miles) from there. Do these otter families overlap during their morning or evening fishing trips?

The most accurate way to learn this would be through radio- or GPS-based telemetry. But for radiotelemetry, I would need to live-capture the target otters, give them an anesthetic, and surgically implant the transmitter. In addition to the specialized equipment and, of course, the aid of a wildlife veterinarian, I would also have to contend with the risks of injury or death for perfectly healthy otters just so I can learn where, how far, and with whom they travel. In other words, radiotelemetry is high-impact.

GPS telemetry is somewhat less invasive. Because it requires an external antenna, it doesn't involve surgical implantation, but you still have to capture the otter (and, for some methods, capture it a second time to retrieve the data from the device). This means you run the risk of causing a health condition called *capture myopathy*, which happens when the animal overexerts itself trying to escape, resulting in metabolic and lactic acidosis, hyperkalemia (high potassium), shock, and even death. As a behavioral ecologist who studies animal wellness in both captive and wild populations, I give both telemetry options a hard pass.

A truly noninvasive method is studying *environmental DNA*, or eDNA, genetic material that can be collected from the environment rather than directly from the animal. Think of it like an investigation on a crime show in which forensic scientists use DNA left at the crime scene to identify the killer. Biologists do the same in the field—but it's much harder than in crime shows, as the eDNA doesn't stick around for very long and is easily contaminated. It's also not cheap.

This is why I rely so heavily on photos and videos. I can still run density estimates using established algorithms; they're less precise, but still acceptable within wildlife science. Of course, those algorithms are based on the number of latrines, which is why I always feel like the Patron of Poop, the Scat Scientist, the Lady of the Latrine, as I study romp overlap and every other aspect of otter life on Whidbey.

5.

Fur, Feathers, Shells, and Scales

What Otters Eat

It's January. I spend the morning, as I spend many mornings, at the lake with Patches and her girls—but no Swoosh. I haven't seen him since before the storm in December, and I'm trying not to let my worries get the best of me. After the otters finish their morning swim, I go for a run, come home, and take a shower. And then, as soon as I step into the kitchen, there he is. Swoosh is in the bay!

I grab my camera and dash out the door, still wet from the shower, in only a robe and slippers. I hope my neighbors are still in bed as the mist of the morning marine layer chills my bare legs.

As I lift my camera to my face to get a better view, I wonder: What the hell is Swoosh eating? He's chomping open-mouthed on an orangish-brown, wriggling . . . snake? There are no sea snakes in Admiralty Bay or any waters in the Pacific Northwest. It's also not an eel or even one of the local wolf eels, which are technically not eels at all but saltwater ray-finned fish (much like koala bears are not bears but marsupials and killer whales are actually dolphins). I extend my lens and see that Swoosh's catch, now headless, is indeed not a wolf eel but a crescent gunnel, another long, eel-like fish roughly the size and shape of a hot dog—far more manageable for an otter.

Swoosh polishes off the gunnel and tucks his head beneath the water in a dive. I begin to count: *One, two, three, four* . . . I have no idea where he'll pop up again, and in my haste to get a look at him, I didn't bring my notebook to document dive times. So, I wait, camera in hand, standing like a goober in my bathrobe and slippers.

Patches's pups are edging toward a year old, when they'll no longer be considered pups, but they also won't be sexually mature for another year. As the equivalent of a teenager, Swoosh is going the way of young otter bachelors everywhere, exploring and having adventures on his own. He may run across other male adolescents on an otter version of Rumspringa, and they might begin hunting and resting together, learning the essential skills of adulthood like finding a mate and establishing territorial boundaries.

Piercing the quiet is the staccato, high-pitched piping of a bald eagle. Bald eagle females are about 25 percent larger than the males, and this one is signaling her readiness to mate with a chatter call. Using my camera as a scanning scope, I follow her distinctive *kwit, kwit, kwit, kee-kee-kee-ker* to a Douglas fir. About 150 feet up the trunk, she stands atop her enormous nest, a platform of twig, sod, and moss. She's multitasking, calling to her mate between housekeeping responsibilities. She works a branch free from the platform with her beak and unceremoniously lobs it off the edge. It's the tail end of eagle breeding season. Perhaps a little nursery remodel was in order.

Soaring above Admiralty Bay, just off the shore, is her mate. His broad wings glide over the bay as he scans the tide, his white-feathered head pointed downward, following a thread of bubbles where Swoosh resurfaces. Slowly, I stalk south, tracking the bubbles' progress through my camera's viewfinder.

A wet otter head breaches the surface. Swoosh has two gunnels between his teeth. Judging by their lifeless bodies, it appears he dispatched them at the bottom. Crunching on his catch, he chews fast, and within seconds, both fish are gone. Back down he goes. I start counting again, and after roughly three minutes, he's back at the surface, this time with a starry flounder clamped just behind the head. It's a big one, the size of an oval-shaped place mat, with a chestnut-striped fin on either side. Starry flounders are named for the rough, raised, star-shaped scales on the dorsal surface of their bodies. My dad used to call them "rough jackets," their nickname among fishing people, descriptive of the scales' texture rather than their shape.

Swoosh changes course. Instead of moving farther south, he tacks toward the concrete culvert currently exposed in the low tide. It's just feet from where I'm standing. I back away slowly. I don't want to displace him from the safety of the culvert, which is a good spot for him to eat his meal. But he looks right at me and doesn't change course. We hold each other's gaze for a few seconds, until I reluctantly look away, breaking eye contact.

Animals, like humans, have cultural behaviors, some universal and some regional. Among many predators—wolves, big cats, and nonhuman primates, for example—direct eye contact is a challenge, a way to establish dominance. I don't know if this is also true for otters, but I would rather act on what I know than what I don't. Regardless, Swoosh is unbothered. He doesn't seem to care about how close I am to him or who is dominant. He has camped out on the shore, not particularly aware of or concerned about his surroundings, though he's close enough to bolt back to the concrete culvert if need be.

His mother, Patches, is also in the habit of bringing her larger catches to shore rather than eating them in the water. But unlike her son, she doesn't get lost in the food. Gauging where the threats are, she'll tentatively swim along the intertidal zone until she finds a site she feels is safe. She stays alert, wary of every noise and interloper. Swoosh's eagerness to eat has overridden his caution, but at least he's positioned himself for a quick exit if he needs it. Perhaps he has internalized this lesson from Patches after all.

Swoosh's fishing success has garnered the attention of a great blue heron balancing atop an undulating raft of bull kelp in the bay. She relocates to the beach, just feet away from Swoosh, who doesn't give her a second glance. I don't think she's close enough to rob him of his catch, but she's eyeing it. Without blinking, she inches her long neck forward. In slow deliberation, she raises her left leg, as if practicing tai chi, then lowers it, a foot closer to Swoosh and his catch.

"Come on, Swoosh, move!" I whisper. "You're gonna lose your breakfast."

At that moment, the heron lunges for the flounder's tail. Swoosh snarls and bites down on his catch, dragging it as he bounds up the bank into the culvert. His fast reaction startles the heron, and with a banshee screech, she is aloft.

"Well done," I murmur. I wait, watching as the heron pilots toward the lake, the entry point of the culvert. Could she be anticipating where Swoosh will emerge? I consider heron intelligence. In animal cognition, the ability to take the perspective of another being and anticipate its behavior is referred to as *theory of mind.* Animal cognition psychologists have studied nonhuman animals' theory of mind for fifty years, and only a handful of mammals (like primates, bottlenose dolphins, and elephants) and birds (primarily parrots and corvids) are thought to have this ability. But if the heron is predicting where Swoosh will exit the pipe, maybe herons are capable of theory of mind as well. Swoosh's head peeks out of the duct again on the same side he went in, just his muzzle and whiskers exposed from the circular concrete. He has outfoxed the heron.

Swoosh glances around, ducks back into the culvert, and scales the concrete conduit to the rim, dragging the flatfish between his teeth. Perched in a huddle, protectively shielding his catch from the aerial pirate, he works quickly, biting off big pieces of the tail into ingestible chunks. Relaxing his posture, he tilts his head back, directing the fall of masticated meat into his throat.

I raise my camera to my eye just as a flurry of dark feathers descends—the bald eagle has moved in on Swoosh and his breakfast! Swoosh, surprised, protectively lands on his fish. The eagle makes another pass. This time, Swoosh takes what's left of the mangled flatfish and tucks back into the outflow pipe, just as he did with the heron. The eagle appears to surrender, gliding away and landing on his nest beside the female. Swoosh has outmaneuvered his second avian looter of the morning.

This kind of thievery between species, called *kleptoparasitism*, is a common threat for all otters, which share their habitats with many opportunistic predators. In fact, coyotes in Point Reyes, California, were documented over seven years scavenging local river otter caches of brown pelicans stashed along the bank of a lagoon. In one instance, a coyote stole a recently killed coot, a dark gray waterbird with a distinctive white beak, from six river otters who attempted to defend their cache, but with no success. The coyote absconded with the coot, and the otters had one less bird in their larder.

I've never seen Whidbey otters stash prey in this way, which illustrates otters' regional adaptability. But I have seen them take down birds. On Christmas Eve, I watched a lone otter surreptitiously slip beneath a group of sea ducks called surf scoters. Rather than absconding with a drab female, he went for a more lavishly adorned male. On each side of the males' vibrant orange bills is a white spot with a black dot in its center, like a talisman against the evil eye. But that talisman provided no protection. The otter grabbed one of the duck's feet, and held it under as it thrashed until it eventually drowned. Exhausted, the otter slowly swam to shore, dragging the dead duck by the foot, a Christmas canard for an epicurean otter.

North American river otters are not alone in their opportunistic bird predation. In March 2023, a Cape clawless otter was documented for the first time actively hunting and killing an African penguin along the Cape Peninsula near Simon's Town, one of two mainland colonies of penguins in South Africa. These critically endangered birds, with fewer than 800 breeding pairs, have been the targets of other terrestrial predators like Cape leopards, caracals, domestic dogs, and grey mongooses; now they've become a target of otters as well.

Despite these avivorous examples, otters' preferred prey is thought to fall within two *trophic groups*, or dietary specializations. Most of the world's otter species are fish specialists, including North American river otters, Eurasian and southern river otters, neotropical otters, smooth-coated otters, giant otters, spotted-necked otters, hairy-nosed otters, and marine otters. The rest are invertebrate specialists, which prefer to eat mud- or bottom-dwelling mollusks, snails, insects, worms, or amphibians. This diet requires greater tactile sensitivity for mining the mud or using tools. This is evident in the unique anatomy of the invertebrate specialists' claws, which can be reduced (Asian small-clawed otters), absent (Congo and Cape clawless otters), or semi-retractable (sea otters).

Always the odd ones out, the sea otters are the only otter species that is almost entirely aquatic, the only species with semi-retractable claws, and the only durophage among the lutrine subfamily. From the Latin *durus* ("hard") and *phage* ("eat"), *durophagy* is the consumption of hard food such as shells or bones. Durophages evolved to overcome the physical defenses of their prey with strong teeth, muscular jaws, and a viselike bite force. Other durophages include wolf eels, wolverines, and hyenas, the latter of which eat and digest all parts of their prey, including bones and horns, leaving only hair, hooves, and the keratin sheath covering antlers. There are also herbivorous durophages that eat woody or fibrous vegetation, like the giant panda.

Sea otters' preferred food—hard-shell clams, mollusks, and chitons—are primarily *sessile*, meaning they're attached to something else and can't easily swim away, but the cost of this diet is a greater effort in consumption. Sea otters frequently use tools to extract their food, leaving *middens*, or piles of shell fragments, along the shore in their preferred foraging areas.

Hand-oriented and/or tool-using otters' reliance on touch requires specialization not just in their claws but also in their neural architecture. In the 1960s, the esteemed paleobiologist Leonard Radinsky used latex to make casts of the inside of carnivore skulls, revealing the anatomy of the brain based on the grooves of the skull. He found that the somatosensory cortex—a region of the brain that processes touch—varied in otters depending on their preferred prey. Fish-eating otters have a larger somatosensory area for input from whiskers; they use their long vibrissae to detect the hydrodynamic vibrations of fish swimming through the water. Meanwhile, invertebrate-eating otters, whose meals are either buried in mud or attached to rocks, have a larger area dedicated to forepaw touch. This helps explain why, if you give a fish-eating, mouth-oriented river otter a fish, it will reach for it with its mouth. But offer a fish to one of the invertebrate-eating, hand-oriented otters, like the Asian small-clawed otter, and it will grab it between its hands.

Sea otters appear to be an exception to the rule, as usual. Although their forepaw sensitivity is prioritized over that of their whiskers, their whisker region is still disproportionately large compared to that of terrestrial mustelids, including other otters. Their whiskers are not merely thick hairs but sensory antennae whose follicles are irrigated by blood and supported through dense connective tissue and nerve cells. Pinnipeds, too, have ten times the whisker-related nerve connections of land mammals; harbor seals, for example, use their 88 vibrissae to follow their prey's swim path, allowing them to quickly identify a fish's location. By comparison, sea otters have 120 vibrissae—more than harbor seals and three times as many as dogs.

And yet, despite the keenness of their whiskers, their forepaws are so sensitive that studies suggest their skills in object identification may exceed even those of humans, a species known for fine motor and sensory control. In 2016, at the University of California, Santa Cruz, a small sample of humans and a rescued southern sea otter named Selka were trained to discriminate between a series of resin plates with different ridges, bumps, and grooves. Both the humans and Selka learned to identify the different plates using touch alone, either in the air or underwater. Selka's accuracy was on par with the humans', but she could discriminate between the plates thirty times faster than people when using her forepaws (and fifteen times faster when using her whiskers).

Sea otters' need for speed in tactile discrimination is based on where they live. Blood flow to the limbs and peripheral structures is reduced in cold temperatures. This is a challenge for sea otters, since they forage both during the day and at night, when temperatures are typically coldest. To further complicate energy conservation, they lack fat, and their fur must remain clean in order to retain air and provide insulation. All of this confers unique selection pressures on sea otters. Their world is aqueous, cold, and turbulent, often with low light and poor visibility. Speedy discrimination of food is crucial, since, on a given day, sea otters must eat 25 percent of their body mass, and their preferred prey, shellfish, offer less energy per kilogram than fish. To adequately meet these metabolic needs, sea otters spend roughly half their day diving for invertebrates, restricting their range to nearshore areas with brown and red seaweed, where their food is reliable and the dense kelp forests provide protection from predators.

Because of their fidelity to place, sea otters have had to adapt to the extreme challenges of life exclusively at sea. These adaptations include specialized teeth, webbed hind feet, and large kidneys that allow them to drink salt water, which would cause severe dehydration for most terrestrial mammals. They have also evolved more efficient oxygen storage, allowing them to stay underwater longer and adjust their flotation while diving—usually in waters less than 65 feet deep, although one account documented a sea otter foraging dive at almost 300 feet. When river otters prepare to dive, they hold their breath, slowly releasing it as they ascend to the surface, naturally avoiding the bends. But for sea otters, that would present two problems: buoyancy (which could interfere with their dive) and increased pressure (which could cause equalization problems, lung collapse, and decompression issues when they return to the surface). To compensate, sea otters have muscular and efficient lungs, which can exhale up to 90 percent of their body's air, reducing problems with buoyancy and pressure.

Most otter species, however, are more flexible about both habitat and diet. Otters within the mouth-oriented specialization are known for their unfussiness when it comes to foraging. The giant otters of Brazil's southern Pantanal region change their foraging habits seasonally, eating more piranhas during the flooding season and hunting eels in the mud during the dry season. When the dry season extends into prolonged droughts, they've been observed hunting and eating yacare caimans, freshwater crocodilians found throughout South America.

The dietary flexibility of fish-eating otters allows them to forage in the ocean, in brackish water, in fresh water, and on land, both at sea level and at higher elevations, as long as water is available. For example, the spotted-necked otters of central and southern Africa occupy coastal areas, but also live at altitudes as high as 2,500 meters. These semi-social otters are the third smallest member of the otter subfamily (after the marine and Asian small-clawed otters), weighing around 8 pounds and stretching no more than 3 feet long. They get their name from the mottling or splotches on their neck and chest, which are unique to each animal, much like the saddle blazes on orcas, coloring on the tails of humpback whales, or fingerprints on humans.

The fish-eating otters, with their whiskers so sensitive they can feel the undulations of fish in the water column, have such hunting prowess that some human fishing cultures have learned how to exploit their skill. The Sundarbans, a protected preserve of mangrove forests on the Bay of Bengal in India and Bangladesh, are home to many endangered predators, including Bengal tigers, estuarine crocodiles, and three otter species: the Eurasian otter, the Asian small-clawed otter, and the smooth-coated otter. It is this last species, the smooth-coated otter, that is used by the *malo jele*, the fisherman community that employs the traditional practice of otter-assisted fishing. They take trained otters out on boats with them and use them to herd fish into their nets. It's a mutualistic relationship; both humans and otters catch more fish with less effort than they would otherwise.

Likely originating in China, otter-assisted fishing practices date back hundreds of years. But they are now dying out, and in the last several decades, the malo jele has been the sole surviving culture that collaborates with otters in this way. As recently as the 1990s, around five thousand communities in and around the Sundarbans were involved in otter fishing. But by 2022, those numbers dwindled to just fifteen families in two areas of Bangladesh using around forty smooth-coated otters.

This may seem like a win on the surface. Don't conservationists usually frown on domesticating endangered wildlife for economic benefit? But in this case, there's more to the story.

Because of their mutualistic relationship with otters,

the marginalized and economically disadvantaged rural peoples in the Sundarbans traditionally protect the smooth-coated otters in the wild. The fishermen train them by bringing juvenile otters out on fishing expeditions with adults, so the otters form attachments with kin, learn to hunt through social learning, and can survive in the wild. Thus, the malo jele otters bred in captivity actually support the endangered population. According to Mohammed Feeroz, a conservation zoologist at Jahangirnagar University and founder of the Wildlife Rescue Centre (WRC), "the tradition of otter-assisted fishing plays a vital role in conserving otters in Bangladesh through reintroduction, breeding, and rehabilitation of the species."

The dramatic reduction in otter-assisted fishing is attributable to the usual suspects. Declining fish populations, pollution, sedimentation, and other factors have made it hard to earn a living through fishing, and young people, particularly those with an education, pursue other work. The International Union for Conservation of Nature's Red List designates a species as Endangered if its population has declined by 50 to 70 percent over the past ten years or if its current population is fewer than 250 animals. By this metric, the malo jele communities are also critically endangered, and the practice may soon be extinct.

North American river otters adapt and adjust their diet depending upon the available forage. I'm interested in what Whidbey otters in particular are eating. Is there a pattern to when they hunt in freshwater areas versus when they hunt in marine bays? Is their choice of foraging area influenced by weather, human activity, season, or other variables? What is their preferred prey?

In an effort to better understand the breadth of Whidbey otters' diet, I find myself setting twenty-five Petri dishes in five rows atop a picnic bench on Admiralty Beach. These containers hold a dazzling array of bones, scales, and fur from soaked, cleaned, treated, sifted, dried, and labeled otter spraint. Each shallow dish contains the undigested bits of an otter's food, reflecting the diversity of the otter's palate and the most readily available meals. Several containers are embellished with button-sided vertebrae no larger than my smallest fingernail. Among the demure piles of bones and shells are cervical spines as thin and delicate as a single strand of hair. I marvel at the kaleidoscope of bits and pieces in virtually all hues: matte bone fragments; scraps of opalescent mussel shells in magenta, deep blue-gray, and mother-of-pearl; silver fish scales in translucent half-moons; dried sprigs of tawny fur lying like rosemary stems among shards of dull orange crab carapaces.

These samples were collected over several months from twenty-two different otter latrines, some by me and others by island residents. If I was the one who collected the specimen, I processed it immediately, immersing the fecal sample in distilled water and isopropyl alcohol, giving the excrement a week to break down. If I received the specimen as a "gift" from a volunteer who collected it on their property or on a hike somewhere on the island, it was frozen until I could drive to the volunteer's house to get it.

Initially, these transfers felt awkward, almost surreptitious. From the outside, the process probably looks like a drug deal, but it's actually much weirder. I drive to the home of a volunteer collector and knock on the door. They answer with a paper bag containing one or more specimen jars of frozen poop. I hand them a new collection kit, including a data sheet that asks for GPS coordinates, an explanation of the habitat where the specimen was collected, the date and time of day, the weather, the number of spraints present at the latrine, and if the volunteer happened upon otters during their collection. I say, "Thank you," and then . . . what? There is no standard etiquette for collecting scat from a stranger.

I fumbled the first handful of these exchanges until it dawned on me that, of course, the kind of people who are willing to collect scat are the kind of people who are curious about the natural world, open to new experiences, and generally have fascinating life histories. After I realized this, these interactions were no longer awkward. Curiosity was our shared language, and poop brought us together.

Neighbors and vacationers are walking Admiralty Beach, so they see me as I clean the samples at the picnic bench, transferring the soggy piles of wet fur, scales, or bones into Petri dishes to dry. The winter humidity is high here—a damp cold—and moisture is the enemy of cataloging. Before I can send the samples on to the zooarchaeologist who identifies the prey items within them, they have to dry for two weeks to dehydrate fully. At this stage in processing, I can't decipher the bits and pieces beyond "bird," "fish," "mammal," and "insect."

Two women walking their dog saunter up the beach to see what I'm doing. One of them comments on how beautiful my craft project is. Given the density of art galleries in Whidbey and throughout Puget Sound, she understandably assumes that I'm making artwork with the local beach treasures. And in a way, I am. Scat *is* a treasure.

According to veterinarian David Waltner-Toews, author of *The Origin of Feces*, a comprehensive and often funny account of the value of excrement in science, conservation, and history, excrement is 75 percent water. The remaining 25 percent includes a variety of microorganisms (such as bacteria, yeast, shed parasites, and archaea) and metabolic waste products (such as red blood cells, bile, and a bile pigment called stercobilin that's responsible for scat's brown color). There is also, of course, undigested carbohydrates, fiber, protein, and fat; dead epithelial cells; and anything an animal ingested that cannot be broken down, like feathers, fur, bones, scales, and exoskeletons. In the case of my golden retriever, Gracie, these undigested materials occasionally include a puff of polyester from the bowels of a forbidden plush toy gifted to her on the sly by my indulgent dad. Those indigestible parts are what make fecal analysis so useful in animal science.

Most mustelid species produce an anal-gland secretion, a strongly scented substance with a consistency ranging from oily to paste-like. They also extrude a mucus called *scat jelly* or *anal jelly*, though I find the latter term confusing because this material is not manufactured by the anal glands but by oil glands and apocrine glands (the same type of glands that produce earwax, sweat, and breast milk). Both male and female otters secrete these smelly jellies, which are scientifically valuable because the sloughed cells they contain offer information on otter DNA, hormones, and accumulated contaminants. For example, they're a much better source of environmental DNA than feces, which contain a hodgepodge of DNA from otter, prey, and whatever is on the ground around them. The jellies are not always present and appear, among some otter species, only seasonally, but they convey a wealth of information such as age, sex, and endocrine cues related to mating.

A study of the chemical compounds found within otter scent glands identified 47 organic volatile substances. These are the type of quickly evaporating compounds often associated with strong odors, like the acetone in nail polish remover. Among the scent-centric otters, spraint volatility matters; it means the chemical compounds vaporize in the air and dissolve in water. According to their findings, the most abundant compound was benzaldehyde, a flavoring agent naturally found in almonds, cherries, peaches, and other stone fruits, and used in countless commercial products from baked goods to beverages to cosmetics.

It strikes me that *castoreum*, the scent-marking substance produced by beavers, was once widely used in perfumes and even some food products because of its vanilla-smelling compounds. In fact, in 1965, the Food and Drug Administration listed castoreum as a "generally recognized as safe" food additive and considered it a "natural flavor"—which does give me a bit of pause when consuming foods that list "natural flavors" in their ingredients. Luckily, to my knowledge, otter scat jelly has not been used in the same way.

Sea otters are the only otters that don't scent-mark. Since they only defecate in water and rarely congregate on land, scent-marking has no utility. But they do still communicate through scent in the form of *pheromones*, the small, volatile molecules released in urine, sweat, and other bodily secretions. Pheromones are produced by exocrine glands (like the scent sacs of otters, the anal glands of dogs, and the castor sacs of beavers) and detected by a special structure called the *vomeronasal organ* that is present in most reptiles, amphibians, and mammals, though notably not in humans. Most mammals rely on pheromonal communication. Perhaps the most recognizable form is when dogs sniff each other's butts in greeting at the park, exchanging information about each other's health, age, reproductive status, and more.

Between pheromones and scent-marking, otter latrines are more than toilets; they're communication stations for other otters, predators, and other scent-marking species, like raccoons and beavers. They also communicate territorial boundaries. And though otters don't recognize human property lines, often letting loose a slurry of sewage under someone's deck, they are attentive to each other's territory.

Regardless of the species, the point of establishing territories is to avoid conflict. If I know you're hunting in this area, I won't risk a fight with you by hunting in it myself—unless there's a compelling reason to do so. An animal might challenge the boundaries of another animal's territory if the resources within that territory are scarce and, therefore, valuable. It can be the difference between a full belly and starvation, reproductive options and isolation, safety and vulnerability.

Among humans, establishing territories begins almost as soon as we can talk. A toddler declares a plush toy "mine." Their parents do the same through fences, property laws, and real estate transactions, or, at a larger scale, through colonization and war. Otters' territorial claims are much narrower than ours and rarely result in altercations. Their boundaries are not closely guarded, but they are monitored. These property claims are more like labels calling dibs on food, mates, and denning and couching sites. These labels are visual and fragrant.

Otter marking on Whidbey is seasonal. It begins in the fall and extends into the mating season in late winter and early spring. During mating season, the removal of spraint samples could theoretically influence otter behavior by altering the scent-based messages they're sending and receiving. In a novel field experiment at Humboldt State University, researchers evaluated the effect of foreign and familiar scat on river otter scent-marking in the Arcata Marsh wetlands. They removed all existing scat and scat jellies from five of the most reliably used latrines and placed a five-centimeter layer of local beach sand over them. Then they added foreign otter scat collected from a different latrine site, local otter scat gathered from the same latrine, or no new scat. The otters' reaction to the foreign scat was surprising. They didn't overmark, as one might expect them to do if an interloper had violated their territorial boundary. Instead, they explored the scat, sometimes displacing it from where it was. Otherwise, they toileted normally, with some extra urine and scat jelly if the site had been completely cleared.

Although this study found no evidence that otters would leave or stop using a site when scat was removed, I never removed all spraints from a latrine on Whidbey, for fear of disrupting the otters' scent-marking. I had another motivation as well. Since coastal river otters eat marine fish and invertebrates, their waste provides marine-derived nitrogen, which is great for fertilizing plants. This is why, if you use a commercial fertilizer on your houseplants, there's a good chance it's a nitrogen-rich fish emulsion. Like bat guano, otter spraints are ecosystem jewels. In their daily habits, as they move between sleeping and feeding grounds, river otters fertilize new grass, nurture blooming flowers, support healthy soil, and return nitrogen to the ecosystem.

For the latrines where I take samples, I sprinkle my pink biodegradable glitter on top of the old piles to distinguish them from the new. I frequently wonder, as I scatter sparkles, what Patches and her kin think of their newly accessorized poo piles. If the otters are confused by the excreta embellishments, it doesn't seem to affect their activity at the latrines. From studies of otter vision, we know that sea otters have dichromatic color perception, similar to that of humans with red-green color blindness. If North American river otters are also red-green deficient, they can't distinguish pink from gray, so my disco-pink overmark likely just looks like dirt.

I send my spraint samples out for identification in February. The results return to me in March. I open the box, unwrapping blankets of bubble wrap from my Petri dishes, which are now retaped with handwritten numbers and notations on my typed labels. Tiny vertebrae are sealed in empty vitamin capsules, the gelatin casing protecting their delicate neural spines from damage in shipping.

A data file accompanies the samples. It's all becoming real now. I have butterflies in my stomach as I whisper a little prayer to the universe: "Please don't let there be endangered prey among these samples."

Most of the time, otters seem to be the public's favorite animal. Who doesn't love an otter? But that changes when you live in an area where they can be a messy nuisance or, worse, aggressive, protecting their offspring with a defensiveness they've learned from one too many encounters with curious or antagonistic dogs. Worst of all, the otters might represent competition for fish.

In a study of river otters in the San Juan Islands just north of Whidbey, investigators found rockfish in up to 22 percent of the scat they studied. Rockfish, like salmon, are an economically valuable fish stock, but their numbers have been in decline, due in part to overfishing. They're one of many diminishing species that spurred the creation of Washington's marine protected areas, which limit what people can take from the sea. It's not the otters' fault, but if otters are eating the rockfish, they become a scapegoat. Scapegoats do not receive a warm welcome in fishing spots. Sea lions, another scapegoat, are frequently found shot on navigation buoys.

Sitting at my computer, I open the data file to a spreadsheet listing line after line of prey species. All the fish, birds, invertebrates, amphibians, and mammals from the otters' meals are identified, a written catalog of all the beautiful, glittering parts. As I scan the data, I see that each collection contains not just one meal but the accumulation of several meals, like Swoosh's foraging bout of crescent gunnels chased with a starry flounder.

I sort the spreadsheet by abundance, with the most frequently occurring species at the top and the least frequently occurring at the bottom. I look at the column labeled "Common Name" and start scrolling. Stickleback, sculpin, gunnel, vole, flatfish, tadpole, sand lance, high cockscomb, pipefish, perch, sand dab, poacher. Down and down I scroll, through collections from Admiralty Bay, Admirals Lake, Lake Pondilla, Deer Lake, Strawberry Point, and on and on. I am relieved to find that even among the infrequently occurring species, there are no rockfish in the data.

At the very bottom of the list is a single instance of a fish identified as "Salmon, Species Unknown." Salmon is the only other fish I was concerned about finding. Widespread declines of wild salmon have negatively affected fisheries, the cultural heritage of Indigenous tribes, and the well-being of other marine species, including the critically endangered Southern Resident killer whales, who rely on the Chinook for 100 percent of their diet in the spring and up to 50 percent in the winter.

But this unknown salmon species, collected from Mutiny Bay, is probably not the endangered Chinook. More likely, it's a pink salmon, which are far more abundant, or maybe a coho; the collection date in late September coincides with the fall run of coho, when the scads of seasonal fishermen who clean their catch on the beach offer fortuitous forage for an opportunistic otter. No matter the species, the island otters' single salmon catch is harming neither the human fishery nor the forage of endangered predators in the Salish Sea.

6.

Sliding, Rock Rolling, and Wrestling

What Is Otter Play?

From behind a stand of frozen lupine, Patches, Crest, and Slash emerge onto the wetland. Moonshine reflects off the newly fallen snow, illuminating the predawn hour with a supernatural brightness. The three female otters surf the snow, their forward momentum pulling them across the slick surface like kids on a Slip 'N Slide: lope-lope-slide, lope-lope-slide. They halt beside a corrugated metal culvert, side by side, until Patches lurches forward and leaps onto the bank of Admirals Lake. Her landing fractures the frozen lakeshore, stamping an otter-sized divot. The two girls follow behind her, each landing with a loud crunch, leaving star-shaped bull's-eyes in the ice. The otters are out early, exploiting the cold; an icy lake makes for sluggish fish.

Patches points her nose toward a stand of bare willow cane and releases a rasping hiss. Another romp of five otters cautiously bumbles out from behind a cleaver of stiffened goosegrass, each scenting the air. I don't recognize these new otters. Their coats are lighter in color, and the smallest has a pronounced limp favoring its right hind leg, though there's no blood trail in the snow.

From my vantage point about fifty feet away, I wait to see what the otters will do, trying not to make any noise. But these unfamiliar otters must pose a more immediate threat to each other than the human standing nearby. They pay me little mind.

In a flash, a sixth otter I have not seen leaps out from behind the newcomers. He releases a series of chirps, passing all five in a rush. Without hesitation, he bounds at Patches and her girls. His vocalizations transition to a buzzing hum. Crest and Slash scamper forward, chuffing and purring. This is not attack behavior. This is a solicitation to play.

The three otters meet in a tackle, a jumble of tails and feet, chuckles and chirps. Patches, unperturbed, directs a passing glance toward the newcomers and begins to groom her fur. The otter must be Swoosh, but his Nike-logo muzzle mark is fading, as often happens when river otters reach maturity. I'm feeling celebratory, too, as it's been a few months since I last saw him and I thought perhaps he'd left the cove. His young-adult coloring has darkened, filling in most of the wavelike band I used to identify him in the fall.

Slash, her dark stripe still prominent on her face, tumbles into Swoosh. Swoosh snorts and nips at the air above Slash's head just as Crest straddles Slash's back sidesaddle. Slash rolls over, displacing her sister, who stumbles into one of the smaller newcomers, who rolls into a sapling, causing the snow load to fall to the ground in a thud. Swoosh and the girls move their wrestling alongside Patches until Swoosh, realizing he's beside his mother, stops his horseplay and gently headbutts her muzzle. Patches stops grooming and leans into him. Like two cats, they nuzzle and rub cheeks. The girls let him go. They're in their own world, wriggling on their backs and making otter-shaped snow angels.

The new otters, still observing the reunion from the sidelines, are more relaxed. One of the bigger newcomers eases over to Swoosh and throws himself on his back, landing on Swoosh's tail. I'm not sure about the sexes of these five newcomer otters, but given their behavior, I suspect they're all bachelors who have formed a temporary social group of young males, a phenomenon occasionally observed among marine-foraging river otters. These social coalitions offer advantages to young male otters, especially soon after they've been evicted from their family groups, when their fishing skills are still in the rookie range. In a social group, male river otters may cooperatively forage, maximizing their success in capturing larger and higher-quality fish. These Lost Boys have weathered storms, surf, and now snow.

Crest and Slash clamber onto the lake, then back again, almost as if testing the structural stability of the ice. The Lost Boys join in, nipping, rolling, tackling. And then, all at once, they dance—the scat dance of marching, scratching, digging, marking, and sniffing.

This is otter play, one of the many metrics used to gauge animal health and intelligence. And if play hints at health, these otters have it in spades.

Otters and play are closely linked in our imaginations. Whether they're sliding in the snow, juggling rocks, grappling with and chasing each other, or pounding abalone shells with stones, everything otters do seems somehow playful. Even otter pooping is referred to as a "dance," and of course, we call a group of them a "romp."

But otters are not *only* playful. And when we think of all otter behavior in those terms, we forget they're complex carnivores, part of the same family of accomplished predators as the weasel, badger, and wolverine. They protect their young, hunt, fish, and forage. When threatened, they can attack dogs or humans; one sea otter in Santa Cruz, California, became famous for aggressively stealing the surfboards of unsuspecting surfers. There are even accounts of Eurasian and giant otters killing and cannibalizing other otters.

It's easy for us to misunderstand otters' behavior as playful because of their *neotenous*, or baby-like, features.

Their large foreheads, eyes, and pupils, paired with the soft, downy fuzz of their round faces, engage our parenting and nurturing instincts. However, to understand the true nature of otter behavior, scientists and enthusiasts alike must take care not to interpret other animals' experiences through a human lens. Anthropomorphism, the attribution of human characteristics or behavior to nonhuman animals, constrains what we can truly observe and learn. This is a challenge for everyone, including wildlife scientists.

Play is especially difficult not to anthropomorphize because it's entrenched in the human experience; we're so obsessed with it that we've built multibillion-dollar industries around it in the form of sports and video games. Play is also one of those behaviors, like love, that are hard to define, but we feel we know it when we see it. Appearances can be deceiving, though, when we're looking at animals very different from ourselves.

On the other hand, we'd be foolish to completely ignore play behavior or dismiss it as "marshmallow science," as ethologists did for many years. An early trailblazer who helped reverse this trend was ethologist Robert Fagan, author of *Animal Play Behavior,* who found that play among juvenile brown bears was correlated with longer and healthier lives. Marc Bekoff, another animal play pioneer, who researches dogs, coyotes, and wolves, concluded that play is practice, improving the skills needed for other biologically relevant behaviors.

According to Jaak Panksepp, a prominent neuroscientist, play is aerobics for the brain. Panksepp identified seven primal brain circuits that motivate purposeful behavior; play is front and center, as are care, lust, panic, fear, rage, and seeking (i.e., curiosity). But the neural mechanisms for rough-and-tumble play are critically important, not only for development of social skills but also for social joy. This suggests that play is part of a broader cognitive framework involving *social intelligence*, an animal's ability to learn, solve problems, and adapt to novel circumstances relevant to their social world.

So how do we know that what we see as otter play is really play behavior? And is that behavior something that all otters do? Or is it malleable, changing with the context, the species, or the individual?

In 1973, Nikolaas Tinbergen shared the Nobel Prize in Physiology or Medicine with Karl von Frisch and Konrad Lorenz for their joint contributions to the "organization and elicitation of individual and social behavior patterns." While von Frisch discovered the "waggle dance" honeybees use to communicate the location of flowers and Lorenz studied avian imprinting in geese, Tinbergen's investigations led to his famous "four questions" for understanding animal behavior. These questions ask about a given behavior's (1) function, (2) development, (3) mechanism, and (4) evolution.

When looking at otter play, we might apply those questions like this:

1. Why do otters perform a particular play behavior?
2. How does the play behavior develop over the otter's lifetime?
3. What causes the otters' play behavior to occur?
4. How did the play behavior evolve over time?

These lines of inquiry help us think about the ultimate reasons for otter play. Does it confer some adaptive advantage? Is it practice for hunting or mating, as the practice hypothesis of play suggests? Does it train otters in social competency, as the socialization hypothesis of play suggests?

Hans Kruuk's book *Otters: Ecology, Behaviour, and Conservation*—probably the most well-worn book in my library—is the academic authority on all the world's otters, but despite the animals' playful reputation, it doesn't have a single chapter dedicated to play. In the early 2000s, when it was published, there were too few peer-reviewed studies on otter play to justify a devoted chapter. Even now, two decades later, there are fewer than twenty published articles dedicated to understanding the very behavior otters are most celebrated for.

It's impossible to nail down a universal, comprehensive definition of play because it can vary so widely based on factors like anatomy and environment. For example, an otter and an octopus have very different bodies and habitats—the way the former plays might look nothing like the way the latter plays, yet both may be exhibiting forms of play. Social behavior can be quite different even between closely related species. For example, some otter species are highly social, others less so. If some otters engage in social play, that doesn't mean otters engaged in solitary or object play aren't also playing.

Fortunately, ethologist Gordon Burghardt established five criteria, similar to Tinbergen's four questions, as a baseline for establishing if behavior is play:

1. "The performance of the behavior is not fully functional in the form or context in which it

is expressed; that is, it includes elements, or is directed toward stimuli, that do not contribute to current survival."

2. "The behavior is spontaneous, voluntary, intentional, pleasurable, rewarding, reinforcing, or autotelic ('done for its own sake')."
3. "Play . . . differs from the 'serious' performance of ethotypic behavior structurally [in form] or temporally [i.e., timing] in at least one respect," such as being "incomplete . . . exaggerated, awkward, or precocious."
4. "The behavior is performed repeatedly in a similar, but not rigidly stereotyped, form during at least part of the animal's ontogeny [e.g., rocking or pacing]."
5. "The behavior is initiated when an animal is adequately fed, healthy, and free from stress (e.g., predator threat, harsh microclimate, social instability), or intense competing systems (e.g., feeding, mating, predator avoidance)."

Additionally, play is more likely to evolve among animals with greater parental care, because when parents provide resources the young would otherwise have to provide for themselves, they have more downtime to horse around. Most animal experts have adopted these five criteria because they can be identified in any species or behavior system.

Common examples of otter play include behavior that mimics foraging (e.g., biting and grabbing), fighting (e.g., wrestling and posturing), fleeing (e.g., rolling and tumbling), and even courtship (e.g., mounting). Each behavior may improve the otter's success in the biologically relevant situation. Social play is also thought to nurture attachments and connections within a community or between animal pairs, and to encourage the development of social competency, teaching animals across species to read behavioral signals and respond in a way that limits conflict and increases survivability. Social play can occur between two or more otters, or even between an otter and a different animal, like a dog.

In the northwest corner of the Olympic Peninsula, 135 miles from Seattle, is Clallam Bay, one of Shawn Larson's sea otter survey sites near the Neah Bay Makah Indian Reservation. This remote area of northwest Washington is rich in food, which is one of the reasons why, in 1969 and 1970, fifty-nine sea otters were reintroduced there from Amchitka Island, Alaska. The otters Larson and her collaborators research today are the descendants of the original survivors of those translocations. I first met Larson, the senior conservation research manager at the Seattle Aquarium, years ago during one of the aquarium's biennial sea otter conservation meetings, a conference Shawn has organized since the late 1990s.

Today, a sunny afternoon in October 2024, we stand side by side on the rocky riprap of a viewing area along the highway. Using high-powered telescopes, we observe a social group of juvenile male northern sea otters playing in the kelp. With her trademark energy and enthusiasm, Larson offers her spot at the telescope to a passing tourist, who explains she came all the way from Australia hoping to spot the sea otters, only to realize that she didn't have the necessary equipment. Larson explains that young sea otters are easy to identify by their dark faces, which become blond or grizzled as they age.

Whidbey's ocean-foraging river otters are always within meters of shore, and there are many areas in California, like Monterey, where you can sip a glass of wine and watch a sea otter or two swim beneath a nearby pier. This is not the case for Washington sea otters. Nearshore kelp beds, where sea otters spend most of their time, can be 1 to 2 kilometers (roughly a mile) from land-based observers, especially at low tide. In 2022, the Washington state sea otter survey—an annual collaborative effort between biologists, volunteers, state and federal agencies, and the Quinault Indian Nation—observed some sea otters up to four miles offshore. On the upside, sea otters' fidelity to foraging areas means you usually know where they'll be. As long as you have the right equipment and the weather is fair, there's a good chance of collecting data. And unlike with Whidbey's river otters, you can get up at a civilized hour, since observing sea otters from a distance requires daylight.

Larson and her colleagues visit one or more of the twenty-nine sea otter sites along the Olympic Peninsula each month. For two days, they record dive intervals, foraging success, food type, and other relevant information in an *ethogram*, a data sheet used among animal scientists to inventory behavior. This afternoon, Clallam Bay harbors a bachelor pad full of juvenile males. Young male sea otters leave their natal area when they're around six months old, which means they still have about four years before they reach reproductive age. During their nonbreeding or juvenile independence, males form bachelor groups outside of the territorial breeding areas of sexually mature males.

There are, by our count, eleven boys in the bay today. This is a modest bachelor *raft*, the collective noun used for sea otters, just as *romp* is used for groups of terrestrial otters (and *tangle* is used for terrestrial otters when they're mating or socializing in water). Larger rafts, like the so-called Jetty Road Boys near Monterey, can reach 100 sea otters. But in August 2019, the Jetty Road Boys "suddenly dispersed" and did not return. Why? Gena Bentall, marine biologist and founder of the nonprofit program Sea Otter Savvy, posits an array of factors that may—individually or in combination—cause sea otters to abandon a location, including poor prey availability, predator avoidance, human disturbance, and a changing environment. In the case of the Jetty Road raft, the specific reasons are uncertain, but Bentall theorizes that the initial dispersal may have been caused by a single male driving off the others in an attempt to establish a territory.

Among the dark faces in Clallam Bay, there is no dominant territorial male, just the jocular frolicking of ten juveniles and one white-faced old guy, merrily chomping on butter clams and urchins, aged out of competing for female attention. The younger males also pause their playing and take a snack break, munching on tube worms, their heads and shoulders remaining stationary while their trunks swivel as though attached to ball bearings. Heads and hands above water, they logroll, occasionally pulling a new morsel from their armpit pockets. Yet another unique sea otter adaptation, these long folds of skin are the perfect place to stash food and implements for opening stubborn shells.

Suddenly, play spreads through the group, and the clowning recommences as if on cue. A male otter curls into a forward dive, emerging seconds later to yank the flipper of a distracted playmate and pull him under the waves. Another otter, a few feet away, torpedoes out of the water, landing on the torso of the flipper tugger. The senior sea otter, still on his back, grooms by scrubbing his cheeks with his paws. His flippers also rub against one another, slowly propelling him out of the melee. Somehow, I missed the communicatory signal that said, "Let's get back to playing." But it was there.

Consider your dog. It might invite you to play with a "play bow," head lowered, forelimbs extended, tail wagging in the air. It may even run at you, then pivot and run away, as if to say, "Chase me!" Play begins if the dog's play target (canine, human, or otherwise) reciprocates with a similar stance or behavioral patterns. After a few minutes of playing, the dog might repeat the play bow. Ethologist Marc Bekoff, who has extensively studied social signaling in dogs, refers to this as the *maintenance of play behavior*, a way of communicating, "I still want to play with you."

Among river otters, social play is signaled through scent, the absence of stress hormones, and play posture. During play, playmates may temporarily stop to scent each other. To us, this might look like distraction—like they're interrupting their play bout because they smelled something compelling. But for animals, this is deliberate play management, the equivalent of dogs continuing to play-bow every few minutes. They scent and nuzzle; one otter rolls onto its back, belly-up in submission: "I still want to play with you. Do you still want to play with me?" Social play-fighting among Asian small-clawed otters is frequently signaled through a relaxed posture and open-mouthed face, without the typical flattening of ears that happens during an aggressive fight. This is called a "play face" and is well documented in primates as well, especially bonobos and chimpanzees.

I never tire of observing otters. It doesn't matter the species. Larson and I have been here for two hours, easily an hour and a half longer than I would ever get with the quick in-and-out efficiency of foraging river otters. Getting this much time in a single otter observation almost feels indulgent. I realize I'm in the throes of a giggle—and so are Larson and her two research trainees. It doesn't matter how accustomed we are to observing animals in the field, the sea otter boys' antics have infected us with their joy. And that's one of the notable things about social play: It's contagious.

But not all play involves a playmate. *Solitary play* may occur with others around, but it does not directly include them. It might involve running, jumping, or sliding (which are called *locomotor play*), or playing with food, a rock, or some other item (which is known as *object play*). When your dog gets "the zoomies" and runs frenetically around the house, that's an example of solitary play, though it may turn into social play if another dog (or human) joins in.

When otters bodysurf down snow-covered trails or muddy hills, are they engaging in locomotor play, or is it just the quickest way to get where they need to go? It certainly looks playful, and it has been characterized that way since at least 1828, when naturalist John Godman gave this account:

> Their favourite sport is *sliding*, and for this purpose in winter the highest ridge of snow is selected, to the top of which the otters scramble, where, lying on the belly, with the fore-feet bent backwards, they give themselves an impulse with their hind-legs and swiftly glide head-foremost down the declivity, sometimes for the distance of twenty yards. This sport they continue, apparently with the keenest enjoyment, until fatigue or hunger induces them to desist.

More recently, researchers' trail cameras in Pennsylvania's Ohiopyle State Park caught footage of three river otters sledding in much the same way Godman described. The otters slid down a snow-covered embankment sixteen times consecutively over five minutes. Over and over, they climbed back to the top and coasted back down on their bellies. The researchers argued that this sledding was not simply moving from point A to B with as little energy as possible. They actually expended extra energy; it's not exactly efficient to spend five minutes running up and down a hill without acquiring food, finding a reproductive partner, evading predators, or otherwise supporting critical biological needs. Sometimes the simplest explanation is the correct one: *Playing in the snow is fun for otters.*

Even though the Ohiopyle otters slid down the hill individually, they soon shifted to playing together, wrestling and chasing each other. This illustrates the blurriness of play designations. What starts as solitary play can morph into social play and back again.

Otters may also play with playthings, like the Asian small-clawed otters who "juggle" rocks. This object play emerges among juveniles around weaning at four months of age. Though less common among other species, rock handling has been observed among eleven of the fourteen global otter species. It's not quite juggling in the way a circus performer would toss pins in the air. Rather, the otter handles a rock or stone close to the body, quickly passing it between the forepaws, armpit, and/or mouth. Of course, it can be difficult not to anthropomorphize rock juggling, right down to its very name. Is it actually a play behavior, or does it just seem that way to us humans?

To learn more, researchers at the University of Exeter studied groups of otters at zoos and wildlife parks in the United Kingdom. They enlisted four groups of Asian small-clawed otters, the most well-known rock handlers, and two groups of smooth-coated otters, which also juggle rocks, but not as frequently. The scientists hypothesized that rock handling was related to food handling, so they predicted that the Asian small-clawed otters with their hand-oriented, invertebrate-eating diet would engage in more rock juggling than the mouth-oriented, fish-eating smooth-coated otters. They also predicted that younger otters would juggle more than adults (based on the practice hypothesis of play) and that there would be more male jugglers than female (based on field observations and the overrepresentation of play among male otters). Finally, they predicted that if rock juggling was indeed an artifact of food handling, it would occur more often if time between feedings were longer, acting as a motor distraction when food was anticipated but not immediately forthcoming.

The researchers designed three novel food puzzles to test the otters' skills at extractive foraging, putting meat in screw-top medicine bottles, in green tennis balls with crosshatches cut into them, and between paired bricks. Their results were surprising. Despite the differences in feeding styles and rock-juggling frequency, Asian small-clawed and smooth-coated otters were equally adept at extracting meat from food puzzles; the Asian small-clawed otters had no advantage. Equally surprising, the adults juggled more than the juveniles, and the females juggled more than the males. The scientists did predict one thing correctly: All otters rock-handled significantly more before feeding than when they were satiated, supporting the hypothesis that perhaps rock juggling is associated with the anticipation of food. But is it play behavior? It's impossible to say definitively, and this ambiguity is characteristic of studying play in otters.

In human-care facilities like zoos and aquariums, there are fewer "do-or-die" stressors than in the wild. Otters and other animals need not worry so much about finding food, avoiding predators, or surviving disease, like they would in their natural habitat. However, what they do experience is anxiety—not acute fight-or-flight stress, but rather prolonged anxiety induced by under- or overstimulation.

Understimulation occurs when animals are not free to exercise their species-typical behaviors, like managing territory, migrating, finding food, parenting, mating, etc. This is especially true for isolated social species. (During the isolation of the global COVID-19 pandemic in 2020, humans, a social animal, experienced the highest historic rates of clinical depression and anxiety diagnoses.) *Overstimulation*, in contrast, occurs when there is too much sensory input, as is often the case in zoos—too much noise, too many people, and no way to escape it all and get some peace and quiet. The consequence of this anxiety is *abnormal repetitive behaviors* (ARBs), which act as a form of self-soothing. If you've ever chewed your nails, twiddled your thumbs, or jiggled your leg, you've engaged in an ARB. You may have seen ARBs among animals in a captive environment in the form of a big cat pacing back and forth or a gorilla overgrooming.

ARBs aren't always a big problem among zoo- or aquarium-housed animals. They can be simple reactions to feeling bored or anxious in the moment. In fact, they often occur just before a scheduled feeding, acting as more of an anticipatory behavior than a stress response. But prolonged boredom or overstimulation, limited space, lack of social interaction, or poor conditions can turn benign forms of self-regulation into neurological changes that can cause harm, like when parrots pluck out their own feathers.

This is why play is such a critical component of wellness for otters and other animals in captivity. In fact, there are cortical and neural connections within the brain that mediate play behavior, in terms of both the motivation to play and the process of socialization and attachment. In a study of play among rats, neuroscientists found that "rats that play as juveniles are more socially competent as adults." Conscientious zoos and aquariums provide opportunities for otters to exercise their creativity, curiosity, and problem-solving skills, alone (solitary play), with other otters (social play), and with toys and games (object play), mimicking experiences they might have in the wild.

One example is the Oregon Coast Aquarium (OCA)

in Newport, a conservation- and education-based non-profit with half a million annual visitors. Like the Clallam Bay Boys that Shawn Larson and I watched through telescopes, the three sea otters at the aquarium are a bachelor raft. In 2023, they became part of a comparative longitudinal study that I began in 2016 with the male and female sea otters at the Oregon Zoo. The study expanded to include the exclusively female sea otters at the Monterey Bay Aquarium during 2020, when web cameras allowed us to continue to observe captive otter behavior during lockdown. Together, these three groups let my students and me evaluate if behavioral wellness indicators differed between rafts of otters that were mixed-sex (Oregon Zoo), all-female (Monterey Bay Aquarium), and all-male (OCA).

The OCA Boys showed virtually no ARBs during our observation times, and they engaged in the most play of any of the three groups. Sex was not the only disparate variable, but given that all three groups were similar in terms of age and enrichment activities, and all were rescued populations, sex may help explain their behavioral differences. In the wild, preadult male sea otters may have more time to play. The formation of bachelor groups confers safety in numbers, particularly when the otters are nearshore. If their main concern is feeding and they don't have to worry too much about safety or mating, then they have time to play between foraging and sleeping.

The enrichment offered to all three sea otter communities included creative toys and games to exercise the otters' brains and bodies. Eddie, an elderly male sea otter in the mixed-sex group at the Oregon Zoo, was even trained to "shoot hoops" to help combat arthritis in his elbows and shoulders. This capitalized on a natural behavior of sea otters called the "spy hop," in which they elevate their shoulders above the water's surface to improve their view or to investigate something they can't see while on their backs. Eddie's miniature basketball hoop was set up in a behind-the-scenes training pool, around 40 to 60 centimeters above the water's surface—just low enough for an aging otter to raise his shoulders above the water and extend his front limbs to sink a small plastic ball through it.

A series of videos showing this physical therapy made Eddie quite famous for his dunking skills, so much so that the local NBA team, the Portland Trail Blazers, gave him an upgraded hoop with their logo on it. After he died in 2018, another otter, Juno, was also trained to engage with the basketball hoop. She added her own "spin" on it by occasionally twirling as she dunked. Although there is no way to know definitively if an otter *enjoys* shooting hoops, Eddie's and Juno's willingness to spend some of their "activity budget" on it is a good sign of their engagement. They're certainly doing their part to uphold otters' playful reputation.

7.

Otter Smarts

How Otters Learn and Remember

Outside the Oregon Coast Aquarium's sea otter habitat, Brittany Blades, the marine mammal curator, points out the three members of the resident bachelor raft: Oswald, Schuster, and Earle. We're standing at the observation window along an expansive pool with a mock-rock perimeter. Earle leaps like a dolphin out of the water toward a pile of ice along the ledge. Ice is a favorite treat, especially when mixed with shrimp and mollusks.

It's September 2024, and all three otters are on exhibit this morning. Earle is the easiest to identify, since he's smaller than Oswald and Schuster and lacks the mature white felting on his face. He has crafted an architectural pile of ice on his chest, and with both hands, he scoops pieces up to his mouth to crunch on. When finished, he dives beneath the water, about twelve feet to the bottom, scanning for residual bivalves that may have sunk there.

Oswald, an older, more robust otter, follows behind in a sloppy imitation of Earle's swim sequence: forward dive, roll, side swim, bottom scan. In a moment of showmanship, he pirouettes, a salvaged clam in hand, making eye contact with Blades and me, and then dives back beneath the water.

Schuster has less gusto. Content to hang out by the feeding station, he picks through shellfish scattered along the terrestrial part of the habitat. As he eats, he performs cleansing rolls. His head and hands stay stationary above the water as his body rotates, allowing shell fragments to fall away from his chest into the water.

Blades takes me to the off-exhibit space that houses the aquarium's sea otters, sea lions, and harbor seals. This is a behind-the-scenes area not open to the public, full of elevated pools and an outbuilding with a curving tank just behind it where the animals can transfer from their on-exhibit (public) habitats to their off-exhibit spaces. It's a lot of industrial concrete and stainless steel—freezers, commercial sinks, thick hoses with spray nozzles. Two of the aquarium mammalogists pull a wagon stacked with Bundt pans full of ice-ensconced crab, clams, and mussels: an ambrosia salad for sea otters. Dry-erase boards with schedules and codes keep track of each animal's enrichment goals.

Enrichment refers to activities, objects, or environmental modifications designed to stimulate animals' physical and cognitive well-being, particularly in *ex situ* (non-wild) settings like aquariums and zoos. The goal is to mimic as closely as possible an animal's wild habitat so it can engage in natural behavior, like foraging, problem-solving, or, in the case of sea otters, tool use. The main purpose of enrichment is to prevent boredom, but it may also promote coping behavior if the animal is stressed or scared. Tactile enrichment figures prominently in sea otter care and includes puzzles, food hidden in ice or containers, live prey like fish in a bucket, and imitation kelp made from a durable nylon.

It can be hard to know if enrichment is "working." You can measure certain physiological markers with blood tests, but they're cumbersome and expensive, and it takes several days to get results. In an effort to monitor the efficacy of sea otter enrichment programs in a different way, the Georgia Aquarium joined forces with researchers at the Georgia Institute of Technology to put sensors in their sea otters' enrichment devices. The sensors can't measure biomarkers like blood tests can, but they can measure in what ways and for how long the otters manipulate the item—kind of like a sea otter Fitbit. These "smart" enrichment devices may be the future of evaluating physical, cognitive, and mental health for otters in human care.

At the Oregon Coast Aquarium, each sea otter has its own unique approach to enrichment. Earle, the youngest of the raft, leverages his youthful energy to declare dibs on his favorite treats by getting to them before Oswald and Schuster, who are older and more, shall we say, full-figured. Earle has no problem jumping onto land if it means he might persuade the care staff to offer him a side treat. Despite the mammalogists' best efforts to provide equal-opportunity enrichment, Earle has figured out that he can get more for himself if he picks up an ice mold and drops the entire thing onto the ground, shattering the ice and liberating whatever ocean treasures are encased inside.

Schuster, the oldest of the OCA Boys, has his own strategy for commandeering favored edible enrichment. He rushes the enrichment piles, squirreling as many of the treats as possible into his armpit pockets. Diving to the bottom of the pool like a sea dragon guarding his hoard, he off-loads his pockets into an underwater pile.

Less greedy, Oswald solicits audience participation, much to the delight of his adoring public. He waits patiently until he can sneak in and grab Earle's leavings, then swims to the viewing glass and whacks the ice against the window to get at the goodies inside.

All the OCA Boys' strategies for engaging in enrichment are examples of sophisticated otter problem-solving. In order to reliably liberate food from containers, the otters have to apply the right amount of force with the right kind of motion, something that changes depending on the container. They also have to anticipate what their companions will do and take countermeasures to get enough food for themselves. This theory of mind, or ability to imagine other beings' perspectives, is one of the hallmarks of higher cognition.

Charles Darwin noted that selective pressures favor animals with the ability to learn, understand, and adapt to new and changing circumstances. Although intelligent behavior is best documented in primates, many other animals also have impressive cognitive abilities. Dolphins, for example, can mentally represent and manipulate symbol systems, understand symbols as references to tangible objects, learn abstract concepts, use referential pointing, and exhibit self-perception. Various other learning and memory skills have been documented in sea lions, African gray parrots, bonobos, elephants, New Caledonian crows, and even octopuses, whose behavioral flexibility is legendary.

There are two types of learning: *non-associative learning*, which happens through exposure, and *associative learning*, which happens by linking two stimuli or a stimulus and a response.

Non-associative learning is the simplest form of behavioral or cognitive change. It occurs when an animal's reaction to a repeated event or stimulus changes over time, either by becoming stronger (which is called *sensitization*) or by becoming weaker (which is called *habituation*). An example of this is when wildlife becomes habituated to the presence of humans. When river otters repeatedly encounter humans without negative consequences, non-associative learning teaches them that we're not a problem, and they become accustomed to being around us. They may then act bolder and less fearful, emerging to forage during hours they otherwise wouldn't.

Associative learning is more complex. A classic example is the dogs in Ivan Pavlov's experiment, who learned to associate the sound of a bell with receiving food and eventually began to drool whenever they heard the bell, even if there was no food presented. The smooth-coated otters used by fishermen in the Sundarbans exemplify a more complex form of associative learning called *operant conditioning*. They learn to herd fish into nets at the fishermen's commands, and, more impressively, they learn they'll ultimately get to eat more fish if they wait to be rewarded with a share of the harvest rather than opportunistically taking the catch on impulse. Delaying gratification in this way is a cognitive skill even small children have difficulty with, but these otters have mastered it.

But before they learned any of that, the Sundarban otters, like most otters, had to learn to swim. With the exception of sea otters, otters aren't born ready to swim. They have the innate physical ability, but they require maternal encouragement to enter the water. They first begin to swim, dive, and hunt through a form of associative learning called *social learning*, in which one animal observes and imitates another—in this case, its mother.

Social learning was famously documented in the 1950s among Japanese macaques, also known as snow monkeys. Eight years before Jane Goodall went to study chimpanzees in Tanzania, a yearling female monkey on Koshima Islet was observed taking sweet potatoes to the edge of the bay, then using one hand to dip the potato in water and the other to brush sand off of it. This monkey, nicknamed Imo, was the first to do this behavior, but ten more monkeys soon followed her lead. After a decade, almost all of the island's monkeys engaged in sweet-potato washing, except the much older adults—because sometimes you can't teach an old monkey new tricks.

The social transmission of sweet-potato washing probably wouldn't have occurred if Japanese macaques were a solitary species rather than a highly social one. A century of research has led to the *social intelligence hypothesis*, which posits that social complexity selects for cognitive complexity, or more thoughtful learning, problem-solving, and communication. So it's unsurprising that the animal cognition literature is filled mainly with social species.

This includes otters. Nine of the fourteen global otter species are *gregarious*, meaning they form social groups. The cohesion of these groups varies and often involves *fission-fusion dynamics*, in which animal groups alternately split into smaller units (fission) and come back together (fusion). Some otters form long-term social groups, like the Asian small-clawed and giant otters. Others, like the Eurasian, spotted-necked, and marine otters, establish sociality based on matrilines, meaning female offspring stay with their mothers, at least for a while. Social groups of extended families, or family units, also occur, like in the smooth-coated, African clawless, and North American river otters. Sea otters exhibit *intrasexual sociality*, meaning they generally gather in same-sex rafts. Within these closer-knit social groups, social learning is more likely to occur.

One study of social transmission in otters looked at two gregarious otter species that live in stable family groups and rely on each other for foraging and safety: smooth-coated otters and Asian small-clawed otters, or ASCOs ("AZ-kohs") for short. The researchers studied twenty-four otters of mixed sex and varying ages in zoos and wildlife parks in the UK. They tested the otters' ability to solve novel foraging tasks by giving them food inside clear plastic containers that had to be opened in different ways, some more complex than others. Some containers had lids that clipped on, some required a quick tug to break a seal, some had screw tops, and some required a bamboo rod to be lifted in a particular way. The researchers predicted that all otters would have more difficulty solving the more complex puzzles and, under those circumstances, would be more likely to imitate each other's solutions.

Using modeling software to make sure their findings were statistically significant, the researchers found that the smooth-coated otters interacted with virtually all group members, though some individuals were more social than others. The smooth-coated otters solved all the foraging tasks, regardless of complexity, by copying each other's solutions. Additionally, the younger otters solved the tasks faster than their parents. This was not the case for the Asian small-clawed otters. Their social networks were more homogenous, with less variability in social interaction, and they were more likely to figure out solutions alone rather than relying on social information. Fewer than half of the ASCOs solved the most complex tasks, the screw-top lid and bamboo rod.

Considering the foraging behavior of both species in nature, there may be an explanation for this. Smooth-coated otters live in family groups with an adult female and several litters of offspring, and they coordinate their behavior to cooperatively hunt and deter threats. ASCOs live in large social groups of fifteen animals or more, and while they show group defense against predators, they forage individually for shellfish. Even though smooth-coated and Asian small-clawed otters live in similar family groups, the cooperative hunting and foraging strategy of the smooth-coated otters lends some credibility to the social intelligence hypothesis that social cohesion selects for cognitive complexity, at least in the social transmission of novel, puzzle-like tasks.

But perhaps the foraging self-reliance of the Asian small-clawed otters nurtured a secondary skill set: tool use. ASCOs' forelimbs are much smaller than those of other otter species, allowing them to catch and handle crabs, their preferred forage, more efficiently. Like sea otters, they rely on hard-shell prey, and thus, like sea otters, they're skilled at object manipulation. They utilize rock tools to crack shellfish carapaces, a skill that requires problem-solving and adaptability.

We've celebrated tool users since Louis and Mary Leakey's discovery of the human ancestor *Homo habilis*, in northern Tanzania in the 1960s. Emblematic of early hominin intelligence, *H. habilis* was credited with developing the earliest known tools, simple stone choppers and flakes dating back 2.6 million years. At the same time, just 560 kilometers away, Leakey's research assistant Jane Goodall observed a community of chimpanzees using tools; specifically, a big male she named David Greybeard stripped leaves from flexible twigs and used the twigs to fish termites from their mounds as part of his food-foraging repertoire.

But Goodall's clever chimpanzees were not actually the first scientifically documented animal tool users. That designation goes to southern sea otters observed along Bixby Creek in Monterey County, California. In the late 1930s, another important but lesser-known female naturalist, Edna Marie Fisher, described the sea otters' habit of diving and retrieving mussels and stones from the bottom of the bay, returning to the surface to float on their backs with the mollusks on their bellies, and using stone tools to break open the hard shells.

Since Fisher's early account of sea otter tool use, many others have described the flexibility and breadth of sea otters' ingenuity in excavating hard-shell prey using larger shells, bottles from human litter, or rocks. Sea otter use of tools takes three forms: using a rock underwater to pry food loose from a hard surface, pounding food with a rock on their chest while floating on their back, or pounding food directly against a rock. The latter type is what Oswald at the Oregon Coast Aquarium did when he smashed his frozen treats against the visitor viewing window. It's called *emergent anvil use*, because the rocky outcroppings, boat hulls, and concrete docks (or viewing windows) that otters use as makeshift anvils stick out, or *emerge*, from the water. In each instance, sea otters conform to the definition of tool use or, at the very least, proto-tool use, which involves "an animal solving a problem for which evolution has not provided a rigid morphological or behavioural adaptation," potentially making use of "general cognitive abilities, like learning and reasoning."

And sea otters don't simply *use* tools; they appear to *select* them. They shop for the best tool, given the size and shape of their prey and its abundance within a specific ecological niche. A sea otter may carry a rock to the surface, realize it's too light for the task at hand, and swap it out for a heavier rock that better meets their need. In a longitudinal study of 196 radio-tagged sea otters along the California coast, eighty-five years after Fisher's first observations of sea otters using tools, researchers found that tool use conferred advantages by allowing the otters to process hard-shell, energy-rich prey like clams and crabs—or energy-poor but abundant snails—when their preferred prey, the less-armored abalone or urchins, were scarce.

Interestingly, not all sea otters use tools. For example, sea otter tool use is more common among females, who live in larger rafts, where competition limits the abundance of prey choices and thus the otters need greater problem-solving and adaptive strategies to get enough food to eat.

Since tool use is purposeful and goal-directed, animal cognition researchers and behavioral ecologists cite it as evidence of higher-order cognition. But it's not the only form of intelligence, and we have to be careful not to privilege it over other forms just because we humans are such adept tool users. Thomas Zentall, an animal cognition researcher at the University of Kentucky, argues that humans typically place themselves at the top of the evolutionary scale by overvaluing our rule-based communication and ability to modify our environment and undervaluing the limits of our vision, olfaction, audition, and touch relative to other organisms. In doing so, we minimize the exceptional sensory and cognitive skills of different animals.

Consider, for example, the remarkable spatial memory of Clark's nutcracker, a member of the intelligent Corvidae, the family that contains crows, magpies, jackdaws, and jays. This caching bird hides up to 25,000 pine seeds in as many as 5,000 locations and can recall where they are, and how many seeds they have removed from the caches, up to nine months later. This ability to navigate the world and return to specific locations has been demonstrated in species in every taxonomic class, including insects, fish, cephalopods, amphibians, reptiles, and mammals. Animals need to remember where food sources are so they can find them again. And yes, this includes otters.

One of the most common ways to study spatial memory is with one of two kinds of mazes. The first is a box maze, which requires the animal to move from a starting point to an end point, learning to avoid dead ends that don't produce a reward. This is the type of maze you might find in a botanical garden, a children's educational magazine, or *The Shining*. The second kind is a radial arm maze, which consists of a small central area with several arms projecting from it, some of which contain a food reward. The participant's job is to remember which arms are baited and which have already been emptied of food. This tests spatial *working* memory (which lets animals remember the locations of the baited food) and spatial *reference* memory (which lets animals remember which arms are depleted of food).

In a study at Zoo Atlanta involving four male and five female Asian small-clawed otters, investigators adapted a radial arm maze methodology, affixing eight "feeders" made of PVC pipe elbows to a concrete floor in an equidistant circle. The otters couldn't identify if the feeders were food-baited by sight, and all eight feeders were also rubbed with fish, so smell wouldn't guide their performance, either. Four of the eight feeders were randomly selected for bait before the foraging sessions. All otters were tested individually and allowed to explore each feeder. The goal was to see if the otters would correctly identify and later remember which feeders were baited and which were not. They found that the Asian small-clawed otters were significantly more likely than chance to visit baited locations and to remember those locations across conditions; furthermore, the otters made fewer errors as the sessions progressed.

There is evidence that during foraging, otters rely most on their sight, though of course touch is also crucial. All otters have a specialized reflective structure behind the retina called the *tapetum lucidum*. Made of green and blue iridescent tissue that amplifies light, it helps otters, as well as other nocturnal and crepuscular species, see in low-light conditions. Based on anatomical and behavioral studies, Lutrinae appear to have dichromatic vision, similar to that of humans with red-green color deficiency. Studies also indicate Eurasian otters can discriminate between blue, green, and differing shades of gray, color variations that convey information about habitat suitability, with cool colors like blues and greens indicative of wetter and therefore more desirable habitats. But how exactly do otters privilege different visual features in their decision-making? To what extent do they rely on shape, color, spatial distance, and other visual factors to find food, latrine sites, and dens?

Caroline DeLong, a comparative cognitive scientist at the Rochester Institute of Technology, has devoted her career to understanding animal cognition, specifically concerning memory, perception, and concept learning. For the last decade, in collaboration with the Seneca Park Zoo, she and her colleagues have studied comparative tool use in Bornean orangutans and human children, trained olive baboons to solve cognitive problems using touchscreen computers, investigated the perception of rhythm in African penguins, and examined the visuoperceptual discrimination of North American river otters. In the latter, her goal was to identify which visual features, like color and shape, are most adaptively important to otters.

In 2023, DeLong and her colleagues established the ManyOtters project. There are several "Many" projects, including ManyPrimates, ManyDogs, and ManyBirds, all of which focus on connecting different scientists and research protocols with each other to resolve unanswered questions like "How do environmental variables like human proximity and noise affect cognition?" and "How does cognition vary among related species?" Part of the onus of DeLong's ManyOtters work is conservation. Understanding how river otters perceive their world may help protect the species from further decline and may also support the ex situ populations in human care.

Ultimately, DeLong and her research team wanted to know about river otters' *umwelt*, a German term meaning "surrounding world" introduced by the trailblazing biologist Jakob von Uexküll in the early twentieth century to describe the subjective, perceptual world experienced by any given animal. An umwelt is shaped by each animal's sensory capabilities, physiological needs, and behavioral repertoire; it's the world of signs and signals that an animal perceives and acts upon. Different species can inhabit very different realities, as Ed Yong explores in marvelous detail in his book *An Immense World: How Animal Senses Reveal the Hidden Realms Around Us.*

Consider the difference between your umwelt and your dog's. Even if you're both standing in the same room, you quite literally see the world from different angles and in different colors—and your dog is probably less concerned with what it sees than with a vast array of sounds and scents you can't even detect. Now think of the umwelt of animals even more different from us, like bats, sharks, or worms. We can try to imagine it, but we can never truly understand the umwelt of another creature, be it a dog that lives in our house or an otter that lives at a lake nearby.

In one of DeLong's studies, she and her colleagues tested whether North American river otters could discriminate among objects that varied in color and shape. They gave two otters red, blue, and black circles, triangles, and squares as stimuli. During the training phase, Heather, a thirteen-year-old female, was consistently rewarded for choosing the red circle, while Sailor, a nine-year-old male, was rewarded for choosing the blue triangle. Then, during the test phase, either the color or the shape was removed to see if they could do it better with color alone or shape alone, instead of both color and shape. Heather was very good at identifying the targets and performed equally well at identifying color and shape, individually or combined. Although Sailor learned to identify color and shape together during the training phase, he didn't learn to associate food reinforcement during the test conditions when he had only shape or color as cues. Instead, he preferred whichever stimulus was on the right side, regardless of whether it was the target with the reward.

This side bias is not uncommon among animals, which, just like people, can be right- or left-"handed." Why does handedness matter? Because it's related to brain hemispheric laterality. Brain function in vertebrates is *lateralized*, meaning that the left and right sides of the brain process sensory information differently and control different behaviors. Somewhat counterintuitively, the left hemisphere of the brain controls functions on the right side of the body, and vice versa. It's thought that among animals, including humans, the left hemisphere specializes in the management of routine, self-motivated behaviors such as feeding; this would explain why animals as diverse as fish, reptiles, and toads have been shown to display right-side bias, striking at food on their right side under the guidance of their right eye (and left brain hemisphere).

You already know that 85 to 90 percent of the human population is right-handed. But did you know that great apes often show right-hand preferences for tool use, chickens show right-foot preferences for scratching, and parrots, bucking the trend, strongly favor their left foot for grasping food? In an investigation of the laterality of Massachusetts Bay's humpback whales, scientists found that of the seventy-five whales with jaw abrasions (wear patterns from lunging at fish or krill near the sea floor), sixty showed abrasions on only the right side, while fifteen showed abrasions on only the left—a ratio roughly consistent with that of right- to left-handed humans. They also found a right-side preference in flippering, though not in breaching.

In the study of emergent anvil tool use among the Bennett Slough sea otters near Monterey, investigators found evidence of a right-side bias in handling mussels. When the otters used an emergent anvil, both forepaws held the mussel in the upward swing, but as the arms came down to strike against the rock, the wrist turned just before impact so that the right paw was oriented palm-down on the mussel. They also noted that the shell breakage pattern of the mussels showed consistent fracturing of the bivalves' right side, suggesting a clear right forepaw preference (and, therefore, left brain hemisphere guidance).

Hemispheric specializations allow animal brains to engage in parallel operations, like searching for food with the left hemisphere while screening the environment for threats with the right hemisphere. Additionally, routine communications such as alerting other animals to danger appear to be under the control of the left hemisphere, while the right hemisphere is in control when an animal is conveying emotional cries, threats, or warnings. It's all a part of the rich mosaic of cognition, learning, and memory in otters and other animals.

8.

Tangled Tails and Teeth

Otter Social Behavior, Vocalizations, and Courtship

It is the last weekend in February 2025, the end of Peru's rainy season, and our second day in the Madre de Dios region. I am with the Otter Specialist Group, one of more than 160 specialist groups within the International Union for Conservation of Nature (IUCN), the organization that designates endangered species. Nicole Duplaix, now emeritus faculty at Oregon State University, founded the Otter Specialist Group fifty years ago. At the time, little was known about otters, and virtually no science existed on giant otters, the species Nicole specialized in.

This year, the group's quadrennial meeting is in Lima, and it's my first time attending. I am especially excited for the presentations on the phylogenomics of the newly identified Mesoamerican otter and on recent trail camera sightings of Malaysia's elusive hairy-nosed otter, which, until around a decade ago, was believed to be extinct.

On the last day of the congress, eight of us head to Playa Pucusana, a small bay within the Boquerón del Diablo ("Devil's Mouth"), a stark, treeless area of natural rock bluffs and tunnel formations scoured by the sea. The bay is busy, choked with brightly colored fishing boats and canopied day runners. We find a local captain and manage to say in Spanish, "*Nos gustaría ver una nutria marina.*" We would like to see a marine otter.

The marine otter, or as it's known in Chile, *el chungungo*, is the only otter within the genus *Lontra* that lives entirely in marine habitats. It's also the smallest of the *Lontra* species and the second smallest of all the lutrines, at 86 to 114 centimeters (34 to 45 inches) from nose to tail. With the feather weight of just 4.5 to 5 kilograms

(9 to 11 pounds), it's no wonder its Latin name is *Lontra felina*, or "cat otter."

As our small boat jockeys through the bay, we pass South American sea lions, with their flattened faces and enormous bodies, basking on the docks. I expect them to bark or wail like the California sea lions I'm accustomed to in Oregon and Washington, but they're a silent bunch, perhaps too hot in the Peruvian sun to offer us more than an uninterested glance. We spend an hour passing Guanay cormorants, Peruvian pelicans, blue-footed boobies, and diminutive Humboldt penguins huddled in caves. But as we begin our return journey, still no marine otters. As biologists and behavioral ecologists, we all know this is the risk of a wildlife trip: Wildlife doesn't always show.

But then, just as we're about to give up, a marine otter swims in front of us, casually going about her day. Another flat head pops up beside her, mouth open and chewing. The two spot us and dive beneath a private dock to our left. Our little boat follows, and we ask the captain to hang back a little. We don't want to crowd them. They've made their home in the bustle of the harbor, and we're just visiting. Later, when reviewing photos, I'm struck by how much the marine otters resemble North American river otters. If I were just looking at the photos and hadn't seen how small the pair were, I could easily mistake them for marine-foraging river otters like the ones on Whidbey. They are part of the same genus, *Lontra*, so it makes sense that they look alike.

We leave the pair, delighted to have seen our first in-person otter of the congress, but also a little disappointed we didn't have more time to sit and watch. Tomorrow, we depart for the jungle in southeast Peru.

There are more than 10,000 plant species in Peru's Tambopata National Reserve. As we hike through the jungle, it feels as though they're all represented on the muddy trail, crammed together, competing for the sun's attention. My favorite is *Socratea exorrhiza*, known in Spanish as *palmera caminante*, the "walking palm." The tree's exposed roots look like thick fingers with tiny, scalelike teeth that protect them from being savaged by insects (or the careless grasp of a human hand). It was once thought that this tree "walked" toward the sunlight shining through gaps in the dense canopy, but in reality, the roots just grow toward any available light—no walking involved, but the process is still intriguing.

Our guides, Jhordy and Eddy, grew up in a small village near here and have an encyclopedic knowledge of the local plants, birds, insects, and fungi. I take photos and type notes in an app on my phone as we hike. As I type, in my peripheral view, I see a tiny convoy of leaf parts held aloft by marching ants. Leafcutter ants, one of the many mutualistic species in the Amazon basin, carefully cut leaves and carry them back to their colony, where they use them to cultivate a fungus to feed their larvae. The fungus benefits not only from the food source but also from a bacterium that lives on the ants' bodies that helps keep it free of disease. This interspecies harmony also creates a habitat for the leaf-litter frog, which stays safe from predators by living within the ant colony and secreting chemicals that prevent the ants from attacking it. As the path bends, I also see the web of an orb weaver spider, at least five feet wide—but no spider. We had a lot of rain last night, so it's probably tucked under a leaf along the lacy tethers of its net.

Finally, we reach our destination: Tres Chimbadas, one of the preserve's many oxbow, or U-shaped, lakes, which form when seasonal rains cause sedimentation that builds up until it cuts off a coil of tributary from the main river. Though it's about two kilometers long and less than four meters deep, it is home to a group of giant river otters. It's hard to imagine that this narrow lake can support a family of otters, but the biodiversity here is intense. I'm accustomed to the silence and calm of remote areas of Puget Sound. Here, the world is noise and color and smell, the air heavy with moisture. Even the song of the russet-backed oropendola, a native blackbird, sounds like the *drip, drip* of water from a faucet. There is a constant hum of insects, punctuated by the chitter of nervous squirrel monkeys jumping from branch to branch overhead.

We file onto a boat, this one a cross between an oar-driven punt and a floating dock; no motorized vessels are allowed on Tres Chimbadas. In front of me, perched on the front bench, peering through binoculars, is Jim Bodkin, a longtime sea otter researcher from Washington. "Otters," he says with the nonchalance of someone who has been otter spotting for decades, pointing to the two o'clock location in front of our boat.

I hear them before I get a good look, but sure enough, there they are. We're still far enough away that, without binoculars, the otters are just moving lines in the water. Our oar-driven floating dock is slow, and I'm nervous that the otters will shift their behavior before we can truly observe them. I feel conflicted, knowing we must maintain a safe distance, but also desperately wanting to see these giants in their native habitat. If we get too close, we'll flush them, and they'll dive—and this boat full of conservationists will have to live with the icky feeling of disturbing the local wildlife we've come so far to see.

But the otters don't flee, even as the boat pulls parallel with them.

The only species within the *Pteronura* genus, giant otters have a distinct morphology, with flattened short noses, large eyes, and a long tail that's compressed in the middle, making it look somewhat like the blade of a sword—or a wing, as its scientific name, from the Latin for "wing-tail," indicates. There's nothing fuzzy about these otters. They have brown, chestnut, or gray coloring with splashes of creamy white around the chin, neck, and chest, and a sleek body composition reminiscent of a pit bull. You can identify the muscle insertions beneath their taut skin as they move. But the giant otter is more of a ballet dancer than a bodybuilder. They are both beautiful and menacing—until, that is, we hear their vocalizations, which sound like Chewbacca's. They also make discordant squeaks, coos, purrs, chirps, as well as an oddly mechanical sound like the whirr of a windup toy.

In Brazilian Portuguese, the giant otter is known as *ariranha*, from the Tupi word *arerãîa*, or "water jaguar." In other areas of the Amazon, Orinoco river basins, and the La Plata river system, they are nicknamed *lobos de río*, "river wolves," a nickname based on their hunting style and social structure. Like wolves, giant otters are pack hunters. In fact, of all the fourteen otter species, they are by far the most socially cohesive.

Right now, a family group of eight has converged on a snag—a thick dead tree with the bark worn away, scraped by otter claws. This romp is engrossed in grooming themselves and each other, nuzzling at each other's necks and shoulders, stopping now and then to dig in and separate stubborn clumped fur along a haunch. One of the recipients of such attention looks directly at our odd floating island. We can tell she's a female because she doesn't have the pronounced testicles visible on adult male giant otters. Giant river otters, like most of the lutrines, are sexually dimorphic, so in addition to the differences in genitalia, there are morphological differences based on sex. While females are around 22 to 26 kilograms (48 to 57 pounds), males are slightly larger with noticeably thicker heads and necks, weighing up to 34 kilograms (75 pounds) and reaching lengths of about 1.5 to 1.8 meters (5 to 6 feet).

We're maybe twenty meters—ten otter lengths—away. It feels a little too close, and it is. Our guides, manning a single heavy oar, try to create some distance, but it's too late.

The rest of the romp stops grooming and watches us from the snag. The large female slips into the water, and a second adult follows—presumably the female's mate, as a monogamous breeding pair heads giant otter romps. Like twin torpedoes, the two otters target our platform, swimming toward us. Then, as if choreographed, they split apart. The female otter swims along the starboard side of our platform as the male checks out the forward area. Their family group's chirps and whistles stretch across the lake. It's a good sign that there are no threatening chuff snorts, the warning vocalizations used among several otter species, including the Eurasian, neotropical, and North American otters. These animals appear curious rather than threatened.

The otters are so close now that I can no longer use my telephoto lens and have to switch to my phone. They periscope, exposing white throat patches that look like landmasses on a map. Like the spots on African spotted-necked otters or the tail fluke markings on humpback whales, these white blotches can be used to recognize and census individual otters. Among the reference materials where we're staying is a book called *Giants of the Madre de Dios* by Jessica Groenendijk and Frank Hajek, ecologists who studied giant otters in Peru and other parts of South America. The protagonist of their book is a female they named Arrow based on the shape of her neck markings, much like I named Patches. Arrow is most certainly long gone by now, but I can't help but search for a white arrow on this curious female's neck. Her markings, though, are more like a splatter of paint than a symbol.

She ducks her head beneath the lake's surface, satisfied that we're just weird water primates, no threat to her or her family. The male stays a little longer, swimming back and forth like the pendulum on a grandfather clock. He utters a few final grumbles that sound like a "huff" and follows the female back to their snag.

Even though otter vocalizations contain information, they don't have the kind of structured grammar necessary to be considered a language. They're more like utterances that may also serve as signals. A *call* is a specific type of vocalization that requires a sender and a receiver. It may be used to express concern, issue a warning, show submission, or solicit a callback to inform the sender of the receiver's location, as in the case of a missing pup. There's even evidence that some otters may use unique calls to represent individual animals, the way dolphins use signature whistles.

Using playback recordings of contact calls, researchers found that giant otters use whistles to stay in contact when visually separated and to reaffirm attachments when reunited, while hums are used to direct group movement when in close proximity. They also found that giant otters' contact whistles are individually distinct and may be used among group members to recognize one another.

In Brazil's Pantanal region, scientists recorded nine giant otter groups making more than 6,200 airborne vocalizations over the course of 112 monitoring hours—a task made slightly easier by the fact that, unlike the more crepuscular North American river otters, giant otters are predominantly diurnal, or active during daylight hours. From this data, researchers identified fifteen giant otter calls and vocalization types, seven of which were made exclusively by adult and subadult otters, and one of which was only uttered by cubs, or juveniles. (North American river otter and sea otter young are referred to as *pups*, while the young of other otter species are called *cubs* or *kits*.)

In a similar comparative study of five giant otter romps in Peru and three from German zoos, researchers found twenty-two distinct adult vocalization types (including whines, barks, whistles, and underwater calls) and context-based calls (including a suckling call, contact call, and mating call). They also observed eleven incidents of "babbling," or practice vocalization, among cubs—the first documented otter babbling in the scientific literature.

Based on these and earlier studies of giant otter

vocalizations, the Chewbacca-like utterance we heard at Tres Chimbadas was likely a "coo-hum" the otters make during grooming. The discordant "squeak," which sounds like *w'eet-ooo, w'eeet-ooo,* occurs during close contact, and the toy-motor sound we heard could be a "hum," both of which are typical during close contact, grooming, swimming, and scent-marking. Although we cannot know what the otters were thinking, the adult scout who departed with a "hah" or "huff" was making vocalizations often described as inquisitive calls. If these sounds had escalated to a "snort," "scream," "growl," or "scream-gurgle," they would have signaled to the rest of the romp that we were a threat.

All otters vocalize, and there are similarities and differences among different species' vocalizations. However, the terminology scientists use to describe those vocalizations is not consistent across species. The Congo clawless otters have a largely undocumented vocal repertoire, but we know it includes barks, growls, snorts, hahs, coos, hums, and whistles. Another African otter species, the spotted-necked otter, was documented in Lake Victoria's Rubondo Island National Park paging other otters with a vocal catalog of twelve different acoustic signals that included mumbles, contact calls, warning growls, and screams. In fact, the spotted-necked otters, as the only members of their genus (*Hydrictis*), are unique in many ways, one of which is that they're the only otters that do not engage in the "hah!" alarm call. Cape clawless otters, the third largest species of the otters, found in South Africa, are reported to emit escalating alarm calls from "hah" to the peculiar "ow-ow-ow," as well as grunts, shrieks, and screams. Sea otters, with their ten-call repertoire, also scream, but theirs are distress calls that occur when mothers are separated from their dependent young; a missing pup in the ocean has very little chance of surviving. On a calm day, the spooky sea otter scream can be heard from over a kilometer away.

The variability in otter vocalizations by species likely has to do with differences in their social behavior and ecology. For example, marine-foraging North American river otters can live in large groups of three to eighteen animals, who are not always related to each other. Inland North American river otter groups tend to be smaller and must travel farther to find food during winter freezes. The patchiness of food and territory favors the overlap of otter home ranges. According to the *resource dispersion hypothesis*, this pattern of limited food and territorial resources often results in more social behavioral systems among animals. Social behavior requires communicatory systems, so these otters develop broader vocal repertoires. Two-way calls are the province of family groups, whereas vocalizations are used more among unrelated aggregates to convey intent: "Hey, I'm not a threat! I'm just here for the buffet!"

Social groups don't just evolve communication strategies; they may also evolve cooperative strategies for foraging and defending against threats.

Caroline Leuchtenberger and her colleagues documented three accounts of giant otters acting in cooperative defense against jaguars. *Mobbing* is when a group of animals gang up to collectively harass or attack a perceived threat and drive it away from their territory, young, or food resources, reducing the risk of predation. Although mobbing behavior is most frequently described among birds, Leuchtenberger observed giant otters mobbing jaguars. Just as you might see a group of crows cawing as they swoop and dive at a predator, the giant otters vocalized while mobbing the jaguars from the water, where they're most agile. One of the three events, which involved a group of twelve otters (seven adults and five cubs) and an adult male jaguar, is described here:

> The jaguar approached the otters on land while the entire group was in the water, close to the den. Once the otters perceived the jaguar, all adults displayed the periscope posture, emitting sharp snorts interspersed with hah vocalizations and some isolated hum-growls. The jaguar lunged forward twice towards the otters, growling and exposing its canines, to a distance of about 1 m from the closest animal, but did not enter the water. After 4:05 min of interactions, the jaguar turned to leave the site, but the otters simultaneously lunged toward the cat. The jaguar faced the otters in a stalemate. About 30 s later, the jaguar walked away about 10 m, lay down for 2:18 min, and then left the area. The entire event lasted 9 min.

The defensive stakes are high in the jungle, so it's no small wonder that the South American giant otters require size and numbers to combat predators and protect their vulnerable cubs. Yet, despite all the giant otters' strategies for survival—body size, group numbers, cooperative behavior, and complex vocalizations—there is one strategy they did not evolve: *delayed implantation.*

Delayed implantation, also known as *embryonic dia-*

pause, is a reproductive strategy in which a fertilized egg can lie dormant for several months before implanting in the uterus and developing into a fetus. This adaptive strategy was first documented in roe deer, but also occurs in over 130 mammals, some marsupials, elasmobranchs (sharks and rays), and even reptiles. It's common among mustelids, including North American river otters and sea otters.

The primary evolutionary function for placing a hold on embryonic development is to give birth during favorable environmental conditions. When unfavorable conditions are predictably recurrent—like winter, which comes around every year—an animal can migrate to more advantageous climes, which otters don't do, or use delayed implantation to wait for a better time to have babies. Seasonal diapause is triggered by shorter days during the winter, which initiate a hormonal cascade that suspends the fertilized eggs' development. As the seasons change, the increased daylight triggers hormones to reanimate cellular division, and the fertilized eggs implant in the uterus, ready to be born in warmer weather. Another advantage: If new pups can be delayed until older siblings are independent, there is less food competition within a family group.

Like other otter species, once pregnant, North American river otters have a gestation period of between sixty and sixty-five days, but delayed implantation can postpone this period by nine to twelve months. Typically, North American river otters mate in the late winter to early spring, depending where they live, though in some areas, like Yellowstone National Park, mating season can extend into June, coinciding with cutthroat trout spawning runs.

In contrast, giant otters do not delay implantation, nor are they seasonal breeders. They're always game for a romp (pun intended), because the environmental conditions in tropical rainforests change primarily based on flooding, rather than on food and resource availability. The same is true for Asian small-clawed otters, Cape and Congo clawless otters, smooth-coated otters, and Eurasian otters, though the latter can show breeding seasonality in some northern parts of Europe, where food availability and climate are seasonally variable.

Among most otters, mating is flexible, depending on opportunity and environmental conditions, and is more likely to occur in the water. These couplings are short-lived, with some notable exceptions, like the serial monogamy of smooth-coated otters, Asian small-clawed otters, and giant otters, who live in large family groups with a dominant mating pair.

Unique among the lutrines are, as usual, the sea otters. They lack a formal breeding season, but typically pup in the spring and fall. Their delayed implantation is generally around two to three months, shorter than river otters' nine to twelve months. In captivity, when there is no reproductive partner available, female sea otters can experience false pregnancies, showing physiological and behavioral signs of pregnancy despite not being pregnant. There may be an evolutionary purpose for this; in the wild, when a dominant breeding giant otter becomes pregnant and starts lactating, a second, nonbreeding female will show similar milk letdown, suggesting perhaps a readiness to assume the responsibility of parenting should the pregnant female die.

In their natural habitat, male and female sea otters

spend most of their time with their own sex, though the territories of single-sex rafts do overlap. A sexually mature male, around five to six years old, may form what's called a *consortship* with a receptive female, which lasts about three days. This three-night stand involves multiple copulations in the water, and the male holds on to the female by biting her easiest-to-grab feature: the nose. Rhinarium scarring among adult females is not uncommon; this evidence of their copulatory history can even help researchers identify known female otters in the field.

Yet nose-biting is not the sea otter mating behavior that has scandalized so many people in recent years. What is? I'll let comedian Michelle Wolf explain in a bit from her special *Joke Show*:

> I saw otters in real life, which was very exciting for me. I love otters—big fan. So I post about it on Instagram, because that's how you prove that life happens. And then this woman responds to me. She was like, "You know, I used to love otters, too. But then my husband told me that otters rape baby seals. I just thought you should know. Be better." Okay, a couple things. . . . You don't know me! Maybe that's why I like otters! Maybe I think seals have been getting away with too much for too long! Also, whatever you do, you've got to stop saying "rape"! These are animals!

It is indeed true that there are published accounts of male sea otters copulating with harbor seal pups, sometimes continuing the macabre act days after the pup has died. It's also true that a male sea otter named Ollie, living in a territory off Vancouver Island without available females, was observed for almost a decade killing marine-foraging river otters and molesting the corpses days later. *Davian behavior*, or necrophilia, occurs throughout the animal kingdom, but Ollie's body count, somewhere in the vicinity of twenty river otters, is enough to make even seasoned otter researchers clutch their pearls.

But before we start messaging comedians, it's important to remember that these atypical mating events usually happen only under specific conditions, like restricted range and limited access to mates. They can also happen by accident; sea otter mating is notoriously rough, and when males bite females' faces, it can force them underwater, leading to inadvertent drowning. If a female dies during or shortly after mating, a male might continue copulating with the corpse unknowingly. These salacious stories are irresistible to the media, but they do not accurately reflect typical otter courtship and mating behavior.

Interestingly, the media has also influenced public perception of sea otter mating behavior in quite the opposite direction. It's unlikely anyone would observe the average otter tryst—full of growling, hissing, and biting—and find it romantic. Yet in the popular imagination, sea otters are hand-holding sweethearts. Why? This can likely be traced back to a 2007 viral YouTube video titled "Otters Holding Hands," posted by a visitor to the Vancouver Aquarium. In it, a nineteen-year-old female named Nyac and her seven-year-old male companion, Milo, float side by side in their pool, grasping each other's paws as they sleep. It's an adorable image, but it's not the norm for sea otters. In their native habitat, they sleep with both paws raised in the air, and paw-grasping is not common;

when it does happen, it's usually between two females or between a mother and pup, and it allows them to dock to their raft so they don't float away in the current.

Both these examples—necrophilia and hand-holding—illustrate the hazards inherent in anthropomorphism. As Michelle Wolf pointed out, these are animals, and when we project human characteristics and emotions onto their actions, it can oversimplify the complexity of their behavior. At the same time, humans are animals, too, and we can relate to other animals' desires for safety, food, play, and social interaction. Finding the right balance between objectivity and experience is one of the biggest challenges in wildlife research.

The first day I spot him along Admiralty Bay, he's strolling the beach in front of my cabin, scenting the driftwood and rolling in the sand. It's an unseasonably sunny March afternoon, and this lone male is the biggest river otter I've ever seen. Field scientists evaluate an animal's health using a body condition score from 1 (emaciated) to 9 (obese), and this guy hits a perfect 6, with a healthy muscle balance, sturdy legs, a glossy coat, clear eyes, and no apparent injuries. He's the Jason Momoa of river otters. I call him, perhaps unimaginatively, "Handsome."

Shortly after seeing Handsome, I notice another otter foraging in the bay. It's Patches. I rarely see her hunting in the afternoon; this is unusual. In the mornings, if she comes ashore, it's usually to snack on a sculpin or to take a breather, shake off the water, and blow air into her fur. But today her attention is laser-focused on the tall, dark, and handsome loner sunning himself on the beach. She eases onto the shore in a slow slide with her head down, but her gaze fixates on the big boar. He sees her there, but plays it cool. He begins to roll around in the sand, stopping now and again to peer over at her.

Cautiously, Patches creeps up the beach, her nose directed toward the male. She's maybe twelve meters or forty feet away from him, a driftwood log at her right shoulder as a buffer if she needs it. Then she, too, begins rubbing her head in the sand, digging with her nose in the dirt, and thrusting her shoulders into the newly carved grooves. She flips on her back as though reclining in a beach chair, her shoulders upright with her hind legs and tail resting on the sand, until she, too, wriggles against the sand. Handsome stops his dirt bathing to watch her. His posture is sphinxlike, his stance alert but relaxed. She keeps a coquettish distance, making eye contact, but periodically looking away to groom her fur. After about fifteen minutes of this flirtation—her rolling, him watching, him rolling, her watching—Handsome steps toward the driftwood log. He waits for her reaction, then takes another step, inching closer. Patches stops grooming and gives a short huff, the "hah."

For a whole week, I watch their flirtations. They hunt together in the mornings before nosing around the beach. Then, one afternoon, in a snarling, hissing frenzy like fighting cats, they run toward the bay, biting and thrashing. Handsome grabs her by the neck, and her head goes underwater. She rolls back up to the surface. Handsome hovers above her, his teeth still hanging on to her scruff, and after a handful of intromissions, that's it. They separate.

Patches continues into the bay, diving and surfacing until she catches a flounder and takes it with her to the culvert. Handsome wanders up the shoreline, shakes the water from his fur, and slinks over the road into the prairie marsh of Admirals Lake. I don't see them together again.

Almost one year after her marine tryst with Handsome, Patches's second litter of pups, three or four in total, will enter the world, each weighing 110 to 170 grams, no more than a standard bar of soap. North American river otter pups, like all baby otters, are *altricial*, wholly dependent on their mother, who tirelessly nourishes, grooms, and protects her developing young. As the pups grow, they nurse six to eight times a day, so otter *sows*, or mothers, rarely leave the den. They can't replenish their depleted bodies with an adequate hunt until the pups are between three and five weeks old, which is when they start to open their eyes and orient toward their siblings for warmth. Even then, mom's foraging trips are short and close to the den, as she gobbles down whatever she can find before returning to her pups. By the time they're six to eight weeks old, she can take more extended fishing trips and begin integrating solid foods into their diet by feeding them bits of sculpin or flounder, the otter version of applesauce and pureed peas.

The pups' fur starts out downy and uniform, suited to life in the den. Once they undergo their first molt, at around twelve weeks, their fuzzy coat is replaced with two new fur types: a thick, water-repellent undercoat, sometimes referred to as the *wad*, and the outer guard, or *jar*, hairs that provide the color and texture of their coat. Now they're ready for their swimming lessons. The pups' mother urges them toward the water, but like people, they have different personalities, and one or two may be reluctant to jump right in—and otter moms, like human moms, may grow impatient and haul them in by the scruffs of their necks.

The next lesson for marine-foraging river otters is swimming in the bay. This requires vigilance as they learn to assess tides, adjust their entry and exit points, watch for predators, and learn their prey's daily movements to best time their hunts. By this time, they're around four months, and their mom finally closes the milk bar, as the pups now eat entirely solid foods. However, the mom still stays close to the pups and may cooperatively hunt with them, taking advantage of their numbers to coordinate underwater attacks or confuse their prey, further refining the pups' skills in chase, capture, and consumption.

Once she's confident her pups can navigate the water, the sow reassesses the condition of her den. If she believes a predator—or another otter—has compromised the den, she may move her young to a new location. There is good reason for this: There are documented accounts of male Eurasian otters and giant otters killing unrelated cubs and, in a few cases, eating them.

The social behavior among some other otter species further hints at the risk of infanticide. Spotted-necked otters in Rubondo Island National Park have adapted a social system of short-term congregations called *packs.* These groups consist of individual animals, dyads, triads, same-sex groups, or family romps that associate with each other for multiple days and, on occasion, form *schools*, two or more packs that come together for a short time. In both cases, when spotted-necked otters form packs or schools, moms retreat with their cubs to their dens, potentially recognizing the unpredictability of large, unrelated groups as a danger to their young.

Otters are highly selective when choosing their dens, also called *holts*. Their choices are influenced by factors such as safety, predator protection, and proximity to food and water. Otters typically don't dig their own dens, instead relying on existing natural structures, like rock formations, brush thickets, caves, root wads, or, among Eurasian otters in the Scottish Shetlands, exposed peat burrows. In riparian habitats, North American river otters sometimes use old beaver lodges for den sites, even ousting the current occupants. In 2021, while surveying a Florida cave for roosting bats, biologists were surprised to find a North American river otter mom had settled into a small side chamber with her three pups, the first cave-based natal den ever documented. Along the Puget Sound and the San Juan Islands in Washington, river otters have taken a shine to human-crafted sites, claiming decks, sheds, or boats as their own—and leaving a mess for their hosts in the process.

Sea otters, of course, don't use dens, as they live in the water. But newborn pups can't swim at birth, so they rely on their mothers to carry them on their chests for the first few weeks. They can't regulate their body temperature, either, which means a mother spends around 13 percent of her time during the first two months grooming and blowing insulating pockets of air into her pup's coat, providing both warmth and buoyancy. "Woollies," as they're often called, open their eyes within days of birth, but depend on their mothers for six to eight months, longer than other otter species.

This high maternal care comes with a price. Female sea otters are referred to as *income breeders*. With their high metabolic rate, lack of blubber, and small size, they can't save up energy reserves like some other animals can. This means they need a constant "income" of energy to cover the enormous expense of producing milk for their pups. They do acquire a small stash of fat during pregnancy so they can focus solely on the pup for the first few weeks, but after that, they're back to living paycheck to paycheck—i.e., needing to forage for food.

Though sea otter pups' swimming lessons begin earlier than other otters', they nurse for three to four months longer, which makes the six-month postpartum period a dangerous time for their mothers. Sea otter moms need to eat roughly 30 percent of their body weight in food each day, and if they fall short because they're prioritizing their pups' needs, they become malnourished and emaciated, a condition known as *end-lactation syndrome.* Over half of all adult female sea otter deaths in California are attributed to this condition. Even after her pup is weaned, an otter mom doesn't get much "me time" to recover; once female sea otters reach reproductive age (two to four years), they spend almost all their adult lives either pregnant or providing parental care, giving birth to one pup per year.

Life is no picnic for the pups, either. Despite its mother's careful nurturing, grooming, and protection, a pup has a 30 to 50 percent chance of dying in its first six to eight months, especially if the mom is a first-timer. If separated from its mother by poor weather, strong currents, boat traffic, or fishing entanglement, it can succumb to hypothermia, starvation, or predation within hours to days. In the Aleutian Islands, it's estimated that sea otter pups constitute as much as 15 percent of bald eagles' diet during the nesting season.

The predation risk is not exclusive to pups. Adult otters are also targets of large predators. Among southern sea otters in California, great white shark attacks pose a significant threat, while Alaskan northern sea otters have to contend with the marine-mammal-eating transient killer whales. In fact, in the spring of 2020, the carcass of a killer whale was found washed ashore on Bering Island in Russia with seven sea otters in its stomach. In an ironic twist, one of those otters was found lodged between the orca's pharynx and esophagus. The whale's likely cause of death? Asphyxiation by sea otter.

Even wolves prey on sea otters. Since their early documentation in 2016, a population of coastal gray wolves has been hunting harbor seals and sea otters in the nearshore areas of Katmai National Park. Another wolf pack, located on Pleasant Island in Alaska's Icy Strait, are also known sea otter predators, but their marine foraging comes at a cost: abnormally high mercury levels, not just compared to terrestrial foraging wolves, but compared to all wolves worldwide.

However, as we'll see in the next chapter, the greatest threat to otters isn't sharks, orcas, or wolves. It's humans.

9.

River Otter: $200

Otters, People, and Commerce

In the summer of 2023, while Whidbey's river otters restricted their activity to dawn and dusk hours to avoid people on the beaches, a sea otter in Santa Cruz, California, was out in broad daylight, stealing people's surfboards right out from under them.

Otter 841—or Laverna, as her fans called her, after the Roman goddess of thieves—first came to the public's attention in June, when Santa Cruz photographer and influencer Mark Woodward (@NativeSantaCruz) posted images of a sea otter climbing onto a surfboard at Cowell Beach, saying she "put on quite a show checking out and climbing on multiple boards." Although her unusual behavior initially seemed curious and playful, by July, her antics had escalated. She began chasing surfers, biting longboards, and overturning kayaks. It didn't help that crowds of people flocked to the area hoping to catch a glimpse of the otter celebrity. No one reported an injury, but officials deemed her a public safety hazard and tried to capture her—to no avail.

Perhaps it was in 841's genes. Her mother, Otter 723, was also deemed a public safety hazard after approaching kayaks in Monterey Bay. She was successfully captured, but unbeknownst to the rescue team, she was pregnant, and she gave birth while in human care. The Monterey Bay Aquarium's Sea Otter Program, which is dedicated to rescuing and rereleasing sea otters whenever possible, raised the pup with minimal human contact and released her in 2020, a tracking tag with the number 841 on one of her rear flippers for identification.

Three years later, Laverna, now fully grown, was aggressively looting longboards, and no one was really sure why. Had she accidentally become habituated to humans in her youth, despite the aquarium's best efforts? Had people been illegally feeding her, inadvertently teaching her that humans provided handouts? As it turns out, 841 had something else in common with her mom: At the time of her aggressive behavior, she was pregnant, and her escalating maternal hormones likely accounted for her increased protectiveness. She was strictly policing her territory, giving a whole new meaning to the phrase "Watch out for the fuzz." By October, Laverna had given birth to a healthy, woolly pup.

At the time of this writing, 841's story still has a happy ending, but the situation highlights how complicated human-otter interactions can be. Even with the best intentions, we can inadvertently encroach on their territorial boundaries with our own property (or surfboards), resulting in attacks. While well-meaning people who fail to recognize wildlife boundaries may be merely naive, or at worst, ignorant, there are people with far worse intentions: the capture and purchase of endangered lives.

Otters are adorable. When we see their teddy bear fuzziness and expressive faces, we naturally want to pet and snuggle them. Regrettably, some people commodify that desire, trafficking wild otters as pets or attractions, like for otter cafés—cafés found primarily in Japan that offer visitors the opportunity to pet or cuddle captive otters. The exploitation, commodification, and extermination of otters also occurs in the context of traditional medicines and the fur trade. Despite the dangers it presents to both humans and animals, the wildlife trade is a significant business, generating an estimated $23 billion annually. As with any profitable smuggling operation, trying to stop it is incredibly challenging and requires substantial resources.

In 1973, the same year the Endangered Species Act

was signed into law in the US, the Convention on International Trade in Endangered Species (CITES) was established as an international agreement between governments "to ensure that international trade in specimens of wild animals and plants does not threaten the survival of the species." This legally binding global agreement bans commercial trade for species threatened with extinction, allows regulated trade for species that may become threatened, and permits individual countries to seek international assistance in controlling trade in species they protect domestically. As of today, 185 countries, as well as the European Union, are parties. By joining, the parties pledge to enforce CITES with their national laws, penalizing illegal wildlife trade and confiscating illegally traded items within their borders.

But to effectively enforce laws, you need good information. That's where the Trade Records Analysis of Flora and Fauna in Commerce (TRAFFIC) comes in. Established in 1975 as an IUCN Species Specialist Group, TRAFFIC is like the CIA of wildlife trafficking, collecting and analyzing data on both legal and illegal wildlife commerce, identifying trends, and informing global conservation efforts. They manage extensive databases that document trade patterns, including information on species, products, routes, and countries involved.

In 2018, TRAFFIC published a comprehensive report on the illegal otter trade in Southeast Asia, the principal region of wild otter trafficking. According to the report, "a total of 13 seizure records in four countries (Indonesia, Malaysia, Thailand, and Viet Nam) were recorded from 2015–2017 involving the confiscation of 59 live otters, most of which were juveniles." Additionally, between January and April of 2018, 1,189 otters were observed for sale online, with the majority from Indonesia. The two most heavily trafficked otters were the Asian small-clawed and the smooth-coated otter, though a hairy-nosed and a Eurasian otter were also observed. Social media platforms were identified as key advertising outlets for the illicit trade in otters.

The Asian small-clawed otter is the smallest of all otter species, weighing between 6 and 12 pounds—about the same weight as the average domestic cat. Their active curiosity, frequent vocalizations, humanlike hands, and energetic antics have made them the most commonly smuggled otter in the exotic pet trade. TRAFFIC found ten Japanese otter cafés housing thirty-two ASCOs, and an ASCO owner in Japan frequently posts their "pet" otter's antics to a social media account with 750,000 followers.

But otters of any kind do not make good pets. They have extraordinarily high energy demands, making them voracious feeders, and a bite strength capable of crushing crustaceans. Recall, too, that all otters (except sea otters) are scent markers, so in addition to their frequent and robust evacuations, they leave scat jellies that don't exactly smell like a pumpkin-spice candle. ASCOs are also highly social, and although their claws are small, they're not absent. As semiaquatic animals, otters *require* fresh water, not only for drinking but also to regulate their body temperature.

Records of twenty otters from two Japanese veterinary hospitals show that all of them suffered from at least one chronic disease, including kidney stones, dehydration from pneumonia, and ulcers. Three had bite injuries (one self-inflicted), and five were already dead on arrival. The veterinarians' notes indicate that almost all of them were underweight, one had an enlarged gallbladder from chronic hunger, and two of the dead otters died from hunger. The average age of death was only a year and one month, despite the fact that in zoos, their normal lifespan is ten to fifteen years.

Other, larger otter species are also victims of the illegal wildlife trade, though rather than being sold as pets, they're poached for their pelts. Eurasian otters are taken in North Korea and smuggled for trade. The giant otter has been the target of the illegal fur trade along the Amazon. In East Africa, the fur and the meat of spotted-necked otters have been used in traditional medicine. One Cambodian fisherman reported having hunted and sold forty-nine otters over four years, including twenty-three hairy-nosed otters—a species so endangered that some biologists who study them have only seen them on trail cameras.

In early April, Whidbey Island's Deer Lagoon Preserve is home to a diverse community of migrating waterfowl, shorebirds, passerines, and raptors. It's one of the National Audubon Society's registered Important Bird Areas, with saltwater wetlands separated by a series of aquatic channels and drainage areas. Today I'm hoping to see the great horned owl that frequents this area while I check on two of my trail cameras.

I've been tracking an otter romp in the area. Much like Patches and her pups, this group occupies a brackish lagoon and lake, with outflows into the sea at Useless Bay. Though it was designated a no-hunting area in 2009, that restriction only applies to people. Otters and coyotes frequently tow dead rabbits, ducklings, and fish to and from the lagoon area where I have the cameras planted.

My phone buzzes, startling a kingfisher, who takes off in a whir of wingbeats. I look down and see that Kyle, the stewardship specialist at Whidbey Camano Land Trust, has texted me: *Good morning! Are you still on the island? There's a dead otter along Glendale Beach. It looks pretty recent.*

Kyle explains that earlier this morning, he was leading volunteers on a hike along the Glendale Beach Preserve, at the southernmost end of the island, by the Clinton–Mukilteo ferry landing. While Kyle and the volunteers were checking on the native plants (one of the goals of the Land Trust is to preserve and restore endemic species), they stumbled upon a river otter carcass near the parking lot.

Ever since I gave my first community talk about the otters on Whidbey and asked for citizen science support, I've received several calls about dead otters from locals, but the carcasses have always been in a state of such decomposition that I couldn't do much more than move them off the trail or beach where they were found. In one case, a little girl had seen the otter in her family's backyard pond several times that spring and had named her Penny. Upon the girl's insistence, her parents and I dug a grave for Penny and gave her a burial, complete with flowers.

Just as I pull into the little dirt lot at Glendale Beach Preserve, a front moves in, and it starts to rain—hard. Nevertheless, I grab my permit, field bag, and latex gloves. At least there won't be any beachcombers. I have limited experience with necropsies and need to pay full attention as I move through my checklist.

At the high-water mark, just past the first berm of the parking pullout, the otter is where Kyle said it would be, on its belly, its brown eyes glossy and its coat wet. Given its location, the otter didn't come in on a tide. I'm guessing it died here. I put on my latex gloves and flip the otter over. It's stiff, heavier than I anticipated. Doing some mental math on the timing of rigor mortis, I suspect it died between two and twelve hours ago. My heart sinks as I see two pairs of raised mammary glands. This otter was a mother.

I've directed two decades of dissections in my neuroscience courses: cow eyes, sheep brains, and, at one time, human brains that were donated to the cadaver program at Oregon Health and Science University. But this is very different. This otter did not come from a biological supplier. Her parts are not carefully embalmed in formalin. It feels personal. I have to face the fact of mortality, hers and my own.

I can't do this here, not in the rain, not in the open. With newfound sympathy for the little girl who wanted to give Penny a burial, I place the otter in the only container I have—a garbage bag—and drive home. I wish I were headed to a sterile clinic or my lab, rather than a beach cabin, but I can't worry about that right now. Physiological changes occur almost immediately after death, and rigor mortis has already begun. If I wait too long, the fur will begin to shed in a process called *slippage*, the start of decomposition.

On a foldable table in my garage, I take the otter's measurements: from her nose to the base of her tail, 37 inches; from the base of her tail to its tip, 20.5 inches. I look for parasites but find nothing: no fleas, ticks, shedding tapeworms, or larvae.

As I move toward her armpits, my heart sinks again. There is a tiny hole, an entry wound the size of an apple seed, below her left armpit, and a slight crusting of blood around the fur there. I feel around her back, but find no exit wound. That means somewhere beneath her fur, located within the general area of her rib cage, is a bullet.

I feel anger, sadness, and then, somehow, shame. Shame by association, by history. I stroke her fur and whisper to her, knowing she cannot hear me, but needing to say the words aloud: "I am so, so sorry." Fighting back tears, I recover my resolve. There's work to do.

I look at this beautiful otter on my table and think of all the conservation events I've attended and community talks I've given when curious little kids have approached me and asked: "Are otters the same size as my dog?" "How big are their teeth?" "What does their fur feel like?" I have answers to these questions, but they're unsatisfying for kids who want to see and touch for themselves, to explore the world through all their senses. Given the recency of this otter's death, this may be my only opportunity to salvage a pelt and skull to offer the next kid who wants to see and feel something more tangible than my descriptions. But that means I'll have to do more than just weigh, measure, and take organ samples. A lot more.

Though I grew up in a place where hunting was common, I've never hunted. I resisted it even at a young age. When I went on camping trips with my dad, he would ask if I wanted to bring a deer home for my mom, and I couldn't do it. It was the right decision for me, but it means I don't know the first thing about skinning an animal or tanning a hide, and at this moment, I don't have time to read an article. Ignoring the vehement protests of my inner judge, I search the internet for an instructional video.

By the time I finish, drained and sweaty, it is late afternoon, and I collapse on a dusty folding chair, taking off my gloves and safety mask. The condition of the otter's body beneath the skin was pristine, except for the bullet wound, which left a congealed hematoma. Her pelt is now folded, fur-side up, beside her body, which is swaddled in a towel. There's an array of collection bags with labels like LIVER and TONGUE, as well as the site and time of their sampling. If I have ever been more tired, I cannot remember it.

And there's still more to do. I've finished the abridged necropsy and skinning, but I still have to clean the garage, report the shot otter to the Washington Department of Fish and Wildlife, treat her skull, and take care of her remains. There is also the issue of her hide. So now, my boneless body barely staying on my chair, I do another thing I never thought I would do: I call a taxidermist.

The next day, I drive directly to southeast Portland, to what looks like a set of storage units. As I walk into the small warehouse, I'm met with a full-sized wildebeest mounted on a stand in the entryway and a bobcat in prowl posture on a ledge above a table piled with furs. I've always appreciated subsistence hunters' desire to feed their family through a hunt rather than through factory farming, but these mounts and furs are not subsistence. They are trophies. I feel like I'm fraternizing with the enemy.

When I ring the bell for service, a twentysomething man I'll call Caleb comes out of the backroom in a bun and an ivory cable-knit sweater. I don't know what I expected, but it was not a young, affable hipster.

I set my permit and the cooler with the pelt on a table, and Caleb opens the lid, pulling on a pair of latex gloves. I feel a pang of unease looking at the otter; it's just her skin in the cooler, but it's still her. She doesn't belong here. None of these animals belong here.

We make small talk, and he tells me he's from Montana, where I went to grad school. Despite myself, I'm won over; we spend several minutes discussing the merits of the small local ski area, Snowbowl.

Still holding the otter pelt, he glances up at me and asks, "Is this your work?"

"Yes," I say, almost apologetic. "I thought I should try to salvage the pelt, but I've never collected the skin, and I had to follow a video, and—"

Caleb laughs, holding up both hands. "Whoa, easy! You did a good job."

I relax.

He pulls out a price list and points to a line item. *River otter: $200* . . . And he's lost me again. To see it in print on a cost sheet, like a menu, makes my stomach squeeze. He writes down the price and the date of pickup, three months from now.

Three months and $200—that's what it cost me to process an otter hide. Although I knew there was a fur market, I really didn't know what to expect from it. I don't wear fur, of course, and neither does anyone I know. Yet, as of 2021, forty-one US states have trapping seasons for North American river otters, and every province in Canada allows permitted trapping of otters except Prince Edward Island.

What is the transactional value of a river otter? After seeing the piles and piles of furs in the taxidermy shop, I do a search online and quickly find river otter furs priced between $50 and $150 on a fur trader's website. Scrolling farther down, I find an educational retailer selling a river otter pelt for just over $200. What is the provenance, or source, of these pelts being used as science supplies for kids? Are they vintage (taken from otters killed a long time ago, before current conservation efforts)? Salvage (taken from otters found already dead, like the one I brought to the taxidermist)?

Regardless, these prices are nothing compared to what they were at the height of the maritime fur trade, when sea otter pelts, also called "soft gold," could fetch between $100 and $180—around $6,000 in today's money. By 1910, when the last sea otter was harvested during the maritime fur trade, the pelt earned the hunter $1,000. At the time, it was enough to buy a house.

Although the British king Charles II chartered the Hudson's Bay Company to trade in North American furs as early as 1670, the "soft gold rush" really began to pick up steam in the mid-1700s as the result of a shipwreck.

The Danish-born Captain Vitus Jonassen Bering was tasked by Russian tsar Peter the Great with charting the Northeast Passage into the Americas. His ship, the *St. Peter*, wrecked in 1741 on a small, uninhabited island, some 200 kilometers away from its intended destination on the Kamchatka Peninsula. Many of the crew, including Bering, died there, on what would eventually be known as Bering Island. The others survived by killing and eating local sea otters and sea cows, named Steller's sea cows after the ship's naturalist, the German-born Georg Wilhelm Steller. The crew eventually returned to Russia with 900 otter pelts. When they heard the tales of the docile animals, explorers and traders flooded the area, virtually extirpating its sea otters and fur seals and driving the Steller's sea cow to extinction, just twenty-seven years after they'd learned of its existence.

As the maritime fur trade peaked in the 1780s through the early 1800s, competition among Russian, British, Spanish, and American fur traders intensified. Between 1804 and 1837, it is estimated that American traders alone sold 158,070 sea otter pelts, more than the entire global population of sea otters today (around 125,000, with the vast majority living in Alaska). Sea otters once ranged from northern Japan through Russia's Kuril Islands and Kamchatka Peninsula, across the Commander and Aleutian Islands, and down the west coast of North America, from Alaska all the way to Baja California, Mexico. Indigenous peoples such as the Alutiiq and Ainu hunted them sustainably for centuries. But by the end of the 1800s, the global population of sea otters had shrunk from around 300,000 animals to between 1,000 and 2,000.

Luckily, sea otters have not gone the way of the Steller's sea cow. In 1911, the United States, Great Britain (for Canada), Japan, and Russia signed the International Fur Seal Treaty, the first international treaty to protect and conserve wildlife, which specifically prohibited the commercial hunting of fur seals and sea otters in international waters. Between 1965 and 1972, after decades of failed attempts, just over 700 sea otters were successfully captured from areas where they still lived and reintroduced into the parts of their historic North American range where they had died out. The Washington Olympic Coast sea otters, which started out as just 59 relocated animals in 1971, have stabilized at a population of between 2,500 and 2,800. Now that they're protected under the Marine Mammal Protection Act, sea otters are only permitted to be harvested by Alaska Native peoples, who have hunted them sustainably for thousands of years as part of their cultural heritage.

Although poaching of otter hides persists through the illegal wildlife trade, there are reasons to be hopeful. Several nations have passed legislation to ban the sale or farming of fur, including twenty-two countries in Europe and Japan. Some cities in the US have followed suit, and British Columbia has also taken steps toward a partial ban. And the Hudson's Bay Company, which dominated the trade of otter and beaver pelts for centuries before becoming a retailer, closed its last department stores in Canada in April 2025. Although I sympathize with the employees who lost their jobs, closing the book on the company's legacy feels, to me, overdue.

10.

Clean, Quiet Water

Otter Ecology, Conservation, and Hope

Dating back to the construction of Fort Casey in 1897, Whidbey Island has a rich military history. Three military fortifications—Fort Casey in Coupeville, Fort Worden in Port Townsend, and Fort Flagler on Marrowstone Island—once made up Puget Sound's coastal defense and were collectively referred to as the "Triangle of Fire." During World War I, Fort Casey served as a training facility, preparing soldiers for European combat.

Naval Air Station Whidbey Island (NASWI) is part of that military history. First established in the early 1940s, it is now "the largest single employer on Whidbey Island, with a base population of approximately 10,000 soldiers, civilians, and contractors." New naval pilots from across the country come to NASWI to train on their fleet of EA-18G Growler jets. These flight operations originate at Ault Field, near the north end of the island, and include aircraft carrier touch-and-go practice sessions at the nearby Outlying Landing Field near Coupeville. The training routes cross northwestern Washington, from the Pacific Coast and Olympic Mountains to the Cascade Mountains, affecting several counties, including Clallam and Jefferson, where the entirety of the state's sea otter population is located.

I first experience the Growlers in October 2018, just a few weeks after moving to Whidbey. I'm strapping a trail camera to its security housing in Fort Casey State Park when I hear a low, sonorous growl like an oncoming avalanche. The rumble rolls closer, expanding into a bellow across Crockett Lake and then Admiralty Bay. As the low-flying military fighter jet rockets overhead, there's a noticeable change in air pressure, so that it almost feels like I'm walking through water. I instinctively drop to a tuck, my arms curled around my head, my biceps protecting my ears. At 115 decibels no more than 1,000 feet in the air, the sound is louder than a rock concert, well past the 80-decibel threshold at which hearing damage starts to occur.

Growlers are often described as "thunderous," which is apt, since a thunderclap is around 120 decibels. But standing beneath one, I don't experience it as a single clap; it is an unfurling of sound, and it feels like an attack. The noise itself is not as disorienting as the compression produced by the force of 44,000 pounds of engine thrust, which allows the Growler to reach speeds exceeding Mach 1.8. The jets use approximately 4,000 liters (1,036 gallons) of fuel per hour and produce 12,479 kilograms of carbon dioxide per hour. The engines leave a visible heat mirage that makes the world look like a wet window, while the scent of the afterburn is an acrid scorch of jet fuel, burnt rubber, and ozone.

At that moment, I think of my dogs. Addie and Gracie, who quiver at fireworks, are back in the cabin, alone. I imagine, too, the pair of bald eagles tucked above Admirals Cove in their aerie. The growing eaglets cannot cover their ears. As I run home, I wonder if the adults, frightened by the noise, might abandon their fledglings, or if the fledglings might startle and fall from the nest. My ears throbbing, I open the cabin door and call for the dogs, but they don't come. I walk into the bedroom and see two tails sticking out from beneath the bed. My clever dogs have ducked for cover.

The noise continues for two hours as the pilots take off, fly over the bay, bounce off the runway, and repeat their circular touch-and-go track over and over. I'll soon come to learn that two hours is mercifully short. Sometimes the flight exercises last all day, even into the late night. The navy posts a schedule online, but it's not always reliable; they have the prerogative to change it last minute.

If my dogs hate the racket this much, I can only imagine how the rest of the animals on the island feel. For example, marbled murrelets, diving seabirds less than ten inches in length with narrow wings and dark, slender bills, have a range that extends from central California to Alaska's Aleutian Islands. The Washington population, which includes the birds on Whidbey, relies on the quiet woods of the Olympic Mountains, which are no longer quiet due to the Growlers. In 1992, the species was federally listed as "threatened" under the Endangered Species Act. Despite these protections, various factors, including sensitivity to noise, ultimately led them to be classified as Endangered in Washington. (By the time you read this, the Trump administration may have redefined these categories or dismantled the ESA.)

And, of course, there are the otters. I've never directly observed an otter during the training flights—which is revealing in and of itself—but I do have one trail camera recording of their reaction to the noise. As soon as they hear the jets, they immediately dive into the lake. As my neighbor Bob once remarked to me, "Maybe they're like us. They go indoors." The only problem is that water transmits noise more effectively than air, offering them little protection.

Soon after my first encounter with the Growlers, I attend the Sound Off, one of three simultaneous community events "in protest of the Navy's plans to bring 36 more EA-18G Growlers to Naval Air Station Whidbey Island and to increase the amount of practice at the Outlying Field Coupeville by as much as 370 percent." Five hundred people gather at Crockett Barn, a homestead dating back to the 1850s, to share information, lobby their elected officials, and support the community. There are speeches, letter-writing tables, props, dancing, and musical performances. The attendees are children, parents, grandparents, tribal members, photographers, reporters, teachers, activists, small-business owners, retirees, and veterans. It's not an anti-military protest, nor does anyone propose eliminating the jets altogether; rather, they argue that introducing more jets would be untenable for the already noise-weary community and that other training venues should be used.

Over the next few years, the navy's plans are approved and then halted as it becomes embroiled in lawsuits from Whidbey residents. By 2024, a study identifying the human health impacts of exposure to persistent Growler noise is published, using four weeks of acoustic and flight operation data collected by the navy in 2020 and 2021, as well as data collected by a private acoustics company and the National Park Service along the Olympic Peninsula. To estimate the jet noise exposure of specific communities, the authors mapped noise exposure across the region and, using the World Health Organization's exposure-response models, predicted health risks to over 74,000 people living in high-exposure areas. These health risks included cardiovascular disease, sleep disturbance, hearing impairment, attentional and learning problems, and psychological disturbance, like the exacerbation of symptoms for those with preexisting anxiety and post-traumatic stress disorder diagnoses.

The effects of chronic noise pollution on wildlife are well documented. A noise-induced stress response can lead to problems with fertility, reproductive behavior, foraging, and immune function. In a comprehensive meta-analysis, investigators from Queen's University Belfast reviewed 108 studies assessing the effects of *anthropogenic* (human-caused) *noise* on 109 different species, from mammals to birds, fish to amphibians, mollusks to arthropods. They found that "anthropogenic noise on different species of wildlife can negatively affect the persistence of populations." This is especially true among predatory animals, particularly those that use echolocation. For instance, the hunting efficiency of insectivorous bats was significantly diminished in the presence of traffic noise.

In the most fundamental terms, sound is vibrations that travel as waves through air, water, or solids. It becomes noise pollution when it adversely affects the health, well-being, or survival of living things. Documented noise complaints usually focus on sounds that are loud and/or low-frequency (i.e., low-pitched). Low frequencies also travel the farthest, as is the case with the rumble of jet noise and maritime traffic.

It is no coincidence that I have not observed Whidbey's river otters during periods of high jet activity, as they can relocate to a different part of their territory when flight training is underway. Sea otters, however, are constrained by their nearshore foraging habitat; they cannot simply pack up and move. Instead, as field investigators Shawn Larson, Jim Bodkin, and others have observed, they *flush*, or dive, beneath the water, during low-altitude jet flights along the Olympic Peninsula. Just how much reprieve they get from the jet noise underwater is unclear, as a study of military aircraft noise on

Whidbey Island found that at 30 meters (98 feet) below the sea surface, the jet noise exceeded the noise from ships and other vessels in the area.

But the kelp in sea otter habitats may help attenuate noise. A 2025 study showed that kelp forests reduced the impact of motorboat noise, absorbing and reflecting the sound waves. Aquatic vegetation such as seagrasses have also been shown to dampen ocean noise by as much as 20 to 40 percent. The symbiotic relationship between kelp and sea otters is well known, and indeed, sea otters' keystone species status is attributed to this relationship. When sea otters occupy a nearshore foraging area, they manage the sea urchins that graze on the kelp; without them, kelp forests disappear, overrun by urchins. This means that by supporting the health of kelp, sea otters also support not only blue-carbon sequestration and habitat for a variety of species but also a natural buffer from noise pollution.

How big an effect does noise pollution have on otters? A Danish study of Eurasian otters found that as underwater noise increased, the frequency of their foraging dives decreased. It also took them longer to extract fish from a feeding device under noisy conditions, and they sometimes gave up altogether. Similarly, sea otters near Monterey hauled out less in the presence of noise and human disturbance. Even though sea otters technically don't need to leave the water, hauling out lets them escape predators as well as conserve energy during cold or stormy days. These advantages are compromised in the presence of noise from vessels, highway traffic, and human activity.

If chronic noise is bad, is peace and quiet good? In short, yes. According to studies on lab mice, the absence of ambient noise contributes to neurogenesis (the process by which new brain cells develop) in the hippocampus, the part of the brain responsible for consolidating new memories, facilitating spatial navigation, and to some extent, regulating emotions. A New Zealand study comparing people who lived in quiet areas and noisy areas found that those living in quiet communities scored higher on every health and well-being index, including physical, psychological, and social. These and other studies support the *calm and connection theory*, which posits the importance of calming, quiet natural areas for health and well-being and underscores the need to conserve not just natural habitat but also quiet spaces.

This is all the more urgent considering there are very few quiet places left. According to acoustic ecologist Gordon Hempton, "the extinction rate for quiet places vastly exceeds the species rate." That is, despite the accelerated rate of extinction among plants and animals, quiet spaces—like Washington's Hoh Rain Forest, considered one of the quietest places in the United States—are disappearing even faster, casualties of global habitat loss. Anthropogenic sounds are now twice as prevalent as natural sounds in 63 percent of protected parks and forests. The Salish Sea, with its network of marine protected areas, aquatic reserves, and conservation sites, is dominated by the background noise and the pervasive presence of cargo ships, outboard motorboats, and ferry traffic.

The coastal waters of the Salish Sea are among the busiest waterways in North America, accounting for over 50 percent of the shipping traffic in the United States. In 2019, the *Seattle Times* reported that "more than 300,000 ferry sailings traveled the Salish Sea in 2018, while 6,330 cargo, container and passenger vessels and 1,134 oil tankers and barge tows also entered Washington waters." The ferry systems across the Pacific Northwest have always felt like an extension of home to me. For me, driving onto the deck of a ferry signals the start of a vacation. The ferry represents a promise of escape, a homecoming, and an opportunity to explore somewhere new. For others, the ferry is part of their daily commute. Yet there can be no doubt that for the wildlife beneath the waves, the story is very different.

Along Admiralty Inlet, which abuts the shipping and ferry route, the *mean ambient sound pressure*, or noise underwater, is 117 decibels. Why is this a problem? Since sound travels five times faster in water than in air, and since there's less light the deeper you go underwater, marine animals rely heavily on sound cues to avoid predation, find food, locate mates, navigate, and even communicate. And in aquatic environments, noise doesn't just affect hearing. Since the mechanism of sound is both pressure and vibration, noise also affects marine animals' balance, proprioception, and touch.

In fact, noise has been implicated as the most probable cause of marine mammal mass stranding events (MSEs). In a particularly bad MSE in the United Kingdom, more than fifty short-beaked common dolphins were stranded in the shallows of Falmouth Bay, Cornwall, at least twenty-six of which died before they could be herded back out to sea. According to a report published in *PLOS One*, "international naval exercises did occur in close proximity to the MSE" and were "the most probable cause of the Falmouth Bay MSE."

In her book, *Sing Like Fish*, Amorina Kingdon describes how many fish have the kind of musical vocalizations we normally associate with birds and other terrestrial animals: "Grunt sculpins, well, grunt when they're scared. Black rockfish . . . make low-pitched hums to impress a mate." Noise pollution interrupts all of that. For example, it obscures the high-frequency pulses and clicks of Southern Resident killer whales, affecting their ability to catch fish. A study from the University of Washington's Center for Ecosystem Sentinels found that vessel noise reduced the orcas' hunting success; males missed their targets more often when hunting at greater depths, while females were less willing to hunt at all, forgoing foraging opportunities in favor of traveling to quieter waters.

This might sound like good news for the SRKW's favorite prey, the Chinook salmon—but this endangered fish is also affected by vessel noise. The Chinook has the longest freshwater migration of any salmon species, with populations in Washington and Oregon traveling over 1,400 kilometers (870 miles) and navigating multiple dams to return to their spawning grounds. Although they make use of olfaction and geomagnetic cues while migrating, Chinook, like all fish, also use their lateral line system to detect low-frequency sound waves, vibrations, and water movement, all of which are imperative for navigating their surroundings, detecting predators, and finding prey. Noise pollution disrupts that system.

A study of Atlantic salmon's stress response when exposed to prolonged noise found that they are most sensitive to low-frequency noise, like that produced by large shipping vessels. This is probably true of their Chinook salmon relatives as well. Their reaction to chronic noise is similar to ours: an initial startle response followed by increased cortisol levels and changes in brain activity, which, over time, inhibit the expression of genes related to growth, fertility, and reproduction—which, for Chinook, involves migration. Thus noise pollution makes it harder for Chinook to survive and thrive at every stage of life.

Twenty-eight percent of the 169,400 species on the International Union for Conservation of Nature's Red List are threatened with extinction, including five species of otters that are classified as endangered. Otters, across the subfamily of Lutrinae, are a mirror for watersheds, wetlands, and oceans, reflecting the health of their habitats. Despite global conservation efforts, otters are still in trouble. In many parts of their range, like Southern and Southeast Asia, South America, and parts of Europe, their numbers are critically low. This is due to many reasons, including historic exploitation during the international fur trade and contemporary pressures from wildlife trafficking, road mortalities, pollution, and overfishing of their prey.

But perhaps the greatest threat to otters today is the loss of clean, viable habitat. Between 2009 and 2019, wetlands in the United States shrank by 670,000 acres, which is roughly the land area of Rhode Island. Without additional conservation actions to protect these ecosystems, this loss will continue, resulting in reduced habitat for wildlife and plants. This is a loss for the environment, of course, but it is also a loss for people. Wetlands safeguard us. They're a cultural treasure for many Native American tribes and serve as natural filters, protecting the watershed by trapping pollutants and excess nitrogen and phosphorus from agricultural runoff. They prevent flooding, store water for aquifers, control erosion, and sequester carbon.

Wetlands aren't the only habitats at risk. In 2020,

the world had approximately 9 billion acres of natural forest, covering around 28 percent of its land area. By 2024, it had lost around 26.7 million hectares (66 million acres), equivalent to 10 trillion kilograms of carbon dioxide, due to deforestation (human-caused) and tree-cover loss (climate-related). And according to the Canadian Interagency Forest Fire Center, in 2024, Canada lost 93,000 square kilometers of forests to fires, an area roughly equal to that of the state of Indiana.

There are so many cautionary tales, tragedies that have devastated habitats and wildlife. The infamous *Exxon Valdez* oil spill is a well-known example. On March 24, 1989, in an attempt to avoid icebergs in Alaska's Prince William Sound, the *Exxon Valdez* oil tanker collided with Bligh Reef, spilling 10.8 million gallons of crude oil into the sound. It was the worst oil spill in US history at the time (and is still the second worst, after the *Deepwater Horizon* spill in 2010), covering 2,100 kilometers (1,300 miles) of shoreline and killing an estimated 250,000 sea birds, 3,000 otters, 300 seals, 250 bald eagles, and 22 killer whales.

The spill prompted a massive cleanup effort. Exxon paid $2 billion for oil remediation, which involved manually wiping oil from rocks, mechanical tilling, skimming the sea surface, applying chemical dispersant sprays, and high-pressure hot and cold seawater washing. Although the hot-water washing was effective in removing oil, it also effectively killed shocked plants and animals that had already been affected by the oil. Acute oil exposure in sea otters resulted in lung, liver, and kidney damage, and the otters had poor survival rates, even when placed in aquariums.

Annual oil surveys in Prince William Sound, conducted over fifteen years later, found that oil persisted on beaches and in subsurface sediments, but it was sequestered or buried, isolating it from the recovering ecology. Further, surveys of Prince William Sound suggest some sea otter populations have been steadily recovering at a rate of about 4 percent per year. Despite the egregiousness of this environmental catastrophe, I am still hopeful, always rooting for the resilience of nature. I continue to keep an eye on the ecology articles for evidence of a slow and cautiously optimistic recovery of the Sound.

The importance of science funding, advocacy, and conservation to continue habitat recovery efforts is critical. Progress in technology may provide some of the solutions we need. Artificial intelligence, for example, has been used in conservation research to enable more extensive exploration of the ocean, support genomics, and facilitate the identification of wildlife populations. Although cloud data centers have high power needs, consumer demand to use sustainable energy alternatives is pressuring companies like Facebook to use wind and solar sources for their energy consumption. Additionally, Washington state aims to reduce both carbon emissions and anthropogenic noise by switching from diesel ferries to hybrid ferries. If we use technology in the right ways, we can develop better environmental and health policies, enhance the speed of legislative action, and foster international collaboration toward those solutions.

We have seen how effective efforts like these can be since the 1950s, when countries in Europe began to build green bridges, overpasses, and underpasses to protect wildlife in areas with heavy motor traffic. One of the earliest examples of these "ecoducts" was the Terlet Wildlife Crossing in the Netherlands, which facilitated the safe passage of deer, wild boars, red foxes, badgers, and rodents. It was so successful that more than fifty-six green bridges are in existence today; one such bridge in Sweden saw a 70 percent reduction in road mortality of roe deer.

Meanwhile, in the United States, the average Montanan has a 1 in 53 chance of hitting an animal while driving to and from their place of work, a statistic that prompted the passage of watershed wildlife crossing legislation in 2025. In Colorado, a green crossing on State Highway 9 reduced wildlife road mortality by 90 percent, and wildlife crossings along the Trans-Canada Highway have let bear populations cross the road, allowing isolated populations to breed and furthering their genetic diversity. In the Pacific Northwest, the Washington State Department of Transportation, US Forest Service, community volunteers, tribal groups like the Snoqualmie and Yakama Nation, and conservation groups like Conservation Northwest collaborated on the I-90 Snoqualmie Pass East Project, with multiple under- and overpass crossings along a fifteen-mile stretch. From 2014 to 2023, more than twenty connectivity structures have supported the safe crossings of more than twenty-five thousand animals, including river otters passing from wetlands to Keechelus Lake.

If only there had been a green crossing in Marin County, California, in July 2024, when a romp of three river otters was killed by traffic on Point Reyes–Petaluma Road. Megan Isadore, director of the River Otter Ecology Project, said that "about 90 percent of all otter deaths recorded by [the] organization are due to collisions with vehicles, rather than diseases or other natural causes." Wildlife accommodation through roadside conservation is an investment in our ecology. With an estimated 193 million kilometers (120 million miles) of road spanning the earth, finding ways to prevent collisions is critical.

Despite the extinction of so many species, we are still a diverse planet. Science has only identified an estimated one-tenth of all species on earth, and new ones are discovered every year. Sometimes these are species that we'd observed but didn't know were their own species, like the Mesoamerican otter, previously thought to be a subspecies of the neotropical otter. Other times, these are species we're observing for the first time. And sometimes we think a species is extinct, only to discover that it's actually still around, as with the hairy-nosed otter.

A similar discovery happened in November 2024, when a juvenile Asian small-clawed otter was captured in far-western Nepal, nurtured, and released back into the wild. Though ASCOs weren't thought to be extinct, this was the first time one had been seen in Nepal in just under two centuries. Similarly in India, just two years prior, two confirmed sightings provided the first photo documentation of ASCOs in the Central Himalayas. These new sightings offer hope that, with the right conservation efforts, threatened and endangered otter populations can bounce back.

This may be true for the Eurasian otter as well. Despite its expansive range across Europe, Asia, and parts of northern Africa, its global status is Near Threatened, and it's Critically Endangered in some regions. It was once extinct in the Netherlands and nearly extinct in the UK. However, national and international legislation and legal protections like the European Union Habitats Directive, restrictions or bans on hunting and trapping, and reintroduction efforts have encouraged a tentative recovery in many parts of their range. In 2021, a Eurasian otter skull was even found in Nepal, the first physical evidence of its presence there in three decades.

The endangered smooth-coated otters made a similar return to the Singaporean part of their range in the 1990s, after an absence of over two decades. By the start of the COVID-19 pandemic, their population had recovered enough that, when most of Singapore's humans withdrew indoors, they took the opportunity to descend on vacant shopping centers and local landmarks. One local otter romp, a seven-member family nicknamed the Zouks, raided a pool; another romp of sixteen otters was observed "trying to cut through the lobby of a children's hospital." Like many others during the pandemic, I enjoyed the digital footage of the Singaporean otters on social media. Even now, years after lockdown, smooth-coated otters frequent the urban city center, often among throngs of enthusiastic observers, who, with their phones in hand, document the coexistence of the two species—humans and otters—along the banks of the Singapore River.

As for giant otters, by the late twentieth century, there were only 5,000 left in the wild, due to the international fur trade, deforestation, overfishing, and gold mining and its associated mercury pollution. However, in recent decades, they have begun to return to some parts of the upper Rio Negro and the Araguaia River in Brazil, as well as localized parts of Peru and Colombia, suggesting that conservation efforts are making a difference.

And finally, what about the otters of North America? How have their populations fared over the years? River otters, once extensively hunted and trapped throughout the continent, have recovered much of their historic range thanks to conservation and reintroduction programs like the one in New Mexico, where river otters hadn't lived since 1953. In 2008, New Mexico Friends of River Otters, in collaboration with the nonprofit Amigos Bravos, helped reintroduce thirty-three otters at Rio Pueblo. By 2017, the number of animals had increased to as many as a hundred, and their range had extended along the upper Rio Grande and as far south as Cochiti Lake. The population continues to thrive, supporting the native ecosystem by eating invasive carp and crayfish. In Pennsylvania, river otters "had largely disappeared from the state by the early 1900s," due to overharvest and watershed contamination from coal mining. But through reintroduction efforts beginning in the 1990s and into the early 2000s, as well as watershed cleanup efforts, western Pennsylvania river otters are making a comeback.

Additionally, the endangered sea otter, thanks to reintroduction efforts in the late 1960s and 1970s, has recolonized many parts of its historic range in Canada, Alaska, Washington, and California. In March 2025, after almost a decade of collaborative modeling and habitat assessment by conservation scientists and nonprofit organizations like the Elakha Alliance, the Wildlife Conservation Network announced the Sea Otter Fund, a fundraising effort targeting $40 million in support of sea otter reintroductions in Oregon and Northern California.

Zoos and aquariums are also at the forefront of conservation efforts aimed at mitigating biodiversity loss resulting from climate change, human interference, and habitat loss. The Monterey Bay Aquarium's Sea Otter

Research and Conservation Program is involved in the rescue, rehabilitation, and surrogacy of orphaned and injured sea otters. Likewise, the Seattle Aquarium supports wild populations through monthly surveys of sea otters along Washington's Olympic Peninsula, documenting their foraging behavior and numbers.

Our actions matter for the long-term survival of lutrines. Human activities have pushed otters to the brink of extinction, and yet dedicated efforts have pulled them back, one habitat or population at a time. Otters need our vigilance. They need protection from poaching, the exotic pet trade, retributive shootings, and roadway collisions. And above all, they need clean water. No lifeform on earth can live without water, and for otters, it's home. They need rivers, lakes, and oceans that aren't contaminated by our medications, pesticides, mine tailings, urban runoff, and farm waste.

Calls to action can feel useless in the face of the overwhelming reality of global habitat degradation, especially amid partisan politics, unrest, and uncertainty. Clean water, green spaces, and healthy wildlife should not be political issues; they are shared needs. We may not have the power to solve these problems individually, but together we can work toward enacting the shared values we have in protecting our global home. We can change not only how we shop, how much we consume, and how we travel, but also how we treat and talk to one another, and how we interact with nature. We can inform and advocate. We can support those who protect our sacred spaces and nonjudgmentally encourage others to start making their lifestyles more sustainable. We can elect leaders who recognize the long-term consequences of habitat loss and unsustainable energy and demand those in power remember that the earth is a commons that we all share, not just with humans but with all organisms. As Jane Goodall said, "You cannot get through a single day without having an impact on the world around you." We don't need a "me" and a "you"; we need an "us." This is not a fight, but a global collaboration to meet our united needs for clean water, wild spaces, safe communities, and a future where otters and all animals might thrive.

Epilogue

You have to decide that you care. You have to decide to be optimistic. It doesn't just come naturally. Because the question has been posed to me before: "How do you stay optimistic?" I don't . . . I make a choice every day to live with purpose and to move forward.

—CÉLINE COUSTEAU

I returned to Portland in the fall of 2019, at the end of my sabbatical year. Tom drove up to Whidbey to help me pack up all the camera equipment, a mass of scuba gear, and seventy-five fecal samples that hadn't been processed.

The day we left, I got up at four, headed to the lake, and waited for Patches. She and I were old friends now, in a well-worn pattern, like ladies who lunch. She wasn't wary of me, and I sat far enough back that I wasn't a threat. I would miss this: sitting at the lakeside with my camera in hand, my phone at the ready just in case I wanted to switch from stills to video. Patches emerged solo shortly after I arrived, cutting a V in the water. She threw her flat head back as she worked a freshly caught fish, then dove back down to find a second helping. We were companions, separate but together.

As Tom and I drove onto the Coupeville–Port Townsend ferry, my chest cleaved, and I felt an overwhelming sense of loss. I didn't know why. We weren't *leaving*, not really. We could come back, and we would. The otters were fine. Patches did her job. Her three pups had grown and left her care, establishing their own territories outside Admirals Cove.

We ascended the ferry stairs, making our way to the galley for a tradition we observe every ferry ride that isn't catastrophically stormy: a cup of coffee and a Beecher's mac and cheese. It occurred to me why I was feeling unsettled. It wasn't that I was leaving; I was upset because I was returning—to a city.

On impulse, as Tom forked mac and cheese into his mouth, I blurted out, "What do you think about moving?"

"What do you mean? Move to Whidbey full-time?"

"No," I said. "I mean out of the city, to the country."

"I guess we could. Not ready to go back to the city?"

"I'm not. But I'm surprised that you're not protesting."

He shrugged. "I've been living in the city for the last year, and without you, it hasn't felt like home. If we moved to the Willamette Valley, you'd have a shorter commute to Forest Grove."

"What about your work?" I asked. "You'd be farther from jobs in Portland."

"I have jobs all over the city. I'd just have to work out scheduling by geography."

I looked back at the harbor shrinking from us as we moved into the sound. A small flock of white pelicans flew over Crockett Lake. They're a celebrated migratory bird on the island, but this was the first time I'd seen them. As the sun sank below the trees, it cast a golden glow across the ferry's stern, reaching over the harbor and into Admirals Cove. I wondered if Patches was there, swimming through the remaining streamers of sunlight, catching her dinner.

By Labor Day, our floating home in Portland was for sale, all of our nonessentials in storage. It sold during the peak of the pandemic. Some other city dwellers decided they, too, needed natural things, and floating atop the Columbia River during the shelter-in-place would suit.

They moved in, and we moved out, to a place in the Willamette Valley, deep in the heart of Oregon wine country. It's an old homestead on 70 acres of unfarmable land, bisected by a creek. Skeletal pilings are all that remain of an old bridge long washed away, but you can still cross the creek by foot when the water runs low. I needed no excuse to plant a dozen trail cameras among the blackberry cane and in the understory of old oaks and cherry trees.

Today, I still make it to Whidbey every month, but I no longer see my friend in the bay, her patchy muzzle markings wrapped around a flounder, an eye to the beach as she swims toward the safety of her culvert.

In the early spring of 2023, I received an email from a neighbor saying that she'd found a female otter lying dead on her property. She asked if I wanted to come to Whidbey to collect the body. By that time, Patches would have been at least eight years old, nearing the end of the typical lifespan of wild river otters. But I had just lost my dad to liver cancer two months earlier, and I didn't have the heart to lose another friend. Resisting the urge to ask for a photograph, I asked my neighbor to bury the otter.

There is a new romp of otters in Admirals Cove these days, another kin group of an adult female and three juveniles. I wonder if this romp belongs to Crest or Slash and I just don't recognize them in their adult fur, without their namesake markings. Unlike Patches, they're leisurely, entering the bay around nine in the morning and sometimes showing up again in the afternoon, preferring to stay in the lake for dinner. I'm not surprised they have their own way of doing things. Whidbey is special: its people, its geography, its wildlife, and of course, its otters.

Acknowledgments

I am deeply indebted to all the people mentioned in this book. My introduction to otters, studying their behavior, learning about their ecology, and appreciating the breadth of my actions in their future, is owed to many people. Of those people, I owe Jenna Land Free of Folio Literary Management a unique debt, not just for her extraordinary advice, advocacy, and encouragement, but also for her friendship; without her, this book would not have been written. Equally true, if Pacific University had not supported my research through sabbaticals and grants, I would not be writing this book, either. I am grateful to be part of such a wonderful liberal arts community.

My heart expanded the day I was introduced to Whidbey Island. In many ways, this book is a love letter to Whidbey, the San Juans, Alaska, and more broadly, the Pacific Northwest—the beauty of the area, all the wildlife, their advocates, my neighbors, new friends, and most especially Whidbey Camano Land Trust. I am so appreciative of WCLT's support in connecting me with their conservation community, the speaking invitations, the press, and the stewards for their endless enthusiasm and exceptional correspondence in offering eyes in the field when I could not be everywhere at once. I am also grateful to Sarah Schmidt and Bob Wilbur for their initial read of the Whidbey parts of this book, and to the Washington State Parks and the Washington Department of Fish and Wildlife. I am also grateful to Whidbey's Pioneer Group; all of you gave me a home when I needed it most. Thank you to Seattle Pacific University, including Drs. Baine Craft and Tim Nelson for their warm invitation to study on Blakely Island. I also thank the Oregon Zoo's Research Associate Program and its support of my lab's ex situ otter research.

As I began writing this book, I inquired with Dr. Shawn Larson of the Seattle Aquarium if I might join her in sea otter observation along the Olympic Peninsula. Not only did she welcome me, but I was also invited to contribute by learning their foraging protocols for data collection. Like a mentor, she nurtured introductions to other otter conservation advocates by nominating me to the IUCN Otter Specialist Group, where we traveled together for their triennial congress in Peru. She opened her home to me for the Seattle Aquarium's biennial sea otter workshop a month later. I cannot begin to voice my appreciation for her professional generosity, openness, and friendship.

I discovered, through researching this book, that there is something uniquely special about the international otter conservation community. The scientists, advocates, and volunteers tirelessly devote their time, energy, and enthusiasm to the betterment of wildlife and ecology, extending that respect and care to each other as well. At the OSG, I met Jim Bodkin, Margherita Bandini, Anna Loy, Caroline Leuchtenberger, and Nicole Duplaix, who were extremely generous with their time and encouragement. So were Megan Isadore and Terence Carroll of the River Otter Ecology Project in California, and Tom Serfass of Frostburg State University in Maryland, Jeff Black of Cal Poly Humboldt, Caroline DeLong of the Rochester Institute of Technology, Klaus-Peter Koepfli of the Smithsonian-Mason School of Conservation at George Mason University, Brittany Blades of the Oregon Coast Aquarium, and so many others. I apologize that I cannot list them all here. I hope you know who you are.

This book is the result of contributions from many communities, including those closest to my heart—my family. Many thanks are owed to Tom, my husband, for his patience in serving as a sounding board for the numerous chapter revisions of this book and for knowing me so well that he could make a real estate decision, sight unseen, that would change my life. To my uncle and dive buddy, Jim, for his guidance in the water; to my aunt Judy for her encouragement; and to my mom for being an audience, as I read aloud each chapter for her to listen for errors, and for her reminders that "your dad would be so proud." To my dear friends Michael and Jamie, who regularly checked in, even while they were living abroad, to remind me not to overextend myself. And to Chad Walling, for a lifetime of friendship beginning when we were two tiny deckhands on our dads' boats, and for continuing to offer support and encouragement after forty-plus years, including his review of and suggestions for the introduction.

And finally, to my editor, Lauren O'Neal of Tarcher, who believed in this project and provided the opportunity to write this book, and whose editing and revision suggestions not only elevated the content of this book but also made me a better writer. Her intuitive guidance always hit the mark, both in terms of the nudges I needed to move the story forward and in offering candid, insightful feedback. Thank you.

Global Otter Distribution and Population

Kingdom: Animalia → *Phylum:* Chordata →
Class: Mammalia → *Order:* Carnivora →
Family: Mustelidae ("Mustelids") →
Subfamily: Lutrinae ("Lutrines") →
Otters

Common Name	Scientific Name	Length
1. Sea Otter (Sea Beaver, Kamchatka Otter)	*Enhydra lutris*	67–163 cm
2. Giant Otter (i.e., Ariranha, Lobo de Río)	*Pteronura brasiliensis*	145–180 cm
3. African Clawless Otter (Cape Clawless)	*Aonyx capensis*	115–160 cm
4. Congo Clawless Otter (i.e., Swamp Otter)	*Aonyx congicus*	110–150 cm
5. Neotropical Otter (i.e., Long-Tailed Otter)	*Lontra longicaudis*	90–136 cm
6. Mesoamerican Otter* (i.e., Trans-Andean Otter)	*Lontra annectens*	90–136 cm
7. North American River Otter (i.e., Nearctic River Otter)	*Lontra canadensis*	100–153 cm
8. Eurasian Otter (i.e., Common; Old World Otter)	*Lutra lutra*	102–138 cm
9. Smooth-Coated Otter	*Lutrogale perspicillata*	106–130 cm
10. Southern River Otter (i.e., Huillin, Chilean Otter)	*Lontra provocax*	100–116 cm
11. Hairy Nosed Otter (i.e., Sumatran Otter)	*Lutra sumatrana*	105–113 cm
12. Spotted-Necked Otter (i.e., Water Hyena)	*Hydrictis maculicollis*	95–115 cm
13. Marine Otter (i.e., Chungungo, Gato Marino)	*Lontra felina*	87–115 cm
14. Asian Small-Clawed Otter (i.e., Short-Clawed Otter)	*Aonyx cinereus*	65–94 cm

Organized by weight (largest to smallest), "Otter Species," Otter Specialist Grou[p] International Union for Conservation of Nature (IUCN), accessed May 31, 2025, https://www.otterspecialistgroup.org/osg-newsite/otter-species/.

Weight	Distribution	IUCN Status
23–36 kg	Parts of the North Pacific Rim	**Endangered**
24–34 kg	Andean region, Amazon Basin, and southern South America	**Endangered**
12–19 kg	Sub-Saharan Africa	Near Threatened
12–17 kg	Central and East Africa	Near Threatened
10–14 kg	Central and South America	Near Threatened
10–14 kg	Mexico, Central America, and South America west of the Andes	Data deficient
8–11 kg	North America	Least Concern
4–11 kg	Parts of Asia, Europe, the Middle East, and North Africa	Near Threatened
7–10 kg	South and Southeast Asia, and Iraq	Vulnerable
5–10 kg	Argentina and Chile	**Endangered**
5–8 kg	Southeast Asia	**Endangered**
4–7 kg	Sub-Saharan Africa	Near Threatened
3–6 kg	South America	**Endangered**
2–5 kg	South and Southeast Asia, parts of East Asia	Vulnerable

* Vera de Ferran et al., "Genome-Wide Data Support Recognition of an Additional Species of Neotropical River Otter (Mammalia, Mustelidae, Lutrinae)," *Journal of Mammalogy* 105, no. 3 (2024): 534–42.

Resources

For any readers who are interested in continuing to learn about conservation in general or otters in specific, I've compiled a (non-exhaustive) list of books, websites, and organizations where you can read more and find out how to get involved locally.

Responsible Wildlife Viewing

Best Practices for Social Media Posting and Sharing Wildlife Images

Share Savvy
otterspecialistgroup.org/osg-newsite/wp-content/uploads/2025/03/ShareSavvy-Guidelines.pdf

Marine Mammal Viewing Guidelines

NOAA Marine Mammal Protection Act
fisheries.noaa.gov/topic/laws-policies/marine-mammal-protection-act

Responsible Observation of Wildlife

Audubon Society's Ethical Bird Photography and Videography
audubon.org/photography/awards/audubons-guide-ethical-bird-photography-and-videography

National Parks Service
nps.gov/subjects/watchingwildlife/7ways

Respect the Nap: Sea Otter Viewing Guidelines
seaottersavvy.org/viewing-guidelines

US Fish and Wildlife Guidelines for Ethical Wildlife Observation
fws.gov/story/ethics-wildlife-photography

(Alaska) Sea Otter–Safe Boating: Vessel Guidelines for Boat Operators
fws.gov/sea-otters-boater-guidance

Sustainable Travel

A Beginner's Guide to Sustainable Travel
nationalgeographic.com/travel/article/how-to-travel-better-a-beginners-guide-to-sustainable-travel-in-2023-and-beyond

Calculate Your Eco-Travel Carbon Footprint and Cut Where You Can
sustainabletravel.org/our-work/carbon-offsets/calculate-footprint

Center for Sustainable Tourism
scrd.asu.edu/sustainabletourism

The Difference Between Green or Ecotourism and Sustainable Travel
gstc.org/ecotourism

What You Can Do to Travel Responsibly
gstc.org/for-travelers

Things You Can Do for Wildlife and Watershed Health

EarthDay.org: Many Projects, Tool Kits, and Ideas to Minimize Your Impact to Animals
earthday.org

Oceans Research: Protecting the Oceans; 10 Easy Ways You Can Contribute
oceans-research.com/protecting-oceans-10-ways-to-contribute

One Tree Planted: Nine Tips for Sustainable Eating
onetreeplanted.org/blogs/stories/9-tips-sustainable-eating

Zero Waste: Reducing Your Carbon Impact
zerowaste.org

Recommended Reading and Viewing on Otters

Brown, Nicholas, dir. *Nature.* Season 38, episode 2, "The Serengeti Rules." Aired October 9, 2019, on PBS. pbs.org/wnet/nature/serengeti-rules-dhbtnm/19906.

Collard, Rosemary-Claire. *Animal Traffic: Lively Capital in the Global Exotic Pet Trade.* Duke University Press, 2020.

Cooper, Simon. *The Otters' Tale.* William Collins, 2018.

Darlington, Miriam. *Otter Country: An Unexpected Adventure in the Natural World.* Tin House Books, 2024.

Davis, Randall W., and Anthony M. Pagano, eds. *Ethology and Behavioral Ecology of Sea Otters and Polar Bears.* Ethology and Behavioral Ecology of Marine Mammals. Springer, 2021.

Duplaix, Nicole, and Margherita Bandini. *We Love Otters.* Version 1.0. IUCN-SSC. Otter Specialist Group, Four Corners Institute, 2016.

Estes, James A. *Serendipity: An Ecologist's Quest to Understand Nature.* University of California Press, 2016.

Gibson, James R. *Otter Skins, Boston Ships, and China Goods: The Maritime Fur Trade of the Northwest Coast, 1785–1841.* McGill-Queen's University Press, 1992.

Groenendijk, Jessica. *The Giant Otter: Giants of the Amazon.* Whittles, 2019.

Hajek, Frank, and Jessica Groenendijk. *Giants of the Madre de Dios.* Frankfurt Zoological Society, 2006.

Kenyon, Karl W. *The Sea Otter in the Eastern Pacific Ocean.* North American Fauna, no. 68. Fish and Wildlife Service, United States Department of the Interior, 1969.

Kruuk, Hans. *Otters: Ecology, Behaviour and Conservation.* Oxford University Press, 2006.

Larson, Shawn, James Bodkin, and Erin Foster, eds. *Sea Otter Conservation II: Nearshore Ecosystem Restoration.* 2nd ed. Academic Press, 2025.

Larson, Shawn, James L. Bodkin, and Glenn R. VanBlaricom, eds. *Sea Otter Conservation.* Academic Press, 2015.

VanBlaricom, Glenn. *Sea Otters.* Voyageur Press, 2001.

Werner, Michael James, dir. *Sea Otters v. Climate Change.* KQED. January 14, 2014. Video. kqed.org/quest/65409/sea-otters-urchins-kelp-climate-change.

Williamson, Henry. *Tarka the Otter: His Joyful Water-Life and Death in the Country of the Two Rivers.* G. P. Putnam's Sons, 1927.

Yoxon, Paul, and Grace Yoxon. *Otters of the World.* Whittles, 2019, Kindle.

Other Recommended Resources

Beck, Mary Giraudo. *Heroes and Heroines: Tlingit-Haida Legend.* Alaska Northwest Books, 1989.

Bekoff, Marc, and John A. Byers. *Animal Play: Evolutionary, Comparative, and Ecology Perspectives.* Cambridge University Press, 1998.

Brown, Stuart. *Play: How It Shapes the Brain, Opens the Imagination, and Investigates the Soul.* Avery, 2010.

Burghardt, Gordon M. *The Genesis of Animal Play: Testing the Limits.* Massachusetts Institute of Technology, 2005.

Cousteau, Jacques-Yves, and Philippe Diolé. *Octopus and Squid: The Soft Intelligence.* Translated by J. F. Bernard. Doubleday, 1973.

Cousteau, Jean-Michel, with Daniel Paisner. *My Father, the Captain: My Life with Jacques Cousteau.* National Geographic, 2010.

Earle, Sylvia A. *Blue Hope: Exploring and Caring for Earth's Magnificent Ocean.* National Geographic, 2014.

Goldfarb, Ben. *Crossings: How Road Ecology Is Shaping the Future of Our Planet.* W. W. Norton, 2023.

Goodall, Jane, with Phillip Berman. *Reason for Hope: A Spiritual Journey.* Grand Central, 2000.

Gooley, Tristan. *The Lost Art of Reading Nature's Signs: Use Outdoor Clues to Find Your Way, Predict the Weather, Locate Water, Track Animals—and Other Forgotten Skills.* The Experiment, 2015.

Guss, Elizabeth, Janice C. O'Mahony, and Mary Richardson. *Whidbey Island: Reflections on People & the Land.* History Press, 2014.

Hickel, Jason. *Less Is More: How Degrowth Will Save the World.* Little, Brown, 2020.

Jahren, Hope. *Lab Girl.* Alfred A. Knopf, 2016.

Jahren, Hope. *The Story of More: How We Got to Climate Change and Where to Go from Here.* Alfred A. Knopf, 2020.

Kimmerer, Robin Wall. *Braiding Sweetgrass: Indigenous Wisdom, Scientific Knowledge and the Teachings of Plants.* Milkweed Editions, 2013.

Kimmerer, Robin Wall. *The Serviceberry: Abundance and Reciprocity in the Natural World.* Scribner, 2024.

Kingdon, Amorina. *Sing Like Fish: How Sound Rules Life Under Water.* Crown, 2024.

Kruuk, Hans. *Niko's Nature: The Life of Niko Tinbergen and His Science of Animal Behaviour.* Oxford University Press, 2004.

Mathews, Beth Ann. *Deep Waters: A Memoir of Loss, Alaska Adventure, and Love Rekindled.* She Writes Press, 2023.

Nichols, Wallace J. *Blue Mind: The Surprising Science That Shows How Being Near, In, On, or Under Water Can Make You Happier, Healthier, More Connected, and Better at What You Do.* Little, Brown, 2014.

Pollard, Sandra. *A Puget Sound Orca in Captivity: The Fight to Bring Lolita Home.* History Press, 2019.

Robinson, Mary. *Climate Justice: Hope, Resilience, and the Fight for a Sustainable Future*. Bloomsbury, 2019.

Ruth, Maria Mudd. *Rare Birds: Pursuing the Mystery of the Marbled Murrelet*. Mountaineers Books, 2005.

Samish Indian Nation. *The Maiden of Deception Pass: Guardian of Her People*. Illustrated by Roger Fernandes. Dorsay & Easton LLP, 2019.

Schutt, Bill. *Bite: An Incisive History of Teeth, from Hagfish to Humans*. Algonquin Books, 2023.

Smith, Bren. *Eat Like a Fish: My Adventures Farming the Ocean to Fight Climate Change*. Vintage Books, 2019.

Sound Water Stewards of Island County. *Getting to the Water's Edge on Whidbey & Camano Islands*. 3rd ed. Sound Water Stewards of Island County, 2020.

Stein, William R., and the PBY-Naval Air Museum. *Naval Air Station Whidbey Island*. Images of America. Arcadia, 2017.

Toomey, David. *Kingdom of Play: What Ball-Bouncing Octopuses, Belly-Flopping Monkeys, and Mud-Sliding Elephants Reveal About Life Itself*. Scribner, 2024.

Select Otter Conservation Organizations

Convention on International Trade in Endangered Species of Wild Fauna and Flora (CITES)
cites.org/eng

iNaturalist, Otter Spotting
inaturalist.org/observations

International Otter Survival Fund (Isle of Skye, Scotland)
otter.org/our-work-projects

International Wildlife Coexistence Network
wildlifecoexistence.org/resource

Otter Specialist Group (IUCN, OSG)
otterspecialistgroup.org

TRAFFIC Global Office
traffic.org

African Otters (Spotted-Necked, Congo, and Cape Clawless)

African Otter Network
africanotternetwork.org

Eurasian Otters

Cardiff University Otter Project
otterproject.uk

Cork Nature Network, Eurasian Otter Project
corknaturenetwork.ie/what-we-do/the-eurasian-otter

Mull Otter Group
mullottergroup.co.uk

UK Wild Otter Trust
ukwildottertrust.org

Giant River Otters

Projeto Ariranhas (The Giant Otter Project)
giantotterproject.org

San Diego Zoo Global's Giant Otter Conservation Program (Perú)
cochacashu.sandiegozooglobal.org/giant-otter-conservation-program

Save the Giants (Guyana)
savethegiants.org

Wildlife Giant River Otter (Peru)
peru.wcs.org/en-us/Wildlife/Giant-River-Otter.aspx

Marine Otters

Fundación Chungungo
instagram.com/fundacionchungungo

Hairy-Nosed Otters

Phnom Tamao Rescue Centre (Wildlife Alliance)
wildlifealliance.org/wildlife-phnom-tamao

Neotropical and Mesoamerican Otters

Nutrias de Mexico
facebook.com/NutriasDeMexico

North American River Otters

Amigos Bravos
amigosbravos.org

Rio Nutria Preserve, Nature Conservancy
nature.org/en-us/get-involved/how-to-help/places-we-protect/rio-nutria-preserve

River Otter Ecology Project (ROEP)
riverotterecology.org

Seatuck Otter Watch (SOW)
seatuck.org/otter-watch

Willistown Conservation Trust
wctrust.org

Sea Otters

Alaska SeaLife Center
alaskasealife.org

Elakha Alliance
elakhaalliance.org

Friends of Sea Otter, Defenders of Wildlife
defenders.org/friends-of-sea-otter

Lenfest Ocean Program
lenfestocean.org

Long Beach Aquarium of the Pacific
aquariumofpacific.org/exhibits/otters/southern_sea_otter

Marine Mammal Center
marinemammalcenter.org

Monterey Aquarium Sea Otter Research Center
montereybayaquarium.org/animals/mammals/sea-otter

Nydra Ecological
sites.google.com/view/nhydra-eco

Oregon Coast Aquarium
aquarium.org/support

Sea Otter Foundation & Trust (SOFT)
seaotterfoundationtrust.org

Sea Otter Savvy
seaottersavvy.org

Seattle Aquarium
seattleaquarium.org/conservation/research/marine-populations

Wildlife Conservation Network, Sea Otter Fund
wildnet.org/seaotterfund

Smooth-Coated Otters

Malaysia Otter Network
behance.net/gallery/111687565/Malaysia-Otter-Network

OtterWatch
facebook.com/OtterWatch

Southern River Otters

Fundación Lontra (Chile)
fundacionlontra.org

Select Washington Conservation Groups

Cascadia Research Collective
cascadiaresearch.org

Center for Whale Research
whaleresearch.com

Citizens of Ebey's Reserve
citizensofebeysreserve.com

Conservation Northwest
conservationnw.org/join-us

Friends of the San Juans
sanjuans.org

Port Townsend Marine Science Center
ptmsc.org

Orca Conservancy
orcaconservancy.org

Orca Network
orcanetwork.org

Salish Center for Sustainable Fishing Methods
salishcenter.org/wave-warriors

Salish Sea Indigenous Guardians Association
ssiga.ca

SeaDoc Society
seadocsociety.org

Sound Water Stewards
soundwaterstewards.org

Whidbey Audubon Society
whidbeyaudubonsociety.org

Whidbey Camano Land Trust
wclt.org

Whidbey Community Foundation
whidbeyfoundation.org

Whidbey Environmental Action Network (WEAN)
whidbeyenvironment.org

Whidbey Island Grown Cooperative
whidbeyislandgrown.com

Notes

Chapter 1: Where Are the Otters?

9 **Yet ocean environments:** L. Thompson and L. L. Stelle, "Prey Preference of the North American River Otter (*Lontra canadensis*) Evaluated Based on Optimal Foraging Theory," *IUCN Otter Specialist Group Bulletin* 31, no. 1 (2014): 15–29.

9 **Because coastal areas:** Gail M. Blundell et al., "Effects of Food Resources on Spacing Behavior of River Otters: Does Forage Abundance Control Home-Range Size?," *Biotelemetry* 15 (2000): 325–33.

9 **All of that influences:** Paul Yoxon and Grace M. Yoxon, *Otters of the World* (Whittles, 2014), 43–45.

10 **Although Puget Sound:** Patrick Christie et al., "Marine Protected Areas in Puget Sound," Encyclopedia of Puget Sound, Puget Sound Institute, last modified April 24, 2023, https://www.eopugetsound.org/articles/marine-protected-areas-puget-sound.

10 **In fact, before stepping:** SPU4121, "Blakely Island's History and Architecture," Blakely Island Field Station, accessed June 3, 2024, https://blakely.spu.edu/2018/05/30/blakely-architecture/.

12 **The station's director:** Tim Nelson (director, Blakely Field Station, Seattle Pacific University), personal email communication, September 18, 2018.

18 **This is evidenced:** Larry J. Minter et al., "Digestible Energy Intake and Digestive Efficiency of Human-Managed North American River Otters (*Lontra canadensis*)," *Veterinary Medicine International* 2020, no. 1 (2020): 4307456; Mike Bottini, *The Long Island River Otter Project's River Otter Sign and Survey Manual*, Seatuck Environmental Association, January 2022, 3, https://seatuck.org/wp-content/uploads/2022/02/OtterManual.pdf.

18 **By comparison, humans:** Bottini, *The Long Island River Otter Project's River Otter Sign and Survey Manual*, 3.

19 **A male otter's urine:** Jessica Groenendijk and Frank Hajek, "A Reliable Method for Sexing Giant Otters (*Pteronura brasiliensis*) in the Wild," *Latin American Journal of Aquatic Mammals* 10, no. 2 (2015): 163–65.

19 **Male North American:** Eric J. Baitchman and George V. Kollias, "Clinical Anatomy of the North American River Otter (*Lontra canadensis*)," *Journal of Zoo and Wildlife Medicine* 31, no. 4 (2001): 473–83.

19 **Biologist Scott Shannon:** J. Scott Shannon, "Identifying Individual River Otters," Otters.net, accessed June 22, 2024, https://otters.net/id2.html.

20 **L-25, thought to be:** "Meet the Southern Residents," Orca Conservancy, accessed June 9, 2025, https://www.orcaconservancy.org/meet-the-southern-residents.

21 **Giant otters have:** Jan Reed-Smith et al., "Preliminary Report on the Behavior of Spotted-Necked Otter (*Lutra maculicollis*, Lichtenstein, 1835) Living in a Lentic Ecosystem," *Zoo Biology* 33, no. 2 (2014): 121–30.

21 **Both types of markings:** Jessica Groenendijk, *The Giant Otter: Giants of the Amazon* (Pen and Sword, 2019), 24–25.

22 **Instead, she's traveling:** Andrew Woodin, "Who Is the Fastest Swimmer in the World? Meet Olympian Caeleb Dressel," NBC, May 15, 2024, https://www.nbc.com

/nbc-insider/who-is-the-fastest-swimmer-in-the-world-caeleb-dressel-records-times.

22 **The word *otter*:** "Otter," Etymonline, retrieved June 20, 2024, https://www.etymonline.com/search?q=otter.

23 **Though otter pups:** J. Scott Shannon, "Behavioral Development of Otters (*Lutra canadensis*) in a Marine Coastal Habitat," *IUCN Otter Specialist Group Bulletin* 19A (1998): 312–15.

23 **Depending on food:** Wayne E. Melquist and Maurice G. Hornocker, "Ecology of River Otters in West Central Idaho," *Wildlife Monographs*, no. 83 (1983): 3–60.

24 **Their legs are short:** Léo Botton-Divet et al., "Swimmers, Diggers, Climbers and More, a Study of Integration across the Mustelids' Locomotor Apparatus (Carnivora: Mustelidae)," *Evolutionary Biology* 45, no. 2 (2018): 182–95.

27 **Though these spirits:** Bjorn Dihle, *Haunted Inside Passage: Ghosts, Legends, and Mysteries of Southeast Alaska* (Alaska Northwest Books, 2017), 80.

27 **They "capture those":** Dihle, *Haunted Inside Passage,* 80–81.

27 **They describe seeing people:** Dihle, *Haunted Inside Passage,* 87.

27 **One interviewee, Ethel Lund:** Dihle, *Haunted Inside Passage,* 81–82.

28 **They were also shared:** Daryl C. McClary, "Island County—Thumbnail History," essay 7523, HistoryLink.org, November 14, 2005, https://www.historylink.org/file/7523.

28 **In Salishan traditions:** David M. Buerge, *Chief Seattle and the Town That Took His Name: The Change of Worlds for the Native People and Settlers on Puget Sound* (Sasquatch Books, 2017), 5–6.

28 **According to folklorist:** Michael Dylan Foster, *The Book of Yōkai: Mysterious Creatures of Japanese Folklore* (University of California Press, 2015), 5.

Chapter 2: Whiskers in the Waves

32 **I solicited Jim's support:** Kyle Logan Wilson et al., "Use of Underwater Video to Assess Freshwater Fish Populations in Dense Submersed Aquatic Vegetation," *Marine and Freshwater Research* 66, no. 1 (2014): 10–22.

33 **If the clever otters:** Hans Kruuk, B. Nolet, and D. French, "Fluctuations in Numbers and Activity of Inshore Demersal Fishes in Shetland," *Journal of the Marine Biological Association of the United Kingdom* 68, no. 4 (1988): 601–17.

34 **Otters don't need masks:** "Otter," in Scholarly Community Encyclopedia, last modified May 28, 2025, https://encyclopedia.pub/entry/58397.

34 **They also have strong:** Andrew C. Kitchener, Carlo Meloro, and Terrie M. Williams, "Form and Function of the Musteloids," in *Biology and Conservation of Musteloids*, ed. David W. MacDonald, Chris Newman, and Lauren A. Harrington (Oxford University Press, 2017), 100.

35 **We have to trade:** "Number of Hairs on a Human Head," BioNumbers, https://bionumbers.hms.harvard.edu/bionumber.aspx?id=101509.

35 **In fact, they have:** Kate Riordan et al., "Ontogenetic Changes in Southern Sea Otter (*Enhydra lutris nereis*) Fur Morphology," *Journal of Morphology* 284, no. 9 (2023): e21624.

35 **During the maritime:** Brenda E. Ballachey and James L. Bodkin, "Challenges to Sea Otter Recovery and Conservation," in *Sea Otter Conservation*, ed. Shawn E. Larson, James L. Bodkin, and Glenn R. VanBlaricom (Academic Press, 2015), 63–96.

35 **Like the coats:** Riordan et al., "Ontogenetic Changes in Southern Sea Otter (*Enhydra lutris nereis*) Fur Morphology," e21624.

36 **The hairs' specialized:** John W. Weisel, Chandrasekaran Nagaswami, and Rolf O. Peterson, "River Otter Hair Structure Facilitates Interlocking to Impede Penetration of Water and Allow Trapping of Air," *Canadian Journal of Zoology* 83, no. 5 (2005): 649–55.

36 **The *pelage*, or fur coat:** Hans Kruuk, *Otters: Ecology, Behaviour, and Conservation* (Oxford University Press, 2006), 163–71.

36 **To compensate, they've evolved:** Kruuk, *Otters*, 163–71.

36 **This limits their bottom:** Nicholas T. Zellmer, Lori L. Timm-Davis, and Randall W. Davis, "Sea Otter Behavior: Morphologic, Physiologic, and Sensory Adaptations," in *Ethology and Behavioral Ecology of Sea Otters and Polar Bears*, ed. Randall W. Davis and Anthony M. Pagano (Springer International, 2021), 37–43.

37 **Behaviorally, they spend more:** Traver Wright et al., "Skeletal Muscle Thermogenesis Enables Aquatic Life in the Smallest Marine Mammal," *Science* 373, no. 6551 (2021): 223–25.

37 **This means that shallower:** George A. Antonelis et al., "Activity Cycle and Food Selection of Captive Sea Otters," *Murrelet* 62, no. 1 (1981): 6–9.

37 **Mothers in either habitat:** Zellmer, Timm-Davis, and Davis, "Sea Otter Behavior," 44.

37 **It consists of cleaning:** Lesanna L. Lahner, Pamela A. Tuomi, and Michael J. Murray, "Sea Otter Medicine," in *CRC Handbook of Marine Mammal Medicine*, 3rd ed., ed. Frances M. D. Gulland, Leslie A. Dierauf, and Karyl L. Whitman (CRC Press, 2018), 981–82.

37 **As homeotherms, otters:** James A. Estes, "Natural History, Ecology, and the Conservation and Management of Sea Otters," in *Sea Otter Conservation*, ed. Shawn E. Larson, James L. Bodkin, and Glenn R. VanBlaricom (Academic Press, 2015), 19–41.

37 **They can also use:** Rachel A. Kuhn and Wilfried Meyer, "Infrared Thermography of the Body Surface in the Eurasian Otter *Lutra lutra* and the Giant Otter *Pteronura brasiliensis*," *Aquatic Biology* 6 (2009): 143–52.

38 **I check that:** US Fish & Wildlife Service, *Dive Operations Handbook*, September 2022, 34–41, https://www.fws.gov/sites/default/files/policy/files/Dive_Operations_Handbook.pdf.

39 **Leopard seals are not:** Shona F. Muir, David K. A. Barnes, and Keith Reid, "Interactions Between Humans and Leopard Seals," *Antarctic Science* 18, no. 1 (2006): 61–74.

39 **After several attempts:** Brian Clark Howard, "How a Leopard Seal Fed Me Penguins," *National Geographic*, March 11, 2014, https://www.nationalgeographic.com/adventure/article/140311-paul-nicklen-leopard-seal-photographer-viral.

39 **Yes, they have:** Sarah McKay Strobel et al., "Active Touch in Sea Otters: In-Air and Underwater Texture Discrimination Thresholds and Behavioral Strategies for Paws and Vibrissae," *Journal of Experimental Biology* 221, no. 18 (2018): jeb181347.

39 **Like most mammals:** Magdalena N. Muchlinski et al., "Good Vibrations: The Evolution of Whisking in Small Mammals," *Anatomical Record* 303, no. 1 (2020): 89–99.

39 **The pores that encapsulate:** Robyn A. Grant, Hazel Ryan, and Vicki Breakell, "Demonstrating a Measurement Protocol for Studying Comparative Whisker Movements with Implications for the Evolution of Behavior," *Journal of Neuroscience Methods* 384, no. 2 (2023): 109752.

39 ***Whisking*—the use:** Muchlinski et al., "Good Vibrations," 89–99.

40 **One study of European otters:** J. Green, "Sensory Perception in Hunting Otters (*Lutra lutra* L)," *Otter (Journal of the OtterTrust)* (1977): 13–16.

40 **Whisking within the water:** Tom Hardisky, "River Otter Management in Pennsylvania," Pennsylvania Game Commission, 2013, 8, https://www.pa.gov/content/dam/copapwp-pagov/en/pgc/documents/hunttrap/law/trappingandfurbearers/pa%20otter%20management%20plan%20draft.pdf.

40 **It seems the otter:** Kruuk, *Otters*, 142.

41 **Blue-carbon ecosystems:** Mira Diana Lutz, "A Search for Blue Carbon in Central Salish Sea Eelgrass Meadows," Western Washington University, Summer 2018, https://cedar.wwu.edu/cgi/viewcontent.cgi?article=1780&context=wwuet.

43 **I look at my depth gauge:** "River Otter," Alaska Department of Fish and Game, retrieved July 15, 2024, https://www.adfg.alaska.gov/index.cfm?adfg=riverotter.printerfriendly.

44 **To dive from the surface:** Nicola Chester, *RSPB Spotlight: Otters* (Bloomsbury, 2014), 43.

45 **This involves spreading:** Frank E. Fish, "Association of Propulsive Swimming Mode with Behavior in River Otters (*Lutra canadensis*)," *Journal of Mammalogy* 75, no. 4 (1994): 989–97.

45 **A study of seasonal:** Talitha F. Penland and Jeffrey M. Black, "Seasonal Variation in River Otter Diet in Coastal Northern California," *Northwestern Naturalist* 90, no. 3 (2009): 233–37.

46 **An early river otter study:** Wayne E. Melquist and Maurice G. Hornocker, "Ecology of River Otters in West Central Idaho," *Wildlife Monographs*, no. 83 (1983): 3–60.

Chapter 3: Twitch

52 **It's a 2:** Allison Sundell, Jimmy Bernhard, and Kipp Robertson, "Around 250 Homes Damaged During Tornado in Kitsap County," King 5 News, December 18, 2018, https://www.king5.com/article/news/local/around-250-homes-damaged-during-tornado-in-kitsap-county/281-e118f73d-7503-4611-9e60-4ddc39cc84ee.

53 **They returned to marine areas:** Hilary A. Cosby, "Variation in Diet and Activity of River Otters (*Lontra canadensis*) by Season and Aquatic Community" (master's thesis, California State University, Sacramento, 2013), 25, https://scholarworks.calstate.edu/downloads/zc77ss357.

53 **The habitat is diverse:** *Island County Profile Report*, Economic Development Council for Island County, updated July 2022, https://growthzonesitesprod.azureedge.net/wp-content/uploads/sites/1464/2022/08/2022-Island-County-Profile-Updated-July-2022.pdf.

54 **Washington sea otters:** Nathan L. Stewart, Brenda Konar, and M. Tim Tinker, "Testing the Nutritional-Limitation,

Predator-Avoidance, and Storm-Avoidance Hypotheses for Restricted Sea Otter Habitat Use in the Aleutian Islands, Alaska," *Oecologia* 177, no. 3 (2015): 645–55.

58 **The rear feet look wider:** Mike Bottini, *The Long Island River Otter Project's River Otter Sign and Survey Manual*, Seatuck Environmental Association, January 2022, 3, https://seatuck.org/wp-content/uploads/2022/02/OtterManual.pdf.

62 **When plans were drawn:** Maria Matson, "Whidbey Couple Take a Culinary Leap of Faith," *Everett Herald*, August 31, 2018, https://www.heraldnet.com/business/whidbey-couple-take-a-culinary-leap-of-faith/.

65 **The Land Trust is one of:** "Protected Properties," Whidbey Camano Land Trust, accessed June 17, 2025, https://www.wclt.org/protected-properties/.

65 **At 169 square miles:** "About Whidbey Island," US Navy, accessed May 25, 2025, https://cnrnw.cnic.navy.mil/Installations/NAS-Whidbey-Island/About/.

66 **One of the local theories:** Jessica Larson, "Protecting the Place Where the Lone Elk Plays," *Whidbey Camano Land Trust Newsletter*, June 20, 2016.

67 **There's also Ellie:** Jessie Stensland, "Whidbey Elephant Seal Reveals Aggressive Side," *South Whidbey Record*, January 31, 2023, https://www.southwhidbeyrecord.com/news/whidbey-elephant-seal-reveals-aggressive-side/.

67 **Ellie has birthed:** Sandra Dubpernell and Susan Berta, "Who's Minding the Kids?" Project Report, Central Puget Sound Marine Mammal Stranding Network, December 17, 2020, https://www.globalgiving.org/projects/central-pugetsound-marine-mammal-stranding-network/reports/?subid=140300.

67 **Their repertoire of powerful:** "Timeline of the Marine Mammal Center," Marine Mammal Center, accessed November 12, 2024, https://www.marinemammalcenter.org/timeline-of-the-marine-mammal-center.

68 **Five orcas drowned:** Sandra Pollard, A *Puget Sound Orca in Captivity: The Fight to Bring Lolita Home* (Arcadia, 2019), 20–21.

68 **Found in all oceans:** Phillip A. Morin et al., "Revised Taxonomy of Eastern North Pacific Killer Whales (*Orcinus orca*): Bigg's and Resident Ecotypes Deserve Species Status," *Royal Society Open Science* 11, no. 3 (2024): 231368.

68 **They're now protected:** Marine Mammal Protection Act Policies, Guidance, and Regulations, NOAA Fisheries, https://www.fisheries.noaa.gov/national/marine-mammal-protection/marine-mammal-protection-act-policies-guidance-and-regulations.

69 **Tokitae, who had been:** "Tokitae's Life Now," Orca Network blog, 2021, https://www.orcanetwork.org/tokitaesstory/blog-post-title-three-tslkw.

69 **Often mistaken for albinism:** Brooklyn S. Cars et al., "Island Demographics and Trait Associations in White-Tailed Deer," *Heredity* 133, no. 1 (2024): 1–10.

69 **Given the dearth:** Jessie Stensland, "Piebald Fawn Part of Island Legacy," *Whidbey News-Times*, April 14, 2023, https://www.whidbeynewstimes.com/news/piebald-fawn-part-of-island-legacy.

Chapter 4: What Is an Otter?

73 **This land that the snag:** Terry W. Swanson, "Late Pleistocene Glacial History of Whidbey Island, WA," Field trip handbook, Department of Earth and Space Sciences, University of Washington, 2009, 23, http://faculty.washington.edu/tswanson/302add/Field%20Trips/Trip2009.pdf; Amanuel Beyin, "Upper Pleistocene Human Dispersals out of Africa: A Review of the Current State of the Debate," *International Journal of Evolutionary Biology* 2011, no. 1 (2011): 615094.

74 **Twenty million years ago:** Klaus-Peter Koepfli and Robert K. Wayne, "Phylogenetic Relationships of Otters (Carnivora: Mustelidae) Based on Mitochondrial Cytochrome *B* Sequences," *Journal of the Zoological Society* 246 (1998): 401–16; Annalisa Berta and Gary S. Morgan, "A New Sea Otter (Carnivora: Mustelidae) from the Late Miocene and Early Pliocene (Hemphillian) of North America," *Journal of Paleontology* 59, no. 4 (1985): 809–819; Stéphane Peigné

et al., "Late Miocene Carnivora from Chad: Lutrinae (Mustelidae)," *Zoological Journal of the Linnean Society* 152, no. 4 (2008): 793–846; Camille Grohé et al., "The Oldest Asian *Savaonyx* (*Lutrinae, Mustelidae*): A Contribution to the Evolutionary History of Bunodont Otters," *Palaeontologia Electronica* 16, no. 3, 29A (2013): 1–13.

74 **Alternatively, you could:** Canadian Press, "Ancient Flightless Bird Fossil Found on B.C. Beach Identified as New Species," CBC, December 16, 2015, https://www.cbc.ca/news/science/fossil-bird-bc-1.3367313.

75 **Fortunately, her dad:** Gary Kaiser, Junya Watanabe, and Marji Johns, "A New Member of the Family Plotopteridae (Aves) from the Late Oligocene of British Columbia, Canada," *Palaeontologia Electronica* 18, no. 3 (2015): 1–18.

75 **These are the teeth:** C. Renn Tumlison, Jimmie Harper, and Karson Grant, "A Study of Dental Pathology in River Otters (*Lontra canadensis*) in Arkansas," *Journal of the Arkansas Academy of Science* 76, no. 1 (2022): 8.

75 **If an otter damages:** Tumlison, Harper, and Grant, "A Study of Dental Pathology in River Otters (*Lontra canadensis*) in Arkansas," 8.

75 **Carnassial teeth differ:** R. J. G. Savage, "Evolution in Carnivorous Mammals," *Palaeontology* 20 (1977): 237–71.

75 **By examining wear patterns:** Bill Schutt, *Bite: An Incisive History of Teeth, from Hagfish to Humans* (Algonquin Books of Chapel Hill, 2024), 158–69.

75 **Then there are the sea otters:** John E. Heyning and Gina M. Lento, "The Evolution of Marine Mammals," in *Marine Mammal Biology: An Evolutionary Approach*, ed. A. Rus Hoelzel (Blackwell Science, 2002), 38–72.

76 **Today there are:** Aldo Manzuetti et al., "The Otter Lontra Gray, 1843 (Mustelidae, Lutrinae) in the Late Pleistocene–Early Holocene of Uruguay," *Annales de Paléontologie* 109, no. 3 (2023): 102633.

76 **The Old World otters:** George A. Feldhamer, Bruce C. Thompson, and Joseph A. Chapman, eds., *Wild Mammals of*

North America: Biology, Management, and Conservation, 2nd ed. (Johns Hopkins University Press, 2003), 708; Klaus-Peter Koepfli, personal communication, Otter Specialist Group Congress, International Union for Conservation of Nature, Lima, Peru, February 28, 2025.

76 **But for now, they remain:** Vera de Ferran et al., "Phylogenomics of the World's Otters," *Current Biology* 32, no. 16 (2022): 3650–58.

77 **Mesoamerican otters:** Vera de Ferran et al., "Genome-Wide Data Support Recognition of an Additional Species of Neotropical River Otter (Mammalia, Mustelidae, Lutrinae)," *Journal of Mammalogy* 105, no. 3 (2024): 534–42.

77 **Sea otters have a unique:** Traver Wright et al., "Skeletal Muscle Thermogenesis Enables Aquatic Life in the Smallest Marine Mammal," *Science* 373, no. 6551 (2021): 223–25.

78 **Mitochondrial and nuclear DNA:** Koepfli and Wayne, "Phylogenetic Relationships of Otters," 401–16; Klaus-Peter Koepfli et al., "Multigene Phylogeny of the Mustelidae: Resolving Relationships, Tempo and Biogeographic History of a Mammalian Adaptive Radiation," *BMC Biology* 6, no. 1 (2008): 10.

78 **They're the largest:** Tomohiro Harano and Nobuyuki Kutsukake, "Body Size Evolution in Otters Distinguished from Terrestrial Mustelids," *Journal of Evolutionary Biology* 37, no. 2 (2024): 152–61.

78 **In 2016, a new:** Xiaoming Wang et al., "A New Otter of Giant Size, *Siamogale melilutra* sp. nov. (Lutrinae: Mustelidae: Carnivora), from the Latest Miocene Shuitangba Site in North-Eastern Yunnan, South-Western China, and a Total-Evidence Phylogeny of Lutrines," *Journal of Systematic Palaeontology* 16, no. 1 (2018): 39–65.

78 **Today's sea otters:** Camille Grohé, Kevin Uno, and Jean-Renaud Boisserie, "Lutrinae Bonaparte, 1838 (Carnivora, Mustelidae) from the Plio-Pleistocene of the Lower Omo Valley, Southwestern Ethiopia: Systematics and New Insights into the Paleoecology and Paleobiogeography of the Turkana Otters," *Comptes Rendus Palevol* 30 (2022): 681–705.

79 **Consider for a moment:** Niels Christian Pausch, Franziska Naether, and Karl Friedrich Krey, "Tutankhamun's Dentition: The Pharaoh and His Teeth," *Brazilian Dental Journal* 26, no. 6 (2015): 701–4.

79 **Although they still use their teeth:** J. N. Winer, S. M. Liong, and F. J. M. Verstraete, "The Dental Pathology of Southern Sea Otters (*Enhydra lutris nereis*)," *Journal of Comparative Pathology* 149, nos. 2–3 (2013): 346–55.

79 **It may also explain why:** Nicholas T. Zellmer, Lori L. Timm-Davis, and Randall W. Davis, "Sea Otter Behavior: Morphologic, Physiologic, and Sensory Adaptations," in *Ethology and Behavioral Ecology of Sea Otters and Polar Bears*, ed. Randall W. Davis and Anthony M. Pagano (Springer International, 2021), 23–55.

80 **Since their inception:** Yonca Alkan Göksu, "Per- and Polyfluoroalkyl Substances (PFAS): History, Regulations and Strategies for the Removal," *ITU Journal of Metallurgy and Materials Engineering* 2, no. 1 (2025): 19–28.

81 **According to a *New Yorker* exposé:** Sharon Lerner, "How 3M Discovered, Then Concealed, the Dangers of Forever Chemicals," *New Yorker*, May 20, 2024, https://www.newyorker.com/magazine/2024/05/27/3m-forever-chemicals-pfas-pfos-toxic.

81 **Indeed, "nearly all":** Lerner, "How 3M Discovered, Then Concealed, the Dangers of Forever Chemicals."

81 **These chemicals are toxic:** Jolly Jacob, "A Review of the Accumulation and Distribution of Persistent Organic Pollutants in the Environment," *International Journal of Bioscience, Biochemistry, and Bioinformatics* 3, no. 6 (2013): 657–61.

81 **This additive effect:** Burton C. Suedel et al., "Trophic Transfer and Biomagnification Potential of Contaminants in Aquatic Ecosystems," *Reviews of Environmental Contamination and Toxicology* 136 (1994): 21–89.

82 **In their coastal habitat:** "Toxic Killer Whales," NOAA Fisheries, October 20, 2016, https://www.fisheries.noaa.gov/feature-story/toxic-killer-whales.

82 **In a landmark study:** Jessica I. Lundin et al., "Modulation in Persistent Organic Pollutant Concentration and Profile by Prey Availability and Reproductive Status in Southern Resident Killer Whale Scat Samples," *Environmental Science & Technology* 50, no. 12 (2016): 6506–16.

82 **Further, if an orca:** Kiah Lee et al., "Emerging Contaminants and New POPs (PFAS and HBCDD) in Endangered Southern Resident and Bigg's (Transient) Killer Whales (*Orcinus orca*): In Utero Maternal Transfer and Pollution Management Implications," *Environmental Science & Technology* 57, no. 1 (2022): 360–74.

82 **In fact, in 2014:** "Endangered Orca Calves Exposed to Contaminants Even Before Birth," Wild Orca, March 20, 2023, https://www.wildorca.org/endangered-orca-calves-exposed-to-contaminants-even-before-birth/.

83 **All of Whidbey:** "NPS Geodiversity Atlas—Ebey's Landing National Historical Reserve," National Park Service, June 17, 2024, https://www.nps.gov/articles/nps-geodiversity-atlas-ebey-s-landing-national-historical-reserve-washington.htm.

83 **When the glaciers:** "Whidbey Island State Parks Windows into the Glaciers of Puget Sound Introduction," Friends of Whidbey State Parks, 2024, https://www.friendsofwhidbeystateparks.org/geo-parks.

83 **There are kettle lakes:** Sidney Stevens, "Nine of North America's Most Fascinating Kettle Lakes," *Treehugger*, April 21, 2021, https://www.treehugger.com/north-americas-most-fascinating-kettle-lakes-4869236.

84 **They use a lakeside den:** Brady Blake and Alex Bradbury, "Washington Department of Fish and Wildlife Plan for Rebuilding Olympia Oyster (*Ostrea lurida*) Populations in Puget Sound with a Historical and Contemporary Overview," Washington Department of Fish and Wildlife, 2012, 25.

84 **Seeding fish can be:** Kenneth D. Ham and Todd N. Pearsons, "A Practical Approach for Containing Ecological Risks Associated with Fish Stocking Programs," *Fisheries* 26, no. 4 (2001): 15–23.

85 **There was extensive:** De Ferran et al., "Phylogenomics of the World's Otters," 3650–58.

85 **Even among humans:** Liming Li et al., "Recurrent Gene Flow Between Neanderthals and Modern Humans over the Past 200,000 Years," *Science* 385, no. 6705 (2024): eadi1768.

85 **The likely reason for the otters':** De Ferran et al., "Phylogenomics of the World's Otters," 3650–58.

85 **Just 110 miles:** "Sea Otter (*Enhydra lutris kenyoni*)," Washington Department of Fish & Wildlife, retrieved November 12, 2024, https://wdfw.wa.gov/species-habitats/species/enhydra-lutris-kenyoni.

85 **Before the maritime:** James L. Bodkin, "Historic and Contemporary Status of Sea Otters in the North Pacific," in *Sea Otter Conservation*, ed. Shawn E. Larson, James L. Bodkin, and Glenn R. VanBlaricom (Academic Press, 2015), 43–62.

85 **Though the neotropical otters:** Marcelo Lopes Rheingantz et al., P. 2022. *Lontra longicaudis, Neotropical Otter View* (amended version of 2021 assessment), *IUCN Red List of Threatened Species* (2022): e.T12304A219373698, https://dx.doi.org/10.2305/IUCN.UK.2022-2.RLTS.T12304A219373698.en.

86 **From these extensive:** De Ferran et al., "Genome-Wide Data Support Recognition of an Additional Species of Neotropical River Otter (Mammalia, Mustelidae, Lutrinae)," 534–42.

86 **Although this was big news:** E. Lönnberg, "A New Subspecies of Clawless Otter (*Aonyx capensis congica*) from Lower Congo," *Arkiv för Zoologi* 7 (1913): 1–8, https://play.google.com/store/books/details?id=s7e2LTYkXOMC&rdid=book-s7e2LTYkXOMC&rdot=1&pli=1.

86 **After decades of debate:** H. Jacques et al., "*Aonyx congicus*," IUCN Red List of Threatened Species 2021, e.T1794A164576337, https://dx.doi.org/10.2305/IUCN.UK.2021-3.RLTS.T1794A164576337.en.

86 **A year later, French zoologists:** Hélène Jacques et al., "The

Congo Clawless Otter (*Aonyx congicus*; Mustelidae: Lutrinae): A Review of Its Systematics, Distribution and Conservation Status," *African Zoology* 44, no. 2 (2009): 159–70.

87 **"Genomics has two camps":** Klaus-Peter Koepfli (International Union for the Conservation of Nature, Otter Specialist Group), personal communication, Otter Specialist Group Congress, International Union for the Conservation of Nature, Lima, Peru, February 28, 2025.

87 **For example, the Mesoamerican:** International Otter Survival Fund, Facebook page, June 9, 2025, https://www.facebook.com/InternationalOtterSurvivalFund/photos/what-was-the-answer-to-yesterdays-question-we-hear-you-ask-well-who-nose-thats-r/1106279308206965/.

88 **They both have countershading:** Hannah M. Rowland, "From Abbott Thayer to the Present Day: What Have We Learned about the Function of Countershading?," *Philosophical Transactions of the Royal Society B: Biological Sciences* 364, no. 1516 (2009): 519–27.

88 **Both species have dark:** Jacques et al., "The Congo Clawless Otter," 159–70.

89 **I learned of a:** "Pacific Treefrog (*Pseudacris regilla*)," Living with Wildlife, Oregon Department of Fish and Wildlife, accessed November 18, 2024, https://www.dfw.state.or.us/wildlife/living_with/docs/LWW_Pacific_Treefrog_final.pdf.

89 **Frog feasting is:** Rouhollah Mirzaei, Afshin Danehkar, and Asghar Abdoli, "The Diet of Eurasian Otters in the Jajrood River System, Iran," *Mammal Study* 39, no. 1 (2014): 33–41.

90 **This is especially true:** R. Terry Bowyer et al., "Effects of the Exxon Valdez Oil Spill on River Otters: Injury and Recovery of a Sentinel Species," *Wildlife Monographs* 153, no. 153 (2003): 1–53.

90 **But for radiotelemetry:** Lorenzo Quaglietta et al., "Eurasian Otter (*Lutra lutra*) Density Estimate Based on Radio Tracking and Other Data Sources," *Mammal Research* 60 (2015): 127–37.

90 **it doesn't involve surgical implantation:** Lorenzo

Quaglietta et al., "A Low-Cost GPS GSM/GPRS Telemetry System: Performance in Stationary Field Tests and Preliminary Data on Wild Otters (*Lutra lutra*)," *PloS One* 7, no. 1 (2012): e29235.

91 **This means you run:** Barry K. Hartup et al., "Exertional Myopathy in Translocated River Otters from New York," *Journal of Wildlife Diseases* 35, no. 3 (1999): 542–47.

Chapter 5: Fur, Feathers, Shells, and Scales

95 **Bald eagle females:** David A. Buehler, "Bald Eagle (*Haliaeetus leucocephalus*), Version 2.0," in *Birds of the World*, ed. P. G. Rodewald and S. G. Mlodinow (Cornell Lab of Ornithology, 2022), https://doi.org/10.2173/bow.baleag.02.

96 **Among many predators:** Rolf O. Peterson et al., "Leadership Behavior in Relation to Dominance and Reproductive Status in Gray Wolves, *Canis lupus*," *Canadian Journal of Zoology* 80, no. 8 (2002): 1405–12; Nathan J. Emery, "The Eyes Have It: The Neuroethology, Function and Evolution of Social Gaze," *Neuroscience & Biobehavioral Reviews* 24, no. 6 (2000): 581–604.

98 **In fact, coyotes:** Terence Carroll and Megan Isadore, "North American River Otter (*Lontra canadensis*) Predation on Brown Pelicans (*Pelecanus occidentalis*) at Abbotts Lagoon, Point Reyes National Seashore, California, USA," *IUCN Otter Specialist Group Bulletin* 42, no. 2 (2025): 71–84.

98 **The coyote absconded:** Francis D. Gerraty et al., "Recovering Predators Link Aquatic and Terrestrial Ecosystems: River Otters Subsidize Coyotes with Carrion," *Ecology and Evolution* 14, no. 6 (2024): e11444.

99 **In March 2023:** Albert Snyman et al., "The First Record of Cape Clawless Otters *Aonyx capensis* Predating on African Penguins *Spheniscus demersus*," *Ostrich* 96, no. 2 (2025): 135–39.

99 **These critically endangered:** Snyman et al., "The First Record of Cape Clawless Otters *Aonyx capensis* Predating on African Penguins *Spheniscus demersus*," 135–39.

99 **Most of the world's:** R. Correa and J. Pizarro, "Mortality of *Lontra felina* (Molina, 1782) in Chile (2009–2022) Based on

Reports," *IUCN Otter Specialist Group Bulletin* 40, no. 3 (2023): 144–50.

99 **This is evident in:** Lori L. Timm-Davis, Thomas J. DeWitt, and Christopher D. Marshall, "Divergent Skull Morphology Supports Two Trophic Specializations in Otters (Lutrinae)," *PLoS One* 10, no. 12 (2015): e0143236; Sarah McKay Strobel et al., "Anatomy of the Sense of Touch in Sea Otters: Cutaneous Mechanoreceptors and Structural Features of Glabrous Skin," *Anatomical Record* 305, no. 3 (2022): 535–55.

100 **Always the odd ones:** Leonard B. Radinsky, "Evolution of Somatic Sensory Specialization in Otter Brains," *Journal of Comparative Neurology* 134, no. 4 (1968): 495–505.

100 **There are also herbivorous:** Timm-Davis, DeWitt, and Marshall, "Divergent Skull Morphology Supports Two Trophic Specializations in Otters (Lutrinae)," e0143236.

100 **In the 1960s:** Richard F. Kay, "Leonard B. Radinsky (1937–1985), Radical Biologist," *Journal of Mammalian Evolution* 28, no. 1 (2021): 7–14.

100 **Fish-eating otters:** Ronald J. Schusterman et al., "Why Pinnipeds Don't Echolocate," *Journal of the Acoustical Society of America* 107, no. 4 (2000): 2256–64.

101 **Meanwhile, invertebrate-eating:** Leonard B. Radinsky, "Evolution of Somatic Sensory Specialization in Otter Brains," *Journal of Comparative Neurology* 134, no. 4 (1968): 495–505.

101 **But offer a fish:** L. Wright et al., "*Aonyx cinereus*," *IUCN Red List of Threatened Species 2015*: e. T44166A21939068.

101 **Although their forepaw:** L. B. Radinsky, "Evolution of the Canid Brain," *Brain, Behavior, and Evolution* 7 (1973): 186–202, https://doi.org/10.1159/000124409.

101 **Their whiskers are not:** T. A. Woolsey, "Sensorimotor Integration: Barrels, Vibrissae and Topographic Representations," in *Encyclopedia of Neuroscience*, ed. Larry R. Squire (Birkhäuser Boston, 1988), 601–6.

101 **Pinnipeds, too, have ten:** Guido Dehnhardt et al., "Hydrodynamic Trail-Following in Harbor Seals (*Phoca vitulina*)," *Science* 293, no. 5527 (2001): 102–4.

101 **By comparison, sea otters have:** Christopher D. Marshall et al., "Innervation Patterns of Sea Otter (*Enhydra lutris*) Mystacial Follicle-Sinus Complexes," *Frontiers in Neuroanatomy* 8 (2014): 121.

101 **And yet, despite the keenness:** Sarah McKay Strobel et al., "Active Touch in Sea Otters: In-Air and Underwater Texture Discrimination Thresholds and Behavioral Strategies for Paws and Vibrissae," *Journal of Experimental Biology* 221, no. 18 (2018): jeb181347.

102 **To adequately meet:** Shawn E. Larson, Katherine Ralls, and Holly Ernest, "Sea Otter Conservation Genetics," in *Sea Otter Conservation*, ed. Shawn Larson, James L. Bodkin, and Glenn R. VanBlaricom (Academic Press, 2015), 97–120.

102 **These adaptations include:** Annabel C. Beichman et al., "Aquatic Adaptation and Depleted Diversity: A Deep Dive into the Genomes of the Sea Otter and Giant Otter," *Molecular Biology and Evolution* 36, no. 12 (2019): 2631–55.

102 **They have also evolved:** M. L. Riedman and J. A. Estes, "The Sea Otter *(Enhydra lutris)*: Behavior, Ecology, and Natural History," *Biology of Reproduction* 90, no. 14 (1990): 5–20; Terrell C. Newby, "A Sea Otter (*Enhydra lutris*) Food Dive Record," *Murrelet* 56, no. 1 (1975): 7.

103 **The giant otters of Brazil's:** Caroline Leuchtenberger et al., "Giant Otter Diet Differs Between Habitats and from Fisheries Offtake in a Large Neotropical Floodplain," *Journal of Mammalogy* 101, no. 6 (2020): 1650–59.

103 **When the dry season:** Carolina Ribas et al., "Giant Otters Feeding on Caiman: Evidence for an Expanded Trophic Niche of Recovering Populations," *Studies on Neotropical Fauna and Environment* 47, no. 1 (2012): 19–23.

103 **They get their:** Rowan Jordan, "Spotted-Necked Otter Fact Sheet," International Otter Survival Fund, retrieved December 5, 2024, https://www.otter.org/spotted-necked-otter.

104 **The Sundarbans, a protected:** A. S. M. Helal Siddiqui and M. Masudur Rahman, "Flora of the Sundarbans," *Proceedings of 16th Asian Business Research Conference*, BIAM Foundation (December 27–28, 2019); M. Abdul Aziz, "Notes on

Population Status and Feeding Behaviour of Asian Small-Clawed Otter (*Aonyx cinereus*) in the Sundarbans Mangrove Forest of Bangladesh," *IUCN Otter Specialist Group Bulletin* 35, no. 1 (2018): 3–10.

104 **It is this last species:** Mohammed Mostafa Feeroz, Sajeda Begum, and Md Kamrul Hasan, "Fishing with Otters: A Traditional Conservation Practice in Bangladesh," *IUCN Otter Specialist Group Bulletin* 28A (2011): 21.

104 **Likely originating in China:** Lu Zhang et al., "The Neglected Otters in China: Distribution Change in the Past 400 Years and Current Conservation Status," *Biological Conservation* 228, no. 2 (2018): 259–67.

104 **But they are now dying out:** Eugene Willis Gudger, "Fishing with the Otter," *American Naturalist* 61, no. 674 (1927): 193–225.

104 **But by 2022:** Sumaya Khatun, M. M. Hasan, and M. Abdul Aziz, "A Centuries-Old Otter-Fishing Practice in Bangladesh: Going, Going, Gone," *IUCN Otter Specialist Group Bulletin* 41, no. 4 (2024): 197–205.

105 **According to Mohammed Feeroz:** Feeroz, Begum, and Hasan, "Fishing with Otters," 21.

105 **Declining fish populations:** Khatun, Hasan, and Aziz, "A Centuries-Old Otter-Fishing Practice in Bangladesh," 197–205.

105 **The International Union:** "IUCN Red List of Threatened Species," International Union for Conservation of Nature, retrieved December 30, 2024, https://iucn.org/resources/conservation-tool/iucn-red-list-threatened-species.

108 **According to veterinarian:** David Waltner-Toews, *The Origin of Feces: What Excrement Tells Us About Evolution, Ecology, and a Sustainable Society* (ECW Press, 2018), 17.

108 **They also extrude:** Adegbenro O. Fakoya et al., "Histology, Apocrine Gland," in *StatPearls* (StatPearls Publishing, 2022).

108 **For example, they're:** P. Hájková et al., "Factors Affecting Success of PCR Amplification of Microsatellite Loci from Otter Faeces," *Molecular Ecology Notes* 6, no. 2 (2006): 559–62.

109 **The jellies are not always:** Eleanor F. Kean, Carsten T.

Müller, and Elizabeth A. Chadwick, "Otter Scent Signals Age, Sex, and Reproductive Status," *Chemical Senses* 36, no. 6 (2011): 555–64.

109 **A study of the chemical compounds:** Adeline Bradshaw et al., "Anal Scent Gland Secretion of the European Otter (*Lutra lutra*)," *Chemical Signals in Vertebrates* 9 (2001): 313–19.

109 **Among the scent-centric:** Water Resources Mission Area, "Volatile Organic Compounds (VOCs)," United States Geological Survey, February 27, 2019, https://www.usgs.gov/mission-areas/water-resources/science/volatile-organic-compounds-vocs.

109 **In fact, in 1965:** G. A. Burdock, "Safety Assessment of Castoreum Extract as a Food Ingredient," *International Journal of Toxicology* 26, no. 1 (2007): 51–55, https://doi.org/10.1080/10915810601120145.

111 **Since coastal river otters:** Merav Ben-David et al., "Social Behavior and Ecosystem Processes: River Otter Latrines and Nutrient Dynamics of Terrestrial Vegetation," *Ecology* 79, no. 7 (1998): 2567–71.

112 **From studies of otter vision:** Nicholas T. Zellmer, Lori L. Timm-Davis, and Randall W. Davis, "Sea Otter Behavior: Morphologic, Physiologic, and Sensory Adaptations," in *Ethology and Behavioral Ecology of Sea Otters and Polar Bears*, ed. Randall W. Davis and Anthony M. Pagano (Springer International, 2021), 23–55.

113 **In a study of river otters:** Bobbie Buzzell, Monique M. Lance, and Alejandro Acevedo-Gutiérrez, "Spatial and Temporal Variation in River Otter (*Lontra canadensis*) Diet and Predation on Rockfish (Genus Sebastes) in the San Juan Islands, Washington," *Aquatic Mammals* 40, no. 2 (2014): 150.

113 **Sea lions, another scapegoat:** Kathleen C. O'Neil, J. Michael Hemsley, and L. Allison, "Sea Lions and Buoys, a Battle of Wills and Wit," in *Oceans' 99 MTS/IEEE: Riding the Crest into the 21st Century, Conference and Exhibition, Conference Proceedings*, vol. 1 (IEEE Cat. No. 99CH37008), 1999, 269–72.

114 **Widespread declines of wild:** Lisa G. Crozier et al.,

"Climate Change Threatens Chinook Salmon Throughout Their Life Cycle," *Communications Biology* 4, no. 1 (2021): 222; M. Bradley Hanson et al., "Endangered Predators and Endangered Prey: Seasonal Diet of Southern Resident Killer Whales," *PLoS One* 16, no. 3 (2021): e0247031.

Chapter 6: Sliding, Rock Rolling, and Wrestling

117 **I'm not sure about the sexes:** Gail M. Blundell, Merav Ben-David, and R. Terry Bowyer, "Sociality in River Otters: Cooperative Foraging or Reproductive Strategies?," *Behavioral Ecology* 13, no. 1 (2002): 134–41.

118 **In a social group:** Gail M. Blundell et al., "Kinship and Sociality in Coastal River Otters: Are They Related?," *Behavioral Ecology* 15, no. 5 (2004): 705–14.

118 **When threatened, they can:** Jane Morgan, Michael Belanger, and Carin Wittnich, "Reported Worldwide Otter Attacks on Humans over the Last Decade (2011–2021): Dictated by Human Encroachment or Otter Behavior," *IUCN Otter Specialist Group Bulletin* 40, no. 2 (2023): 80–89; Annie Roth, "She Steals Surfboards by the Seashore. She's an Otter," *New York Times*, July 12, 2023, https://www.nytimes.com/2023/07/12/science/sea-otter-surfboard.html.

118 **There are even accounts:** Cristina Calvo-Fernandez et al., "Cannibalism in Eurasian Otters (*Lutra lutra*)," *River Research and Applications* 40, no. 8 (2024): 1617–20; Guilherme Mourão and L. Carvalho, "Cannibalism Among Giant Otters (*Pteronura brasiliensis*)," *Mammalia* 65, no. 2 (2001): 225–27.

119 **Their large foreheads:** Irenäus Eibl-Eibesfeldt, "Human Ethology: Origins and Prospects of a New Discipline," in *New Aspects of Human Ethology*, ed. Alain Schmitt et al. (Springer US, 1997), 1–23.

119 **An early trailblazer:** "Robert M. Fagen," Play Scientists and Experts, National Institute of Play, retrieved January 25, 2025, https://nifplay.org/play-science/play-scientists-and-play-experts; Robert Fagen and Johanna Fagen, "Play Behaviour and Multi-Year Juvenile Survival in Free-Ranging Brown Bears, *Ursus arctos*," *Evolutionary Ecology Research* 11, no. 7 (2009): 1053–67.

119 **Marc Bekoff, another:** Marc Bekoff, "Social Play and Play-Soliciting by Infant Canids," *American Zoologist* 14, no. 1 (1974): 323–40.

120 **But the neural mechanisms:** Jaak Panksepp, "Cross-Species Affective Neuroscience Decoding of the Primal Affective Experiences of Humans and Related Animals," *PLoS One* 6, no. 9 (2011): e21236, https://journals.plos.org/plosone/article/file?id=10.1371/journal.pone.0021236&type=printable.

120 **This suggests that play:** Andrew Whiten and Carel P. Van Schaik, "The Evolution of Animal 'Cultures' and Social Intelligence," *Philosophical Transactions of the Royal Society B: Biological Sciences* 362, no. 1480 (2007): 603–20, https://pmc.ncbi.nlm.nih.gov/articles/PMC2346520/.

120 **In 1973, Nikolaas Tinbergen:** "Nobel Prize in Physiology or Medicine 1973," Nobel Prize Outreach 2025, retrieved January 29, 2025, https://www.nobelprize.org/prizes/medicine/1973/summary/.

120 **These questions ask:** Dustin Rubenstein and John Alcock, *Introduction to Animal Behavior,* 11th ed. (Sinauer Associates, 2019), 10–11.

121 **For example, some otter:** Thierry Lodé et al., "Solitary Versus Group Living Lifestyles, Social Group Composition and Cooperation in Otters," *Mammal Research* 66, no. 1 (2021): 13–31.

121 **Fortunately, ethologist Gordon:** Gordon M. Burghardt, *The Genesis of Animal Play: Testing the Limits* (MIT Press, 2005), 70–78.

124 **In 2022, the Washington:** Casey T. Clark et al., *Results of the 2023 Survey of Sea Otter Population in Washington State,* U.S. Fish and Wildlife Service, December 29, 2023, 4.

124 **During their nonbreeding:** Marie-Loup Lélias, Alban Lemasson, and Thierry Lodé, "Social Organization of Otters in Relation to Their Ecology," *Biological Journal of the Linnean Society* 133, no. 1 (2021): 1–27.

125 **But in August 2019:** Gena Bentall, "The Jetty Road Boys: Where Are They?," Sea Otter Savvy, accessed April 12, 2025, https://www.seaottersavvy.org/the-jetty-road-boys.

126 **Play begins if the dog's:** Marc Bekoff, "Play Signals as Punctuation: The Structure of Social Play in Canids," *Behaviour* 132, nos. 5–6 (1995): 419–29.

126 **Ethologist Marc Bekoff:** Marc Bekoff, "Playing with Play: What Can We Learn about Cognition, Negotiation, and Evolution?," in *The Evolution of Mind*, ed. D. D. Cummins and C. Allen (Oxford University Press, 1998), 162–82.

127 **Social play-fighting:** Sergio M. Pellis, "Two Aspects of Play-Fighting in a Captive Group of Oriental Small-Clawed Otters *Amblonyx cinerea*," *Zeitschrift für Tierpsychologie* 65, no. 1 (1984): 77–83.

127 **This is called a "play face":** Caroline Loizos, "Play Behaviour in Higher Primates: A Review," in *Primate Ethology*, ed. Desmond Morris (Routledge, 2017), 176–218.

128 **"This sport they continue":** John D. Godman, "Mastology," in *American Natural History*, vol. 1 (H. C. Carey and I. Lea, 1828), 225, HathiTrust digitized copy, accessed January 20, 2025, https://babel.hathitrust.org/cgi/pt?id=nyp.33433010950610&seq=25&q1=otter.

128 **More recently, researchers':** Sadie S. Stevens and Thomas L. Serfass, "Sliding Behavior in Nearctic River Otters: Locomotion or Play?," *Northeastern Naturalist* 12, no. 2 (2005): 241–44.

128 **This object play:** Mirela Cuculescu-Santana et al., "Outdoor Enclosure Use and Behaviour of Adult and Cub Asian Small-Clawed Otters *Aonyx cinereus* in Summer and Winter," *IUCN Otter Specialist Group Bulletin* 38, no. 1 (2021): 3–27.

130 **The scientists did predict:** Mari-Lisa Allison et al., "The Drivers and Functions of Rock Juggling in Otters," *Royal Society Open Science* 7, no. 5 (2020): 200141.

130 **During the isolation:** Shanaya Rathod et al., "Effects of Cumulative COVID-19 Cases on Mental Health: Evidence from Multi-Country Survey," *World Journal of Psychiatry* 13, no. 7 (2023): 461.

131 **The consequence of this:** J. P. Garner, "Perseveration and Stereotypy—Systems-Level Insights from Clinical

Psychology," in *Stereotypic Animal Behaviour: Fundamentals and Applications to Welfare*, 2nd ed., ed. G. Mason and J. Rushen (Cabi, 2006), 121–52.

131 **In fact, they often occur:** Georgia J. Mason, "Age and Context Affect the Stereotypies of Caged Mink," *Behaviour* 127, nos. 3–4 (1993): 191–229.

131 **But prolonged boredom:** Joseph P. Garner, "Stereotypies and Other Abnormal Repetitive Behaviors: Potential Impact on Validity, Reliability, and Replicability of Scientific Outcomes," *ILAR Journal* 46, no. 2 (2005): 106–17.

131 **In a study of play:** Sergio M. Pellis, Vivien C. Pellis, and Heather C. Bell, "The Function of Play in the Development of the Social Brain," *American Journal of Play* 2, no. 3 (2010): 278–96.

131 **One example is the Oregon:** Ashley Korslien, "Oregon Coast Aquarium Estimates Nearly $3M Revenue Loss from Pandemic," KGBW, May 26, 2020, https://www.kgw.com/article/money/business/oregon-coast-aquarium-estimates-nearly-3m-revenue-loss-from-covid-19/283-fe5d430f-2642-403c-865d-e509ec4c1732.

133 **Eddie's miniature basketball:** Lizzy Acker, "Oregon Zoo Otter, Known for Slam Dunking and Self-Pleasuring, Dies at Age 20," updated December 21, 2018, *The Oregonian/* OregonLive, https://www.oregonlive.com/portland/2018/12/oregon-zoo-otter-known-for-slam-dunking-and-self-pleasuring-dies-at-age-20.html.

133 **A series of videos:** "Eddie the Slam-Dunking Sea Otter Turns 20," Oregon Zoo, March 2, 2018, https://www.oregonzoo.org/news/eddie-slam-dunking-sea-otters-turns-20.

Chapter 7: Otter Smarts

138 **These "smart" enrichment:** Charles Ramey et al., "Shelling Out the Fun: Quantifying Otter Interactions with Instrumented Enrichment Objects," *Proceedings of the International Conference on Animal-Computer Interaction*, 2024, 1–10.

138 **He waits patiently until:** "Otter Live Camera," Oregon

Coast Aquarium, accessed October 24, 2024, https://aquarium.org/live-cameras/otter-cam/.

139 **This theory of mind:** David Premack and Guy Woodruff, "Does the Chimpanzee Have a Theory of Mind?," *Behavioral and Brain Sciences* 1, no. 4 (1978): 515–26.

139 **Charles Darwin noted:** Charles Darwin, *The Expression of the Emotions in Man and Animals* (John Murray, 1872), 359–61.

139 **Dolphins, for example:** Louis M. Herman, "What Laboratory Research Has Told Us About Dolphin Cognition," *International Journal of Comparative Psychology* 23, no. 3 (2010): 310–30.

139 **Various other learning:** Ronald J. Schusterman, Colleen Reichmuth Kastak, and David Kastak, "The Cognitive Sea Lion: Meaning and Memory in the Laboratory and in Nature," in *The Cognitive Animal*, ed. Marc Bekoff, Colin Allen, and Gordon M. Burghardt (MIT Press, 2002), 217; Irene M. Pepperberg, "A Communicative Approach to Animal Cognition: A Study of Conceptual Abilities of an African Grey Parrot," in *Cognitive Ethology: The Minds of Animals, ed. Carolyn A. Ristau (*Psychology Press, 2014), 153–86; Sue Savage-Rumbaugh et al., "The Fully Conscious Ape," *International Journal of Comparative Psychology* 31 (2018), https://doi.org/10.46867/ijcp.2018.31.03.03; Joshua M. Plotnik et al., "Self-Recognition in the Asian Elephant and Future Directions for Cognitive Research with Elephants in Zoological Settings," *Zoo Biology* 29, no. 2 (2010): 179–91; Alex Kacelnik et al., "Cognitive Adaptations for Tool-Related Behaviour in New Caledonian Crows," in *Comparative Cognition: Experimental Explorations of Animal Intelligence*, ed. E. A. Wasserman and T. R. Zentall (Oxford University Press, 2006), 515–28; Jennifer A. Mather, "'Home' Choice and Modification by Juvenile *Octopus vulgaris* (Mollusca: Cephalopoda): Specialized Intelligence and Tool Use?," *Journal of Zoology* 233, no. 3 (1994): 359–68.

139 **There are two types:** Anthony Dickinson, "Associative Learning and Animal Cognition," *Philosophical Transactions of the Royal Society B: Biological Sciences* 367, no. 1603 (2012): 2733–42, https://doi.org/10.1098/rstb.2012.0220.

139 **It occurs when an animal's:** Androulla Ioannou and Xenia Anastassiou-Hadjcharalambous, "Non-Associative Learning," in *Encyclopedia of Evolutionary Psychological Science*, ed. Todd K. Shackelford and Viviana A. Weekes-Shackelford (Springer International, 2021), 5419–32.

140 **They first begin to swim:** Sara J. Shettleworth, "Social Learning," in *Cognition, Evolution, and Behavior* (Oxford University Press, 2009), 466–506.

140 **Social learning was famously:** Kinji Imanishi, "Social Behavior in Japanese Monkeys, Macaca fuscata," *Psychologia* 1, no. 1 (1957): 47–54, https://www.jstage.jst.go.jp/article/psysoc/1/1/1_1957.47/_pdf.

141 **After a decade, almost all:** Masao Kawai, "Newly-Acquired Pre-Cultural Behavior of the Natural Troop of Japanese Monkeys on Koshima Islet," *Primates* 6 (1965): 1–30.

141 **A century of research:** Natalia Borrego and Michael Gaines, "Social Carnivores Outperform Asocial Carnivores on an Innovative Problem," *Animal Behaviour* 114 (2016): 21–26.

141 **The cohesion of these:** Thierry Lodé et al., "Solitary Versus Group Living Lifestyles, Social Group Composition and Cooperation in Otters," *Mammal Research* 66, no. 2 (2021): 13–31.

141 **Sea otters exhibit *intrasexual*:** Marie-Loup Lélias, Alban Lemasson, and Thierry Lodé, "Social Organization of Otters in Relation to Their Ecology," *Biological Journal of the Linnean Society* 133, no. 1 (2021): 1–27.

141 **Within these closer-knit:** Thomas R. Zentall, "Mechanisms of Copying, Social Learning, and Imitation in Animals," *Learning and Motivation* 80 (2022): 101844, https://doi.org/10.1016/j.lmot.2022.101844.

141 **One study of social:** Zosia Ladds, William Hoppitt, and Neeltje J. Boogert, "Social Learning in Otters," *Royal Society Open Science* 4, no. 8 (2017): 170489.

142 **Smooth-coated otters live:** Anusha Shivram et al., "Population Distribution and Causes of Mortality of Smooth-Coated Otters, *Lutrogale perspicillata*, in Singapore,"

Journal of Mammalogy 104, no. 3 (2023): 496–508, https://doi.org/10.1093/jmammal/gyad007.

143 **Asian small-clawed otters live:** Ladds, Hoppitt, and Boogert, "Social Learning in Otters," 170489.

143 **ASCOs' forelimbs are much:** Hans Kruuk, *Otters: Ecology, Behaviour, and Conservation* (Oxford University Press, 2006), 8.

143 **Emblematic of early:** Louis S. B. Leakey, Phillip V. Tobias, and John R. Napier, "A New Species of the Genus *Homo* from Olduvai Gorge," *Nature* 202, no. 4927 (1964): 7–9, https://doi.org/10.1038/202007a0.

143 **At the same time, just 560 kilometers:** Jane Goodall, "Tool-Using and Aimed Throwing in a Community of Free-Living Chimpanzees," *Nature* 201, no. 4926 (1964): 1264–66, https://doi.org/10.1038/2011264a0.

143 **In the late 1930s:** Edna M. Fisher, "Habits of the Southern Sea Otter," *Journal of Mammalogy* 20, no. 1 (1939): 21–36.

144 **Sea otter use of tools:** Michael Haslam et al., "Wild Sea Otter Mussel Pounding Leaves Archaeological Traces," *Scientific Reports* 9, no. 1 (2019): 4417.

144 **It's called *emergent anvil*:** Haslam et al., "Wild Sea Otter Mussel Pounding Leaves Archaeological Traces," 4417.

144 **In each instance, sea:** Amanda Seed and Richard Byrne, "Animal Tool-Use," *Current Biology* 20, no. 23 (2010): R1032–R1039.

144 **They shop for the:** Jessica A. Fujii, Katherine Ralls, and Martin Tim Tinker, "Ecological Drivers of Variation in Tool-Use Frequency Across Sea Otter Populations," *Behavioral Ecology* 26, no. 2 (2015): 519–26.

145 **For example, sea otter:** Chris J. Law et al., "Tool Use Increases Mechanical Foraging Success and Tooth Health in Southern Sea Otters (*Enhydra lutris nereis*)," *Science* 384, no. 6697 (2024): 798–802.

145 **Since tool use is:** Erin Elizabeth Frick et al., "Flexibility and Use of a Novel Tool in Asian Small Clawed Otters (*Aonyx*

cinerea)," *International Journal of Comparative Psychology* 29, no. 1 (2016), https://doi.org/10.46867/ijcp.2016.29.00.13.

145 **Thomas Zentall, an animal:** Thomas R. Zentall, "Intelligence in Nonprimates," in *Handbook of Intelligence: Evolutionary Theory, Historical Perspective, and Current Concepts*, ed. Sam Goldstein, Dana Princiotta, and Jack A. Naglieri (Springer, 2015): 11–25.

145 **This caching bird:** Muhammad A. J. Qadri et al., "Examination of Long-Term Visual Memorization Capacity in the Clark's Nutcracker (*Nucifraga columbiana*)," *Psychonomic Bulletin & Review* 25, no. 6 (2018): 2274–80.

145 **This ability to navigate:** S. D. Healy and C. Jozet-Alves, "Spatial Memory," in *Encyclopedia of Animal Behavior*, ed. Michael D. Breed and Janice Moore (Academic Press, 2010), 304–7.

146 **This tests spatial *working*:** Healy and Jozet-Alves, "Spatial Memory," 304–7.

146 **In a study at Zoo Atlanta:** Bonnie M. Perdue, Rebecca J. Snyder, and Terry L. Maple, "Cognitive Research in Asian Small-Clawed Otters," *International Journal of Comparative Psychology* 26, no. 1 (2013), https://doi.org/10.46867/ijcp.2013.26.01.01.

147 **There is evidence that:** Sarah McKay Strobel et al., "Adaptations for Amphibious Vision in Sea Otters (*Enhydra lutris*): Structural and Functional Observations," *Journal of Comparative Physiology A* 206, no. 5 (2020): 767–82.

147 **Based on anatomical:** Joseph T. Svoke, Rebecca J. Snyder, and Jenny Brink Elgart, "Preliminary Evidence for Color Stimuli Discrimination in the Asian Small-Clawed Otter (*Aonyx cinerea*)," *Learning & Behavior* 42, no. 2 (2014): 176–84; Jessica J. Wegman and Caroline M. DeLong, "Investigating Object Recognition Memory Using Sensory Enrichment with a North American River Otter (*Lontra canadensis*)," *Journal of Zoological and Botanical Gardens* 4, no. 2 (2023): 335–63.

147 **Studies also indicate:** Yeong-Seok Jo et al., "Distribution and Habitat Models of the Eurasian Otter, *Lutra lutra*, in South Korea," *Journal of Mammalogy* 98, no. 4 (2017): 1105–17.

147 **For the last decade:** Ashlynn M. Keller and Caroline M. DeLong, "Orangutans (*Pongo pygmaeus pygmaeus*) and Children (*Homo sapiens*) Use Stick Tools in a Puzzle Box Task Involving Semantic Prospection," *International Journal of Comparative Psychology* 29, no. 1 (2016): 29484; Logan R. Brownell, Jessica F. Cantlon, and Caroline M. DeLong, "Hand Preferences in Olive Baboons (*Papio anubis*) during Cognitive Performance on Match-to-Sample Tasks and Natural Behaviors," *American Journal of Primatology* 87, no. 1 (2025): e23728; Irene Ann Fobe, Caroline M. DeLong, and K. Tyler Wilcox, "An Exploration of Rhythm Perception in African Penguins (*Spheniscus demersus*)," *Proceedings of Meetings on Acoustics* 31, no. 1 (2017), https://doi.org/10.1121/2.0000773.

148 **Understanding how river otters:** "Research," Comparative Cognition and Perception Lab, Rochester Institute of Technology, accessed March 11, 2025, https://www.rit.edu/delonglab/research.

148 **An umwelt is shaped:** Jeffrey C. Schank, Meredith C. Lutz, and Sydney Y. Wood, "Information and the Umwelt: A Theoretical Framework for the Evolution of Play," *Neuroscience & Biobehavioral Reviews* 153 (2023): 105349.

149 **Instead, he preferred whichever:** Caroline M. DeLong et al., "North American River Otters (*Lontra canadensis*) Discriminate Between 2D Objects Varying in Shape and Color," *Learning & Behavior* 47, no. 1 (2019): 91–104.

150 **It's thought that among:** Peter F. MacNeilage, Lesley J. Rogers, and Giorgio Vallortigara, "Origins of the Left & Right Brain," *Scientific American* 301, no. 1 (2009): 60–67.

150 **You already know that:** Lesley J. Rogers, Giorgio Vallortigara, and Richard J. Andrew, *Divided Brains: The Biology and Behaviour of Brain Asymmetries* (Cambridge University Press, 2013), 1–16.

150 **But did you know:** Felix Ströckens, Onur Güntürkün, and Sebastian Ocklenburg, "Limb Preferences in Non-Human Vertebrates," *Laterality: Asymmetries of Body, Brain and Cognition* 18, no. 5 (2013): 536–75.

150 **In an investigation:** Phillip J. Clapham et al., "Do Humpback Whales Exhibit Lateralized Behaviour?," *Animal Behaviour* 50, no. 1 (1995): 73–82.

150 **They also noted that:** Haslam et al., "Wild Sea Otter Mussel Pounding Leaves Archaeological Traces," 4417.

151 **Hemispheric specializations allow:** Gesa Hartwigsen, Yoshua Bengio, and Danilo Bzdok, "How Does Hemispheric Specialization Contribute to Human-Defining Cognition?," *Neuron* 109, no. 13 (2021): 2075–90.

151 **Additionally, routine communications:** MacNeilage, Rogers, and Vallortigara, "Origins of the Left & Right Brain," 60–67.

Chapter 8: Tangled Tails and Teeth

154 **I am especially excited:** Klaus-Peter Koepfli, "How Genetics and Genomics Have Enriched Our Understanding of Otter Biology and Phylogeny," in *16th IUCN/SSC OSG International Otter Congress 24–28 February 2025 Lima, Peru—Book of Abstracts* (IUCN/SSC Otter Specialist Group, 2025), 7; Thye Lim Tee et al., "The Current Status and Conservation Effort of Hairy-Nosed Otter (Lutra sumatrana) in Malaysia," in *16th IUCN/SSC OSG International Otter Congress 24–28 February 2025 Lima, Peru—Book of Abstracts* (IUCN/SSC Otter Specialist Group, 2025), 16.

154 **It's also the smallest:** Gonzalo Medina-Vogel et al., "The Natural History of Marine Otter (*Lontra felina*)," in *Marine Otter Conservation*, ed. Gonzalo Medina-Vogel, Liliana Ayala, and Raúl Sánchez-Scaglioni (Springer Nature Switzerland, 2024), 18.

156 **There are more than 10,000:** Jennifer L. Hill and Ross A. Hill, "Ecotourism in Amazonian Peru: Uniting Tourism, Conservation and Community Development," *Geography* 96, no. 2 (2011): 75–85.

156 **It was once thought:** George E. Schatz et al., "Stilt Roots and Growth of Arboreal Palms," *Biotropica* 17, no. 3 (1985): 206–9.

156 **This interspecies harmony:** André de Lima Barros, Jorge Luis López-Lozano, and Albertina Pimentel Lima, "The Frog *Lithodytes lineatus* (Anura: Leptodactylidae) Uses Chemical Recognition to Live in Colonies of Leaf-Cutting Ants of the Genus *Atta* (Hymenoptera: Formicidae)," *Behavioral Ecology and Sociobiology* 70, no. 12 (2016): 2195–2201.

157 **Finally, we reach:** "Oxbow Lakes, Earth Resources Observation and Science (EROS) Center," Earth Shots, retrieved March 3, 2025, https://eros.usgs.gov/earthshots/oxbow-lakes.

157 **Though it's about two:** Jessica Groenendijk and Frank Hajek, *Giants of the Madre de Dios* (Frankfurt Zoological Society, 2006), 89–94.

158 **The only species within:** Nicole Duplaix, "Observations on the Ecology and Behavior of the Giant River Otter *Pteronura brasiliensis* in Suriname," *Revue d'Écologie (La Terre et la Vie)* 34, no. 4 (1980): 495–620.

158 **In Brazilian Portuguese:** Gregory Mann, "Giant Otter," "Ocean Treasures" Memorial Library, accessed July 9, 2025, https://otlibrary.com/giant-river-otter/.

158 **In other areas of the Amazon:** Groenendijk and Hajek, *Giants of the Madre de Dios*, 26–27, 154.

159 **We can tell she's:** Jessica Groenendijk and Frank Hajek, "A Reliable Method for Sexing Giant Otters (*Pteronura brasiliensis*) in the Wild," *Latin American Journal of Aquatic Mammals* 10, no. 2 (2015): 163–65.

159 **While females are around:** Duplaix, "Observations on the Ecology and Behavior of the Giant River Otter *Pteronura brasiliensis* in Suriname," 479–504.

159 **It's a good sign:** Claudio Gnoli and Claudio Prigioni, "Preliminary Study on the Acoustic Communication of Captive Otters (*Lutra lutra*)," *Hystrix, the Italian Journal of Mammalogy* 7, nos. 1–2 (1995): 289–96; Sabrina Bettoni et al., "Airborne Vocal Communication in Adult Neotropical Otters (*Lontra longicaudis*)," *PLoS One* 16, no. 5 (2021): e0251974; Christen Almonte, "Classification of Captive North American River Otters (*Lontra canadensis*) Vocal

Repertoires: Individual Variations, and Age Class Comparisons," *Animal Behavior and Cognition* 1, no. 4 (2014): 502–17.

160 **Like the spots:** Duplaix, "Observations on the Ecology and Behavior of the Giant River Otter *Pteronura brasiliensis* in Suriname," 495–620.

160 **There's even evidence that:** Nicola J. Quick and Vincent M. Janik, "Bottlenose Dolphins Exchange Signature Whistles When Meeting at Sea," *Proceedings of the Royal Society B: Biological Sciences* 279, no. 1738 (2012): 2539–45, https://doi.org/10.1098/rspb.2011.2537.

161 **Using playback recordings:** Christina A. S. Mumm, Maria C. Urrutia, and Mirjam Knörnschild, "Vocal Individuality in Cohesion Calls of Giant Otters, *Pteronura brasiliensis*," *Animal Behaviour* 88 (2014): 243–52.

161 **In Brazil's Pantanal region:** Caroline Leuchtenberger et al., "Vocal Repertoire of the Social Giant Otter," *Journal of the Acoustical Society of America* 136, no. 5 (2014): 2861–75.

161 **They also observed eleven:** Christina A. S. Mumm and Mirjam Knörnschild, "The Vocal Repertoire of Adult and Neonate Giant Otters (*Pteronura brasiliensis*)," *PLoS One* 9, no. 11 (2014): e112562.

162 **If these sounds had:** Leuchtenberger et al., "Vocal Repertoire of the Social Giant Otter," 2861–75.

162 **However, the terminology:** Renata S. Sousa-Lima et al., "Otter Sounds," *Marine Mammal Acoustics in a Noisy Ocean*, ed. Christina Erbe et al. (Springer, 2025), 442, https://www.researchgate.net/profile/Izabela-Laurentino/publication/393361798_Otter_Sounds_6/links/68668cbc92697d42903ce52e/Otter-Sounds-6.pdf.

162 **The Congo clawless otters:** Hélène Jacques et al., "The Congo Clawless Otter (*Aonyx congicus*; Mustelidae: Lutrinae): A Review of Its Systematics, Distribution and Conservation Status," *African Zoology* 44, no. 2 (2009): 159–70.

162 **Another African otter species:** Jan Reed-Smith et al., "Preliminary Report on the Behavior of Spotted-Necked

Otter (*Lutra maculicollis*, Lichtenstein, 1835), Living in a Lentic Ecosystem," *Zoo Biology* 33, no. 2 (2014): 121–30.

162 **In fact, the spotted-necked:** Nicole Duplaix, Phone conversation, July 25, 2025, 13:30–14:00.

162 **Cape clawless otters, the third:** Jan Reed-Smith, "The Cape Clawless Otter (*Aonyx capensis*) in Kenya," *River Otter Journal* 13, no. 1 (2004), 1–12.

163 **On a calm day:** Laura J. McShane et al., "Repertoire, Structure, and Individual Variation of Vocalizations in the Sea Otter," *Journal of Mammalogy* 76, no. 2 (1995): 414–27.

163 **For example, marine-foraging:** Shannon E. Albeke, Nathan P. Nibbelink, and Merav Ben-David, "Modeling Behavior by Coastal River Otter (*Lontra canadensis*) in Response to Prey Availability in Prince William Sound, Alaska: A Spatially-Explicit Individual-Based Approach," *PLoS One* 10, no. 6 (2015): e0126208.

163 **Inland North American river:** Gail M. Blundell et al., "Kinship and Sociality in Coastal River Otters: Are They Related?," *Behavioral Ecology* 15, no. 5 (2004): 705–14.

163 **Two-way calls are:** Dominic D. P. Johnson et al., "Does the Resource Dispersion Hypothesis Explain Group Living?," *Trends in Ecology & Evolution* 17, no. 12 (2002): 563–70.

163 **Although mobbing behavior:** Filipe Cristovão Ribeiro da Cunha, Julio Cesar Rodrigues Fontenelle, and Michael Griesser, "Predation Risk Drives the Expression of Mobbing Across Bird Species," *Behavioral Ecology* 28, no. 6 (2017): 1517–23.

164 **"The jaguar approached":** Caroline Leuchtenberger et al., "Jaguar Mobbing by Giant Otter Groups," *Acta Ethologica* 19, no. 2 (2016): 143–46.

165 **This adaptive strategy:** Marilyn B. Renfree and Jane C. Fenelon, "The Enigma of Embryonic Diapause," *Development* 144, no. 18 (2017): 3199–3210.

165 **As the seasons change:** Renfree and Fenelon, "The Enigma of Embryonic Diapause," 3199–3210.

165 **Typically, North American river:** Jamie R. Crait et al.,

"Late Seasonal Breeding of River Otters in Yellowstone National Park," *American Midland Naturalist* 156, no. 1 (2006): 189–92.

166 **The same is true:** Hans Kruuk, *Otters: Ecology, Behaviour, and Conservation* (Oxford University Press, 2006), 8; Ashley D. Franklin et al., "Biological and Management-Related Predictors of Reproductive Success in North American Ex Situ Asian Small-Clawed Otters (*Aonyx cinereus*)," *Journal of Zoological and Botanical Gardens* 4, no. 3 (2023): 587–612; Jonathan Baranga, "The Distribution and Conservation Status of Otters in Uganda," *IUCN Otter Specialist Group Bulletin* 9 (1994): 4–5.

166 **Among most otters:** Hans Kruuk, *Wild Otters: Predation and Populations* (Oxford University Press, 1995), 89–102.

166 **These couplings are short-lived:** Max De Yuan Khoo and N. Sivasothi, "Observations of the Variation in Group Structure of Two Urban Smooth-Coated Otter *Lutrogale perspicillata* Groups in the Central Watershed of Singapore," *IUCN Otter Specialist Group Bulletin* 35, no. 3 (2018), 148–54; Syed Ainul Hussain et al, "Biology and Ecology of Asian Small-Clawed Otter *Aonyx cinereus* (Illiger, 1815): A Review," *IUCN Otter Specialist Group Bulletin* 28, no. 2 (2011): 63–75; Duplaix, "Observations on the Ecology and Behavior of the Giant River Otter *Pteronura brasiliensis* in Suriname," 495–620.

166 **Their delayed implantation:** Shawn Larson, C. J. Casson, and Sam Wasser, "Noninvasive Reproductive Steroid Hormone Estimates from Fecal Samples of Captive Female Sea Otters (*Enhydra lutris*)," *General and Comparative Endocrinology* 134, no. 1 (2003): 18–25.

166 **In captivity, when there:** John Hammond and Arthur Walton, "Notes on Ovulation and Fertilisation in the Ferret," *Journal of Experimental Biology* 11, no. 3 (1934): 307–19.

166 **There may be an evolutionary:** Jessica Groenendijk, *The Giant Otter: Giants of the Amazon* (Pen & Sword Books, 2019), 70–75.

167 **Rhinarium scarring among:** Heidi C. Pearson and Randall W. Davis, "Reproductive Behavior of Male Sea Otters," in

Ethology and Behavioral Ecology of Sea Otters and Polar Bears, ed. Randall W. Davis and Anthony M. Pagano (Springer International, 2021), 107–23.

167 **"These are animals!":** Michelle Wolf, *Michelle Wolf: Joke Show*, dir. Lance Bangs (Netflix, 2019), streaming video, 59 min., 14:15–15:00, https://www.netflix.com/title/81152788.

167 **It is indeed true:** Heather S. Harris et al., "Lesions and Behavior Associated with Forced Copulation of Juvenile Pacific Harbor Seals (*Phoca vitulina richardsi*) by Southern Sea Otters (*Enhydra lutris nereis*)," *Aquatic Mammals* 36, no. 4 (2010): 331–41.

167 **It's also true that:** Courtney Dickson, "Sea Otter off Vancouver Island Prime Suspect in River Otter Deaths. Researchers Say That's Not Unusual," CBC News, January 31, 2025, https://www.cbc.ca/news/canada/britishcolumbia/sea-otter-river-otter-violence-1.7444982.

168 **If a female dies:** Harris et al., "Lesions and Behavior Associated with Forced Copulation of Juvenile Pacific Harbor Seals," 331–41.

168 **This can likely be traced:** "Otters Holding Hands," YouTube video, 1:41, March 19, 2007, http://www.youtube.com/watch?v=epUk3T2Kfno.

168 **In it, a nineteen-year-old:** Richard Ravalli, *Sea Otters: A History* (University of Nebraska Press, 2018), 103–7.

169 **Field scientists evaluate:** Larry J. Minter et al., "Digestible Energy Intake and Digestive Efficiency of Human-Managed North American River Otters (*Lontra canadensis*)," *Veterinary Medicine International* 2020, no. 1 (2020): 801–8.

171 **Almost one year after her:** Janice Reed-Smith, *North American (Nearctic) River Otter (Lontra canadensis) Husbandry Notebook* (John Ball Zoo, 2012), 93, https://aszk.org.au/wp-content/uploads/2020/06/North-American-River-Otter-Lontra-canadensis-Reed-Smith-J.-2012-Chapters-1-6.pdf.

171 **They can't replenish:** Reed-Smith, *North American (Nearctic) River Otter (Lontra canadensis) Husbandry Notebook*, 92.

171 **By the time they're six to eight:** Kruuk, *Otters*, 79–84.

171 **Once they undergo:** Serge Larivière and Lyle R. Walton, "*Lontra canadensis*," *Mammalian Species* 587 (1998): 1–8.

172 **By this time, they're around:** Wayne Melquist and Maurice Hornocker, *Ecology of River Otters in West Central Idaho* (The Wildlife Society, 1983), 3–60.

172 **However, the mom still:** Melquist and Hornocker, *Ecology of River Otters*, 3–60.

172 **There are documented:** Cristina Calvo-Fernandez et al., "Cannibalism in Eurasian Otters (*Lutra lutra*)," *River Research and Applications* 40, no. 8 (2024): 1617–20; Guilherme Mourão and L. Carvalho, "Cannibalism Among Giant Otters (*Pteronura brasiliensis*)," *Mammalia* 65, no. 2 (2001): 225–27.

172 **In both cases, when:** Reed-Smith et al., "Preliminary Report on the Behavior of Spotted-Necked Otter," 121–30.

172 **Their choices are influenced:** Kruuk, *Otters,* 45.

173 **Otters typically don't:** Thomas A. Gorman et al., "Site Characteristics of River Otter (*Lontra canadensis*) Natal Dens in Minnesota," *American Midland Naturalist* 156, no. 1 (2006): 109–17; Kruuk, *Otters,* 42–44.

173 **In riparian habitats:** Gorman et al., "Site Characteristics of River Otter (*Lontra canadensis*) Natal Dens in Minnesota," 109–17.

173 **In 2021, while surveying:** Lisa M. Smith, Daniel Batie, and Jeffery A. Gore, "First Record of a North American River Otter Using a Cave as a Natal Den," *Southeastern Naturalist* 20, no. 2 (2021): N60.

173 **Along the Puget Sound:** Russell Link, *Living with Wildlife in the Pacific Northwest* (University of Washington Press, 2004), 232.

173 **They can't regulate:** Michelle M. Cortez and Randall W. Davis, "Reproductive Behavior of Female Sea Otters and Their Pups," in *Ethology and Behavioral Ecology of Sea Otters and Polar Bears*, ed. Randall W. Davis and Anthony M. Pagano (Springer, 2021), 125–38.

174 **They do acquire:** Cortez and Davis, "Reproductive Behavior of Female Sea Otters and Their Pups," 125–38.

174 **Though sea otter pups':** Sarah M. Chinn et al., "The High Cost of Motherhood: End-Lactation Syndrome in Southern Sea Otters (*Enhydra lutris nereis*) on the Central California Coast, USA," *Journal of Wildlife Diseases* 52, no. 2 (2016): 307–18.

174 **Over half of all:** Chinn et al., "The High Cost of Motherhood," 307–18.

174 **Even after her pup:** James L. Bodkin, Daniel H. Monson, and Ronald J. Jameson, "Age-Specific Reproduction in Female Sea Otters (*Enhydra lutris*) from South-Central Alaska: Analysis of Reproductive Tracts," *Canadian Journal of Zoology* 71, no. 9 (1993): 1811–15.

174 **Despite its mother's:** Nicole M. Thometz et al., "Energetic Demands of Immature Sea Otters from Birth to Weaning: Implications for Maternal Costs, Reproductive Behavior and Population-Level Trends," *Journal of Experimental Biology* 217, no. 12 (2014): 2053.

174 **If separated from its mother:** Marianne L. Riedman and James A. Estes, "The Sea Otter (*Enhydra lutris*): Behavior, Ecology, and Natural History," *Biological Report* 90, no. 14 (1990): 18.

174 **In the Aleutian islands:** Steve K. Sherrod, James A. Estes, and Clayton M. White, "Depredation of Sea Otter Pups by Bald Eagles at Amchitka Island, Alaska," *Journal of Mammalogy* 56, no. 3 (1975): 701–3.

174 **Among southern sea otters:** James A. Estes et al., "Killer Whale Predation on Sea Otters Linking Oceanic and Nearshore Ecosystems," *Science* 282, no. 5388 (1998): 473–76.

175 **In fact, in the spring:** Daniel H. Monson, "Sea Otter Predator Avoidance Behavior," in *Ethology and Behavioral Ecology of Sea Otters and Polar Bears*, ed. Randall W. Davis and Anthony M. Pagano (Springer, 2021), 167.

175 **Asphyxiation by sea otter:** Monson, "Sea Otter Predator Avoidance Behavior," 167.

175 **Since their early documentation:** Kelsey R. Griffin, Gretchen H. Roffler, and Ellen M. Dymit, "Wolves on the Katmai Coast Hunt Sea Otters and Harbor Seals," *Ecology* 104, no. 12 (2023): e4185.

175 **Another wolf pack:** Gretchen H. Roffler et al., "Switching to Marine Prey Leads to Unprecedented Mercury Concentrations in a Population of Coastal Alaska Wolves," *Science of the Total Environment* 980 (2025): 179542.

Chapter 9: River Otter: $200

178 **Otter 841—or Laverna:** Mark Woodward (@NativeSanta Cruz), "One year ago today," X, June 18, 2024, https://x.com/NativeSantaCruz/status/1803073361041604716.

178 **No one reported:** "Southern Sea Otter 841 Observed with Pup, Wildlife Biologists Encourage Ethical Wildlife Viewing," U.S. Fish and Wildlife Service, October 26, 2023, https://www.fws.gov/press-release/2023-10/southern-sea-otter-841-observed-pup-wildlife-biologists-encourage-ethical.

178 **She was successfully captured:** "Southern Sea Otter 841 Observed with Pup, Wildlife Biologists Encourage Ethical Wildlife Viewing," U.S. Fish and Wildlife Service, https://www.fws.gov/press-release/2023-10/southern-sea-otter-841-observed-pup-wildlife-biologists-encourage-ethical.

178 **The Monterey Bay Aquarium's Sea Otter Program:** "Sea Otter Program," Monterey Bay Aquarium, accessed April 2, 2025, https://www.montereybayaquarium.org/animals/sea-otter-program-timeline.

179 **At the time of her aggressive:** "Southern Sea Otter 841 Observed with Pup," U.S. Fish and Wildlife Service.

179 **Even with the best intentions:** Jane Morgan, Michael Belanger, and Carin Wittnich, "Reported Worldwide Otter Attacks on Humans over the Last Decade (2011–2021): Dictated by Human Encroachment or Otter Behavior," *IUCN Otter Specialist Group Bulletin* 40, no. 2 (2023): 80–89.

179 **Despite the dangers:** United Nations Office on Drugs and Crime, *World Wildlife Crime Report: Trafficking in Protected Species* (United Nations, 2020), 134, https://www.unodc.org/documents/data-and-analysis/wildlife/2020/World_Wildlife_Report_2020_9July.pdf.

179 **In 1973, the same:** "What Is CITES?," CITES, accessed May 28, 2025, https://cites.org/eng/disc/what.php.

180 **This legally binding:** *Convention on International Trade in Endangered Species of Wild Fauna and Flora*, signed at Washington, DC, March 3, 1973, amended at Bonn, June 22, 1979, amended at Gaborone, April 30, 1983, https://cites.org/sites/default/files/eng/disc/CITES-Convention-EN.pdf.

180 **As of today, 185:** "List of Contracting Parties," CITES, accessed May 28, 2025, https://cites.org/eng/disc/parties/chronolo.php.

180 **By joining, the parties:** *Convention on International Trade in Endangered Species of Wild Fauna and Flora.*

180 **They manage extensive:** "TRAFFIC International—the Wildlife Monitoring Network," IWMC, accessed May 28, 2025, https://www.iwmc.org/traffic-international-the-wildlife-monitoring-network/.

180 **According to the report:** Lalita Gomez and Jamie Bouhuys, "Executive Summary," in *Illegal Otter Trade in Southeast Asia* (TRAFFIC, June 2018), vii, https://www.traffic.org/site/assets/files/5228/seasia-otter-report.pdf.

180 **Additionally, between January:** Gomez and Bouhuys, "Executive Summary," vii.

181 **TRAFFIC found ten:** Tomomi Kitade and Yui Naruse, "Executive Summary," in *Otter Alert: A Rapid Assessment of Illegal Trade and Booming Demand in Japan* (TRAFFIC, October 2018), vii, https://traffic.org/site/assets/files/11196/otter-alert-vfinal-web-100.pdf.

182 **The average age of death:** Yumiko Okamoto et al., "The Situation of Pet Otters in Japan—Warning by Vets," *IUCN Otter Specialist Group Bulletin* 37, no. 1 (2020): 71–79.

182 **Eurasian otters are taken:** Joshua Elves-Powell et al., "The Trade in Eurasian Otter, *Lutra lutra,* in North Korea," *IUCN Otter Specialist Group Bulletin* 41, no. 4 (2024): 182–88.

182 **The giant otter has been:** Natalia C. Pimenta et al., "Differential Resilience of Amazonian Otters Along the Rio Negro in the Aftermath of the 20th Century International Fur Trade," *PLoS One* 13, no. 3 (2018): e0193984.

182 **In East Africa:** Janice Reed-Smith et al., "Consumptive Uses

of and Lore Pertaining to Spotted-Necked Otters in East Africa—a Preliminary Report from the Lake Victoria Area of Kenya, Tanzania, and Uganda," *IUCN Otter Specialist Group Bulletin* 27, no. 2 (2010): 85–88.

182 **One Cambodian fisherman:** "The Illegal Trade in Otters: A Global Problem," International Otter Survival Fund, 2014, https://static1.squarespace.com/static/64464f864d53e825428015ef/t/64be4e23758ad423151c42cc/1690193445616/IOSF_Illegal_Trade_in_Otters_Report_2014.pdf.

187 **Yet, as of 2021:** Emily A. Bricker et al., "Conservation Status of the North American River Otter in the United States and Canada," in *Small Carnivores: Evolution, Ecology, Behaviour, and Conservation*, ed. Emmanual Do Linh San et al. (John Wiley & Sons, 2022), 509–35; "North American River Otter: Non-Detriment Finding," Government of Canada, February 17, 2014, https://www.canada.ca/en/environment-climate-change/services/convention-international-trade-endangered-species/non-detriment-findings/north-american-river-otter.html.

188 **Regardless, these prices:** Cameron La Follette et al., "The Invisible Slaughter: Local Sea Otter Hunters on the Oregon Coast," *Oregon Historical Quarterly* 124, no. 3 (2023): 298–323.

188 **By 1910, when:** Shawn E. Larson and James L. Bodkin, "The Conservation of Sea Otters: A Prelude," in *Sea Otter Conservation*, ed. Shawn E. Larson, James L. Bodkin, and Glenn R. VanBlaricom (Academic Press, 2015), 2; Larson, email message to author, July 31, 2025.

188 **The Danish-born Captain:** C. C. Sander, "The Search for the Northeast Passage: The First and the Second Kamchatka Expeditions in the Years 1725–1743," *Studia Humanitatis*, no. 3 (2019): 1.

188 **The others survived by:** Shana Loshbaugh, "Sea Otters and the Maritime Fur Trade," in *Ethology and Behavioral Ecology of Sea Otters and Polar Bears*, ed. Randall W. Davis and Anthony M. Pagano (Springer, 2021), 175–76.

188 **When they heard:** "Vitus Bering," PBS, accessed April 23, 2025, https://www.pbs.org/edens/kamchatka/bering.html.

189 **Between 1804 and 1837:** L. Harrington, J. Marino, and C. King, "People and Wild Musteloids," in *Wild Musteloids: Ecology and Conservation*, ed. L. Harrington and J. Marino (Oxford University Press, 2017), 190; James L. Bodkin, Erin U. Foster, and Shawn E. Larson, "How the History of Harvest and Recovery Influenced Our Understanding of the Ecological Role of Sea Otters," in *Sea Otter Conservation II: Nearshore Ecosystem Restoration* (Academic Press, 2025), 10.

189 **But by the end of the 1800s:** Karl W. Kenyon, *The Sea Otter in the Eastern Pacific Ocean* (U.S. Bureau of Sport Fisheries and Wildlife, 1969), 155.

189 **Between 1965 and 1972:** James L. Bodkin, James A. Estes, and M. Tim Tinker, "History of Prior Sea Otter Translocations," in *Restoring Sea Otters to the Oregon Coast: A Feasibility Study*, ed. M. Tim Tinker et al. (Elakha Alliance, 2023), 7–16, https://www.elakhaalliance.org/wp-content/uploads/2023/03/Ch2-RestoreOtterstoOR-digital.pdf.

189 **The Washington Olympic Coast:** Jessica J. Kyle, Michelle M. Jeffries, and Deanna H. Lynch, "Washington State Sea Otter Survey: Spring 2019," U.S. Fish and Wildlife Service, 2019, https://www.fws.gov/sites/default/files/documents/WASeaOtterSurvey2019.pdf.

189 **Now that they're protected:** Thomas F. Thornton, *Sustainable Indigenous Harvest, Use, and Stewardship of Sea Otter in Sitka Sound and Southeast Alaska*, Sealaska Heritage Institute, June 30, 2025, https://sealaskaheritage.org/wp-content/uploads/2025/09/SHI-Sea-Otter-Final-Report-7.25.25.pdf.

190 **Several nations have:** "Fur bans—FOUR PAWS International—Animal Welfare Organisation," FOUR PAWS International, accessed May 4, 2025, https://www.four-paws.org/campaigns-topics/topics/animals-abused-for-fashion/fur-bans.

190 **Some cities in the US:** "Fur bans—FOUR PAWS International—Animal Welfare Organisation."

190 **And the Hudson's Bay:** "Hudson's Bay Gives Up on Final 7 Stores, Including Canada's Last Saks 5th Avenue Location,"

Retail Dive, April 25, 2025, https://www.retaildive.com/news/hudsons-bay-liquidation-last-stores-canada-saks-5th-avenue/746374/.

Chapter 10: Clean, Quiet Water

192 **First established in:** Lauren M. Kuehne et al., "Above and Below: Military Aircraft Noise in Air and Under Water at Whidbey Island, Washington," *Journal of Marine Science and Engineering* 8, no. 11 (2020): 923.

192 **New naval pilots:** Kuehne et al., "Above and Below," 923.

192 **The training routes:** Giordano Jacuzzi et al., "Population Health Implications of Exposure to Pervasive Military Aircraft Noise Pollution," *Journal of Exposure Science & Environmental Epidemiology* 35, no. 1 (2024): 91–103.

193 **At 115 decibels:** Department of the Navy, Environmental Impact Statement for EA18 "Growler" Airfield Operations at Naval Air Station Whidbey Island Complex, WA, "3: Affected Environment," *NAS Whidbey Island Complex Growler FEIS*, vol. 1, September 2018, 3–38, https://media.defense.gov/2019/Feb/01/2002085194/-1/-1/1/CHAPTER%203%20-%20AFFECTED%20ENVIRONMENT.PDF.

193 **Growlers are often:** "Common Noise Levels," International Noise Awareness Day, accessed May 22, 2025, https://noiseawareness.org/info-center/common-noise-levels/.

193 **The noise itself:** Arnold Engineering Development Center, *Beyond the Speed of Sound* (United States Air Force, 2009), 89, https://www.govinfo.gov/content/pkg/GOVPUB-D301-PURL-gpo70110/pdf/GOVPUB-D301-PURL-gpo70110.pdf.

193 **The jets use:** Citizens of Ebey's Reserve, "CO2 Emissions from an EA-18G Growler," Citizens of Ebey's Reserve, January 1, 2015, https://citizensofebeysreserve.com/2015/01/01/co2-emissions-from-an-ea-18g-growler/.

194 **Despite these protections:** Monique M. Lance and Scott F. Pearson, *2020 Washington At-Sea Marbled Murrelet Population Monitoring: Research Progress Report*, Wildlife Science Division, Washington Department of Fish and Wildlife,

March 2021, https://wdfw.wa.gov/sites/default/files/publications/02263/wdfw02263.pdf.

194 **Soon after my first:** Jesse Stensland, "Whidbey Residents Rally Against Jet Noise," *Daily Herald/HeraldNet,* October 10, 2018, https://www.heraldnet.com/news/whidbey-residents-rally-against-military-jet-noise/.

195 **These health risks:** Jacuzzi et al., "Population Health Implications of Exposure to Pervasive Military Aircraft Noise Pollution," 91–103; Jeffrey Schein et al., "Prevalence of Post-Traumatic Stress Disorder in the United States: A Systematic Literature Review," *Current Medical Research and Opinion* 37, no. 12 (2021): 2151–61.

196 **A noise-induced stress response:** Annebelle C. M. Kok et al., "How Chronic Anthropogenic Noise Can Affect Wildlife Communities," *Frontiers in Ecology and Evolution* 11 (2023): 1130075.

196 **They found that "anthropogenic":** Hansjoerg P. Kunc and Rouven Schmidt, "The Effects of Anthropogenic Noise on Animals: A Meta-Analysis," *Biology Letters* 15, no. 11 (2019): 20190649.

196 **This is especially true:** Kunc and Schmidt, "The Effects of Anthropogenic Noise on Animals," 20190649.

196 **For instance, the hunting:** Björn M. Siemers and Andrea Schaub, "Hunting at the Highway: Traffic Noise Reduces Foraging Efficiency in Acoustic Predators," *Proceedings of the Royal Society B: Biological Sciences* 278, no. 1712 (2011): 1646–52.

196 **It becomes noise pollution:** Enda Murphy and Eoin A. King, *Environmental Noise Pollution: Noise Mapping, Public Health, and Policy* (Elsevier, 2022), 53–77.

196 **Low frequencies also travel:** Jacuzzi et al., "Population Health Implications of Exposure to Pervasive Military Aircraft Noise Pollution," 91–103.

196 **Instead, as field investigators:** Drs. Shawn Larson and Jim Bodkin in discussion with the author, March 23, 2025, Seattle, Washington.

196 **Just how much reprieve:** Kuehne et al., "Above and Below," 923.

197 **A 2025 study showed:** Rayen Olivares et al., "Giant Kelp Forests Act as Natural Barriers to Motorboat Noise," 2025, available at SSRN 5177690.

197 **Aquatic vegetation such as:** Mark S. Fonseca and Jennifer A. Cahalan, "A Preliminary Evaluation of Wave Attenuation by Four Species of Seagrass," *Estuarine, Coastal and Shelf Science* 35, no. 6 (1992): 565–76.

197 **The symbiotic relationship:** Ryan E. Langendorf et al., "Dynamic and Context-Dependent Keystone Species Effects in Kelp Forests," *Proceedings of the National Academy of Sciences* 122, no. 10 (2025): e2413360122.

197 **A Danish study:** Emilie Nicoline Stepien et al., "Response of Eurasian Otters (*Lutra lutra*) to Underwater Acoustic Harassment Device Sounds," *Scientific Reports* 14, no. 1 (2024): 4988.

197 **Similarly, sea otters:** Daniela Maldini et al., "Patterns of Sea Otter Haul-Out Behavior in a California Tidal Estuary in Relation to Environmental Variables," *Northwestern Naturalist* 93, no. 1 (2012): 67–78.

197 **According to studies:** Imke Kirste et al., "Is Silence Golden? Effects of Auditory Stimuli and Their Absence on Adult Hippocampal Neurogenesis," *Brain Structure and Function* 220, no. 2 (2015): 1221–28, https://link.springer.com/content/pdf/10.1007/s00429-013-0679-3.pdf.

198 **A New Zealand study:** Daniel Shepherd et al., "Do Quiet Areas Afford Greater Health-Related Quality of Life Than Noisy Areas?," *International Journal of Environmental Research and Public Health* 10, no. 4 (2013): 1284–1303, https://www.mdpi.com/1660-4601/10/4/1284.

198 **These and other studies:** Patrik Grahn, Johan Ottosson, and Kerstin Uvnäs-Moberg, "The Oxytocinergic System as a Mediator of Anti-Stress and Instorative Effects Induced by Nature: The Calm and Connection Theory," *Frontiers in Psychology* 12 (2021): 617814, https://pubmed.ncbi.nlm.nih.gov/34290636/.

198 **According to acoustic ecologist:** Gordon Hempton, quoted in Nicholas Sherman, "One Square Inch of Silence, from the Documentary 'Soundtracker,'" YouTube video, June 7, 2010, http://www.youtube.com/watch?v=a0xHfFC_6n0.

198 **That is, despite the:** "One Square Inch of Silence," One Square Inch of Silence, accessed May 27, 2025, https://onesquareinch.org/.

198 **Anthropogenic sounds are now:** Rachel T. Buxton et al., "Noise Pollution Is Pervasive in U.S. Protected Areas," *Science* 356, no. 6337 (May 5, 2017): 531–33, https://doi.org/10.1126/science.aah4783.

198 **The Salish Sea, with its:** Simone Cominelli et al., "Noise Exposure from Commercial Shipping for the Southern Resident Killer Whale Population," *Marine Pollution Bulletin* 136 (2018): 177–200.

198 **The coastal waters:** Peter Simard et al., "Quantification of Boat Visitation Rates at Artificial and Natural Reefs in the Eastern Gulf of Mexico Using Acoustic Recorders," *PLoS One* 11, no. 8 (2016): e0160695.

198 **In 2019, the *Seattle Times*:** Lynda V. Mapes, "The Roar Below: How Our Noise Is Hurting Orcas' Search for Salmon," *Seattle Times*, May 19, 2019, https://projects.seattletimes.com/2019/hostile-waters-orcas-noise/.

199 **Along Admiralty Inlet:** Christopher Bassett, Jim Thomson, and Brian Polagye, "Characteristics of Underwater Ambient Noise at a Proposed Tidal Energy Site in Puget Sound," in *Oceans 2010 MTS/IEEE SEATTLE* (IEEE, 2010), 1–8.

199 **Since sound travels:** Paul Webb, "Sound," in *Introduction to Oceanography*, last updated August 2023, https://rwu.pressbooks.pub/webboceanography/chapter/6-4-sound/.

199 **Since the mechanism:** Joachim Mogdans, "Sensory Ecology of the Fish Lateral-Line System: Morphological and Physiological Adaptations for the Perception of Hydrodynamic Stimuli," *Journal of Fish Biology* 95, no. 1 (2019): 53–72.

199 **In a particularly bad MSE:** Paul D. Jepson et al., "What Caused the UK's Largest Common Dolphin (*Delphinus*

delphis) Mass Stranding Event?," *PLoS One* 8, no. 4 (2013): e60953, https://doi.org/10.1371/journal.pone.0060953.

199 **According to a report:** Jepson et al., "What Caused the UK's Largest Common Dolphin," e60953.

199 **In her book, *Sing*:** Amorina Kingdon, *Sing Like Fish: How Sound Rules Life Under Water* (Crown, 2024), 15.

200 **A study from the:** Jennifer B. Tennessen et al., "Males Miss and Females Forgo: Auditory Masking from Vessel Noise Impairs Foraging Efficiency and Success in Killer Whales," *Global Change Biology* 30, no. 9 (2024): e17490.

200 **A study of Atlantic:** Frode Oppedal et al., "The Behavioral and Neurobiological Response to Sound Stress in Salmon," *Brain Behavior and Evolution* 100, no. 1 (2025): 11–28; Samara M. Haver et al., "Large Vessel Activity and Low-Frequency Underwater Sound Benchmarks in United States Waters," *Frontiers in Marine Science* 8 (2021): 669528.

201 **Twenty-eight percent:** "The IUCN Red List of Threatened Species," IUCN, n.d., https://www.iucnredlist.org/. Specific species assessments can be found by searching for each scientific name on the website: *Lontra provocax, Pteronura brasiliensis, Lontra felina, Lutra sumatrana, Enhydra lutris, Aonyx cinereus, Lutrogale perspicillata, Lutra lutra, Lontra longicaudis, Aonyx capensis, Hydrictis maculicollis, Aonyx congicus, Lontra canadensis.*

201 **In many parts of their range:** Aarati Basnet et al., "Otter Research in Asia: Trends, Biases and Future Directions," *Global Ecology and Conservation* 24 (2020): e01391.

201 **Between 2009 and 2019:** "Continued Decline of Wetlands Documented in New U.S. Fish and Wildlife Service Report," press release, U.S. Fish and Wildlife Service, March 22, 2024, https://www.fws.gov/press-release/2024-03/continued-decline-wetlands-documented-new-us-fish-and-wildlife-service-report.

201 **They're a cultural treasure:** Megan W. Lang, Jordan C. Ingebritsen, and Rachel K. Griffin, *Status and Trends of Wetlands in the Conterminous United States, 2009 to 2019* (Fish and Wildlife Service, U.S. Department of the Interior, 2024),

https://www.fws.gov/project/2019-wetlands-status-and-trends-report.

201 **They prevent flooding:** David Were et al., "Carbon Sequestration by Wetlands: A Critical Review of Enhancement Measures for Climate Change Mitigation," *Earth Systems and Environment* 3, no. 1 (2019): 327–40.

202 **And according to the Canadian:** M. C. Hansen et al., "High-Resolution Global Maps of 21st-Century Forest Cover Change," *Science* 342 (2013): 850–53, https://doi.org/10.1126/science.1244693.

202 **It was the worst oil spill:** Jesse Greenspan, "Exxon Valdez Oil Spill," History, last updated March 28, 2025, https://www.history.com/articles/exxon-valdez-oil-spill.

202 **Although the hot-water:** Mandy R. Lindeberg et al., "Conditions of Persistent Oil on Beaches in Prince William Sound 26 Years After the Exxon Valdez Spill," *Deep Sea Research Part II: Topical Studies in Oceanography* 147 (2018): 9–19.

202 **Acute oil exposure:** Daniel H. Monson et al., "Long-Term Impacts of the Exxon Valdez Oil Spill on Sea Otters, Assessed Through Age-Dependent Mortality Patterns," *Proceedings of the National Academy of Sciences* 97, no. 12 (2000): 6562–67.

202 **Annual oil surveys:** "Lingering Oil from Exxon Valdez Spill," National Oceanic and Atmospheric Administration, February 26, 2018, https://www.fisheries.noaa.gov/feature-story/lingering-oil-exxon-valdez-spill.

203 **Further, surveys of:** James L. Bodkin, Brenda E. Ballachey, and George G. Esslinger, *Trends in Sea Otter Population Abundance in Western Prince William Sound, Alaska: Progress Toward Recovery Following the 1989* Exxon Valdez *Oil Spill*, Scientific Investigations Report 2011-5213, US Geological Survey, U.S. Department of the Interior, 2011.

203 **Artificial intelligence, for example:** Paul Fergus et al., "Harnessing Artificial Intelligence for Wildlife Conservation," *Conservation* 4, no. 4 (2024): 685–702; Mohammadreza Mohammadabadi et al., "The Role of

Artificial Intelligence in Genomics," *Journal of Agricultural Biotechnology* 16, no. 2 (2024): 195–279; Drew Blount et al., "Flukebook: An Open-Source AI Platform for Cetacean Photo Identification," *Mammalian Biology* 102, no. 3 (2022): 1005–23.

203 **Although cloud data centers:** Chonglin Gu et al., "Planning for Green Cloud Data Centers Using Sustainable Energy," in *2016 IEEE Symposium on Computers and Communication (ISCC)* (IEEE, 2016), 804–9.

203 **Additionally, Washington state:** "Ferry System Electrification," Washington State Department of Transportation, accessed May 30, 2025, https://wsdot.wa.gov/construction-planning/major-projects/ferry-system-electrification.

203 **One of the earliest:** Natural England, "Green Bridges: Safer Travel for Wildlife," Gov.UK, July 31, 2015, https://www.gov.uk/government/news/green-bridges-safer-travel-for-wildlife.

204 **It was so successful:** European Centre for Environment and Human Health, and LDA Design Consulting Ltd., University of Exeter Medical School, *Green Bridges: A Literature Review*, Natural England Commissioned Report NECR181 (Natural England, 2015), https://publications.naturalengland.org.uk/publication/6312886965108736.

204 **Meanwhile, in the United:** Sophie Tsairis, "Montana's New Landmark Wildlife Crossing Laws," *Montana Free Press*, July 22, 2025, https://montanafreepress.org/2025/07/22/montanas-new-landmark-wildlife-crossing-laws.

204 **In Colorado, a green:** Amy Golden, "Study: Crossings on Highway 9 Reduced Wildlife Collisions by 90%," *Sky-Hi News*, June 22, 2021, https://www.skyhinews.com/news/study-crossings-on-highway-9-reduced-wildlife-collisions-by-90/; Michael A. Sawaya, Steven T. Kalinowski, and Anthony P. Clevenger, "Genetic Connectivity for Two Bear Species at Wildlife Crossing Structures in Banff National Park," *Proceedings of the Royal Society B: Biological Sciences* 281, no. 1780 (2014): 20131705.

204 **In the Pacific Northwest:** "Connecting the Wild

Northwest," Conservation Northwest, YouTube video, 5:26, April 26, 2018, https://youtube.com/watch?v=bvj7seHwaZM; "Connecting Wildlife Habitat Under and Over I-90," Conservation Northwest, YouTube video, 4:11, March 31, 2015, https://youtube.com/watch?v=9cO9NXD3Ynw; "I-90 Snoqualmie Pass East: Critter Crossings in the Cascades," Washington Department of Transportation, YouTube video, 19:42, November 3, 2021, https://youtube.com/watch?v=Cf5nMLrlgW4.

204 **From 2014 to 2023:** "Snoqualmie Pass East Project: Performance Analysis," Washington Department of Transportation, accessed July 24, 2025, https://wsdot.wa.gov/about/data/gray-notebook/gnbhome/environment/wildlifehabitatconnectivity/snoqualmiepasseastproject.htm#info.

204 **Megan Isadore, director:** Amanda Bartlett, "'Really Unusual': 3 River Otters Found Dead on Bay Area Road," SFGate.com, July 31, 2024, https://www.sfgate.com/local/article/river-otter-deaths-bay-area-19607909.php.

204 **With an estimated 193:** "Roads and Streets," Britannica Kids, accessed July 4, 2025, https://kids.britannica.com/students/article/roads-and-streets/276743.

205 **Science has only identified:** Katie Hunt, "New Species Named in 2024," CNN, December 31, 2024, https://www.cnn.com/2024/12/31/science/new-species-named-in-2024.

205 **Though ASCOs weren't thought:** Mohan Bikram Shrestha et al., "Confirmation of the Presence of Asian Small-Clawed Otter (*Aonyx cinereus*) in Nepal After 185 Years," *IUCN Otter Specialist Group Bulletin* 42, no. 1 (2025): 3–8.

205 **Similarly in India:** S. Sharma et al., "Photographic Evidence of Incidental Sightings of the Vulnerable Asian Small-Clawed Otter (*Aonyx cinereus* Illiger, 1815) in the Mixed Forest of Darjeeling and Kalimpong District as Part of Central Himalaya," *IUCN Otter Specialist Group Bulletin 41*, no. 3 (2024): 140–53, https://www.iucnosgbull.org/Volume41/Sharma_et_al_2024_a.html.

205 **However, national and international:** Nia Evelyn Thomas et al., "Spatio-Temporal Changes in Effective Population Size

in an Expanding Metapopulation of Eurasian Otters," *Evolutionary Applications* 18, no. 1 (2025): e70067, https://doi.org/10.1111/eva.70067.

206 **In 2021, a Eurasian:** M. B. Shrestha et al., "First Evidence of Eurasian Otter in Nepal in Three Decades," *IUCN Otter Specialist Group Bulletin* 38, no. 5 (2021): 279–91.

206 **One local otter romp:** David Pierson, "Meet the Otters Who Raided a Spa During a Coronavirus Shutdown, Sparking Outrage," *Los Angeles Times*, May 23, 2020, https://www.latimes.com/world-nation/story/2020-05-23/singapore-otters-backlash.

206 **Even now, years after:** Kilian Hughes, Justin M. J. Travis, and Aurore Ponchon, "Modelling the Surprising Recolonisation of an Understudied Aquatic Mammal in a Highly Urbanised Area: Fortune Favoured the Smooth-Coated Otter in Singapore," *Wildlife Biology* (2024): e01200.

206 **As for giant otters:** "Giant Otters," Wildlife Foundation, accessed May 29, 2025, https://wildlife-foundation.org.uk/giant-otters.

206 **However, in recent decades:** Isabella Beltrán-Triana, Ángela Alviz, and Karen Pérez-Albarracín, "The Return of the Giant Otter (*Pteronura brasiliensis*) to Tauramena (Casanare, Colombia): Relative Abundance, Distribution, and Conservation Considerations," *Latin American Journal of Aquatic Mammals* 20, no. 1 (2025): 13–22.

206 **otters, once extensively hunted:** Joanna Zhang, "Returning River Otters to the Gila and How Beavers Can Help," WildEarth Guardians, August 4, 2025, https://wildearthguardians.org/brave-new-wild/where-we-work/new-mexico/returning-river-otters-to-the-gila-and-how-beavers-can-help/.

207 **In 2008, New Mexico:** "Native Species Protection," Amigos Bravos, accessed June 1, 2025, https://www.amigosbravos.org/native-species-protection/.

207 **The population continues:** Griffin Ruston, "New Mexico Game and Fish Works with Nonprofits to Bring Wild Otters Back," KOB4, May 28, 2025, https://www.kob.com/new

-mexico/new-mexico-game-and-fish-works-with-nonprofits-to-bring-wild-otters-back/.

207 **In Pennsylvania, river otters:** Julie Grant, "River Otters in Western Pennsylvania: An Environmental Success Story," *Allegheny Front*, May 30, 2025, https://www.alleghenyfront.org/river-otters-pennsylvania-conemaugh-river.

207 **In March 2025:** Dominique V. Kone, M. Tim Tinker, and Leigh G. Torres, "Informing Sea Otter Reintroduction Through Habitat and Human Interaction Assessment," *Endangered Species Research* 44 (2020): 159–76; Charles Knowles and Paul Thomson, "Catalyzing Sea Otter Recovery: Introducing the Sea Otter Fund," proceedings, Sea Otter Conservation Workshop XVI, Seattle Aquarium, Seattle, WA, March 21–23, 2025, 26.

208 **Research and Conservation Program:** "Sea Otter Program Timeline," Monterey Bay Aquarium, accessed June 1, 2025, https://www.montereybayaquarium.org/animals/sea-otter-program-timeline.

208 **Likewise, the Seattle:** Shawn Larson, "Tracking Wild Sea Otter Populations," Seattle Aquarium, September 27, 2023, https://www.seattleaquarium.org/stories/she-sees-sea-otters-nearshore-tracking-sea-otter-populations-dr-shawn-larson/.

209 **As Jane Goodall said:** "What We Do," Jane Goodall Institute Canada, accessed May 30, 2025, https://janegoodall.ca/our-stories/dr-jane-goodall-quotes-to-guide-you.

Epilogue

213 **By that time, Patches:** Hans Kruuk, *Otters: Ecology, Behaviour, and Conservation* (Oxford University Press, 2006), 91.

Index

About the Author

Heide Island, PhD, is a professor of biological psychology and behavioral ecology at Pacific University and a member of the International Union for Conservation of Nature's Otter Specialist Group. Her research on the welfare of captive and wild otter populations in the Pacific Northwest, including her longitudinal study of Whidbey Island's otters, has been published in peer-reviewed journals and presented at conferences. She splits her time between a cabin on Whidbey Island, Washington, and a farm in McMinnville, Oregon, with her husband, Tom, and their dogs, cats, chickens, ducks, and honeybees.